Cyberculture and the Subaltern

Cyberculture and the Subaltern

Weavings of the Virtual and Real

Edited by Radhika Gajjala

LEXINGTON BOOKS
Lanham • Boulder • New York • Toronto • Plymouth, UK

Published by Lexington Books
A wholly owned subsidiary of The Rowman & Littlefield Publishing Group, Inc.
4501 Forbes Boulevard, Suite 200, Lanham, Maryland 20706
www.rowman.com

10 Thornbury Road, Plymouth PL6 7PP, United Kingdom

British Library Cataloguing in Publication Information Available

Library of Congress Cataloging-in-Publication Data
Cyberculture and the subaltern : weavings of the virtual and real / Radhika Gajjala.
p. cm.
Summary: "Cyberculture and the Subaltern: Weavings of the Virtual and Real, edited by Radhika Gajjala, maps how voice and silence shape online space in relation to offline actualities. Thus, it weaves the virtual and real in relation to so-called old and new technologies using globalization and technology as the frame for examination. Implicit in this investigation is the question of how offline actualities and online cultures are in turn shaped by online hierarchies, as well as different kinds of local access to global contexts. This book reveals the logic of particular global-local directions that emerge within digital, transnational capital and labor flows. To this end, the contributors to this volume examine various sites and intersections through critical lenses enabled by conversations and writings in subaltern studies, affect theory, postcolonial feminist theory, critical cultural studies, communication studies, critical development studies, and science and technology studies. Contexts explored in this collection include microfinance online, handloom contexts from India and Africa in relation to development discourse, new technologies, and virtual world marketing. Through actual auto-ethnographic engagement, Cyberculture and the Subaltern reveals the interdependence of the economic, political, cultural, and social in the production of the subaltern online"-- Provided by publisher.
ISBN 978-0-7391-1853-5 (hardback) -- ISBN 978-0-7391-1854-2 (electronic) 1. Microfinance--India. 2. Microfinance--Africa. 3. Internet marketing--India. 4. Internet marketing--Africa. I. Gajjala, Radhika, 1960-
HG178.33.I4C93 2012
332--dc23

2012038972

™ The paper used in this publication meets the minimum requirements of American National Standard for Information Sciences—Permanence of Paper for Printed Library Materials, ANSI/NISO Z39.48-1992.

Printed in the United States of America

CONTENTS

Acknowledgments

I dedicate this book mainly to Vedula Sathyavathy, my mother, who is entering her ninetieth year and can still spin expertly on the charkha and sing anti-mill songs from pre-1947 socio-political movements as she spins. I also want to note a special dedication to my eldest brother-in-law (Dr. A. Venkatesh) from who (I'm told) I seem to have learned to be a teacher and mentor. And a very special ultra special thankyou to his wife, my eldest sister, Dr. Subbalakshmi Murthy (the most recent family member to become my facebook friend) who has been a female professional model for me all my life. All my other siblings, their spouses, my nieces, nephews, grandnieces and grandnephews are always my inspiration and contribute to my learning experiences from near and far through real and imagined dialogues.performances and debates.

I want to thank all my past RAs and graduate student advisees since 2006 (I mean Candice Munoz, Phyllis Dako-Gyeke, Yahui Zhang, Samara Anarbaeva, Mike Delnero, Melissa Altman, Cassandra Jones, Oh Yeon Ju, Sean Watkins and maybe a couple of others I've surely forgotten to mention) since, even though this book ended up being something else and I did not use what they had collected as data and worked on with me in discussing readings relevant to that other project – those understandings and experiences helped me along in these chapters. I also want to acknowledge members of the seminar on Subalternity and Affect that I taught. And thank you @Greg Seigworth for your reviews of drafts and constant facebook encouragements. I thank Lenore Lautigar for dragging me out of my perpetual doubt and constant need to add more and quietly reminding me of the final deadlines. I would also like to thank Johnnie Simpson and the others in the Lexington Press team that helped behind the scenes.

Thanks to all the young daughters and sons of the handloom weavers in South India. Thanks to the people I met in Semarang and Jogjakarta and the conversations that broadened my understandings of local/global non-profit and for-profit dynamics. Thanks also to all the desi SL avatars, all the SL people who rad ever met and learned from. Thanks goes also to Latha, Syama, Jagada, Durga, Anjali, Annapurna, Sridhar, Vanita, and all the past and continuing officers and volunteers and workers at Dastkar Andhra and workers and managers at Daaram. On this side of the world (NW Ohio) I want to thank Sheila Roberts, Susan Cayton, members of the Toledo, Ohio Weaving Guild and Black Swamp Spinning guild as well as my friends on Ravelry and favorites and others I've transacted with on Etsy.com etc. Special thanks to Franklin and Anca for help with the final formatting and proofing of the manuscript.

In memory of Julie Burke, Seemanthini Niranjana and John T. Warren, each of whom I mourned through obsessive (art) yarn stashing and endless crocheting.

As the spinning goes on and on
This book may tie the yarn into further knots.
Perhaps then, in the next [and then the next] book, I shall unravel it.
Making new friends, maybe disconnecting with older ones.
Carving my words out in digital leaflets and notes on the gadgets that come my way.
Contradicting myself, re-winding, negotiating the "virtual" and "real."
Which is virtual?
The yarn or the word? The image or the body?
Which body? Which thought? Which act?
Whose body? Whose conversation?
Con-sequences
Will I hear it, feel it or see it—how shall I know?

That any book project is "single-authored" is a myth. In the initial stages of work on this book, I struggled to keep up that myth. That anyone writes without multiple conversations in their heads and outside is also a myth. When I write, I have a party in my head. In this book, the voices I encountered were real and through our conversations and the work they contributed to the overall theme of the book, they materialized as real co-authors.

Chapters one and two contain some restructured and revised material previously published as Gajjala R. and Birzescu A. (2011) Digital Imperialism through Online Social/Financial Networks – Special issue of *Economic and Political Weekly* (Edited by Rohit Chopra and Aniket Alam). Thanks to Rohit Chopra for helping us articulate some of these connections.

Chapter three is a reprint of Gajjala R (2011) Snapshots from Sari Trails: Cyborgs Old and New, *Social Identities* (reproduced with permission from Taylor and Francis). Thanks to the unknown reviewers for helping me develop and expand the ideas in the first draft I submitted to that journal.

As always, I am thankful for the support (and tolerance of what can only be termed my madness) provided on a daily basis by Venkat and Pratap.

Radhika Gajjala
Bowling Green, Ohio
May 2012

INTRODUCTION

SUBALTERN EMPOWERMENT, SOCIO-ECONOMIC GLOBALIZATION AND DIGITAL DIVIDES

Theoretical and Disciplinary Intersections

Broadly, in this book I map a particular path in examining how voice and silence shape online space in relation to offline actualities. Implicit in this investigation is also the question of how offline actualities and online cultures are in turn shaped by online hierarchies as well as different kinds of local access to global contexts. Underlying the whole project, of course, is the revealing of a logic of particular "global/local" trajectories that emerge in the context of digital, transnational capital and labor flows. To this end, I have examined various relevant sites and intersections through critical lenses enabled by conversations and writings in postcolonial feminist theory (Spivak, 1988; Mohanty, 1988; Alcoff and Potter, 1993), critical cultural studies, communication studies (Couldry, 2010, Schiller, 1999) development studies (Escobar, 1995, Tirthankar Roy, 2007; Parthasarathi, 2001) and science and technology studies (Latour, 2005; Haraway, 1991). Through interdisciplinary lenses enabled by cultural studies and feminist methodologies, this work looks at online microfinance, new technologies and virtual world marketing, and handloom contexts from India and Africa in relation to development discourse that posits a binary between "tradition" and modernity. Through actual (auto)ethnographic engagement in all these contexts, my collaborators and I reveal the interdependence of the economic, political, cultural and social in the production of the subaltern online. Online microfinance, it turns out, is a move to globalize microfinance and is therefore a bit different in operation and process that offline located microfinance. Therefore claims and observations in this book should not be conflated with microfinance in general.

The ways in which we speak of categories such as "third-world," "South Asia," and even "race" in relation to Internet-mediated online/offline environments have to be much more nuanced than in previous times when we engaged these concepts. There is a continual interplay of economics, politics, culture, and everyday life in these online environments as more and more people—young and old—work and play in these spaces that they inhabit. Cyberspaces have become the nodes at which various locals connect and disconnect in the production of the global. Thus those of us who inhabit online networks are also networked into processes of globalization through interplays of online global audiences and offline located/situated producers and consumers. And no matter where we live in the world we are both—global audiences and located/situated producers—in varying degrees. So rather than say "first world" and "third-world" or even "rural" and "urban" or even global and local, virtual and real, or east and west, we need to develop a different vocabulary to talk about what is happening. Euphoria about "new" media and Internet connectivity is concealing the crucial political and economic shifts that are enabled by the ways in which digital technologies have become key players in processes of globalization. For instance, in our academic investigations of identity online, we rarely link the fact that financial transactions occur through digital networks and the specific ways that that impacts who is online and why. In our celebration of online youth cultures and simultaneously the social panics around teens and children having online access we sideline issues related to how the Internet and related media shape future generations of consumers.

Thus implicit in the investigations and conversations in this book are questions about the so-called subaltern, labor, affect and political economy. What technologies of power, literacy, and culture play into the "inter-nets" that weave the online and offline through the rural and urban, through the private and the public, through the nation-state and scattered hegemonies? When, how, and why do these "inter-nets" contribute to the production of "trans" flows of capital. What kind of communicative and technical labor shapes and structures these so-called "flows"? When is the subaltern brought online and for what purpose? For the subaltern to access capital or for capital to access the subaltern? Chapters 1 and 2 take a look at this in relation to microfinance online. The issues raised include further questions. My co-authors and I[1] continue to ask about the in/visibility of the subaltern body and context that exist simultaneously with the hypervisibility of particular images and constructs of "the subaltern."

Further, does the mere act of claiming/naming of erasure and the noting of invisibility and absence in itself produce the possibility of a subaltern subject position? Yet what layers of cultural and material capital allow this naming and what layers of disadvantage permit it to be framed/disciplined so the subaltern voice is not heard but reinterpreted in an elsewhere that the subaltern has no claim to? Thus in white male (and upper-class) privilege, the bisexual male may claim his bisexual erasure—and this produces the struggle and visibility of such a subject position from a comparative position of authority. But would a fat black woman of lesser material privilege in global hierarchies (for we cannot assume all such women lack material and cultural authority in global hierarchies either, can we?) be able to produce this authority through the naming of her erasure as complexly and intersectionally interpellated and accountable? Or would she, when placed online, get stereotypically deployed as a signifier of underprivilege and come to symbolize a token Other and native informant for a particular thus far "erased" subject position (that she may or may not have historically occupied in actuality) within the global marketplace? Can the well-meaning nonprofit workers avoid this trap? Should they? Or would they in their locally situated mode of production realize how this woman's image would travel as a signifier of authenticity in ways they did not mean it to represent her? Further, what's at stake in this kind of discursive search and revelation of the authentic subaltern voice and location? What are the voicings permitted or unwittingly produced and circulated—where are they located? Once voiced—does speech always lose bearing and location? Why, how, and when? Is the concept of voice in itself not "disembodied"? If so—how are we articulating this notion of disembodiment? How does the noting of erasure produce subaltern citizenship? What sorts of speaking locations does it produce and under what conditions?

In attempting to investigate socio-economic formations and cultural practices around technology in relation to global/local contexts, I engage in partnerships (local and international). Thus the projects that chapters in this book draw-from come under the broad heading of "Globalization and Technology," where technology stands not just for digital and "new" digital technologies alone, but also for spindles, looms and such. The conversations and explorations, which engage issues of agency, representation and voice in relation to globalization and technology, are informed and interlaced through an exploration of development practice, capacity building with nongovernmental organizations in the U.S. and India and knowledge building within nongovernmental organizations (NGOs). Thus my collaborations include those with members of nonprofit and nongovernmental organizations in the US and India while drawing on understandings produced through collaborations initiated and in progress in Indonesia, and a range of collaborations and conversations (and ethnographic investigations) with development workers, with software workers, with students, academic colleagues, fiber and related handmade enthusiasts in NW Ohio and with a variety of people who hang out in virtual worlds for work and play. I follow the principle that theory must clearly be built through an involved and location-aware, self-reflexive engagement with contextual practice (Mamidipudi and Gajjala 2008; Gajjala, Rybas and Altman 2007).

This work thus occupies intersections of media and critical/cultural studies and is investigated through critical ethnographic methodologies—under the heading of "cyberethnography" and "epistemologies of doing"—for research and pedagogy at online/offline and global/local intersections and nodes. Communication and the understanding of organizations, as well as the role of culture, politics, economics and everyday life, are central to this research. My collaborators and I conduct ongoing participant and performative ethnographies in emerging socio-political spaces where digital communicative environments impact and shape globalization, and in emerging areas where development work produces unexpected encounters between so-called new and old technologies. For instance, the study of "emerging technocultures" is as much about emerging forms of handloom technologies offline (as is discussed in chapter five of this book), as weavers and marketers of handlooms negotiate how transnational capital flows to and away from them, as it is about the study of emerging forms of digital communicative environments and financial instruments.

It has been widely noted, whether as a critique or in celebration, that current forms of economic globalization require labor forces that are individualized. Often, these are individual workers uprooted culturally, materially and socially (and oftentimes even physically) from within local economies made non-functional through the direct and indirect effects of globalization. Current forms of economic globalization require labor forces that are individualized in a particular manner. Chapters in this book implicitly engage these dilemmas both through visual analyses of online development-oriented portals and in conversation with members of a nonprofit working to maintain handloom weaving as a viable rural Indian livelihood. For instance, we see how the discourse of "Shining India" breaks up these communities through its need to individualize the labor force and draw it into (in)secure low-skilled information technology ("IT") jobs and call center work that will service the global economy and neo-colonial hierarchies therein.

Offline international, national and cross-cultural business and social communicative translations, banking policies, foreign exchange and trade regulations, as well as shifts in everyday practices of users that need to take place to set the stage for the possibility of individual online presence, all play a role in how access and digital divides are reconfigured within these apparently interactive Web 2.0 contexts. Thus, in the case of the third-world subaltern (rural) "Other," there are more learning steps for access and more gatekeeping issues both culturally and technically, in addition to actual material access to the technological artifact itself. In the case of the Western-educated and comparatively materially well-off self (whether located geographically in Western and European nations or in developing world contexts), wireless technology adoption is comparatively more seamless in the context of their everyday lives. These kinds of implicit and explicit embedded hierarchies of literacy and access shape the user base for socio-financial networks celebrated as empowering through their abilities for micro-credit transactions with tools such as paypal. Thus, for instance, networks such as *etsy.com* are accessible to a particular set of craft producer who wishes to reach a consumer market (generationally, geographically, culturally and so on), while shopping portals such as *novica.com* work with another set of craft producers who use the platform to reach global and international consumers. Thus even as both of these are socio-financial online networks set up through online platforms that provide easy use of and access to micro-transactional tools for buying and selling, each one is situated in different hierarchies of literacy and practice. So, for instance, *etsy.com*—mostly viewed as a leader in a now widely prevalent online and offline DIY (do-it-yourself) culture—provides comparatively more direct access to sellers and buyers. However *novica.com*, a portal set up by *National Geographic* with the aim of connecting crafts producers (mostly) from previously colonized locations to first-world collectors and art lovers allows easier access to buyers and consumers than to the actual producers and sellers who are mostly from third-world locations.

Each such network has different rules of engagement and prospective sellers are screened with the use of various kinds of criteria that involve both online and offline processes. In the case of some, the offline screening for sellers is more rigid than in others. So, for instance, while *novica.com* has a rigorous process of examining the prospective seller's products in order to approve them for sale on the *novica* platform, *etsy.com* has seemingly less institutional involvement with examining the actual offline product. Policing the quality of products and the conduct of individual sellers is thus done with varying degrees of online and offline interaction between the owners/producers/managers of the portal and the users of the portal. The gatekeeping and screening processes are not easily understood unless one actually uses the online interface and also interacts offline with and through multiple online and other channels in conversation with sellers and buyers. On the surface it appears that quality control thus is emphasized for material coming from developing world contexts—but these practices of quality control have long colonial histories (see Parthasarathi, 2009 and McGowan 2009). Looking at multiple historical contexts of quality control of crafted products suggests actually that crafts and handmade textiles that are considered as seriously produced for sale—for the market—are to be more closely reviewed by those who take on the task of selling the product. Implicit in the difference of approach to selling/marketing on these portals are layers of histories concerning attitudes toward craft as livelihood and craft as leisure. In future work I hope to investigate more of these issues since, as I point out in the conclusion of this book, the book would need at minimum three more chapters were I to cover the complexity of all that I have encountered during my ethnographies weaving in and out of the virtual and real.

Much of my understanding of how these differences play out is drawn from several years of ethnographic journeying to offline contexts of craft production and marketing both in rural and urban south India and elsewhere in the world. In the current book and chapters that follow, the logic of colonial gaze is what I primarily focus on in looking at global microfinance networks set up through portals from first-world locations such as the US and the UK (for example, *kiva.org*, *microplace.com* and *lendwithcare.org*), and the message of philanthropy is explicit. Even in regard to the negotiation of this colonial gaze by actual grassroots development workers onsite is a whole other aspect that requires more in depth investigation (that I have only just scratched the surface of in my continuing ethnographies and have only touched upon in this book).

There is also a difference in how users are profiled as "agents" in each of these networks. To a large extent, these differences are manifested mostly because of the different degrees of access that particular kinds of users of these platforms have to the technologies and related social, cultural and technical literacy needed for the production of the self online. Some of these social networks and micro-transactional platforms/portals that are set up online implicitly and explicitly make claims of "empowering" the poor of the world financially and socially, and work from a model of what Aradhana Sharma, in her anthropological study of the struggles that NGO (nongovernmental organization) workers face in seeking to empower women rural in India, refers to as "neoliberal logics of empowerment" (Sharma, 2008). This logic functions through the production of premodern subaltern through visual and textual representations that are not just mere reproductions of previously available frames for the representation of the "other" in print media. They mobilize a renewed discourse of agency of the subaltern through the discourse of "empowerment and self-production" that is implicit in how Web 2.0 technologies are described as bringing the "real" and the "authentic" individual into the global interactive space to submit voluntary accounts of themselves—here I invoke Couldry's definition of voice as giving an account of one's self (Couldry, 2010)—through the equalizing interface of the social network online.

Thus, while in actuality there are active processes and practices of both online and offline preparation of how the real and authentic self is performed online, a majority of socio-financial networks online actually serve to essentialize, freeze and visually immobilize subaltern "others," while mobilizing a modern global middle class to participate in philanthropic/entrepreneurial projects made accessible to them via wireless technologies. As a development worker I met in my recent ethnographic explorations in Indonesia noted, the development worker engaged in development practice from within developing world contexts may clearly see the pitfalls of the neoliberal framework of empowerment and of various aid projects coming to developing world locations from first-world donors and funders and altruistic do-gooders. Yet they cannot afford to turn away from accepting any sort of material access or assistance. Thus instead of rejecting and openly questioning the ideologies of and the possible ignorance of the particular donors and funders, the development workers will accept the material assistance and actively reconstruct and negotiate from within unique socio-cultural and economic needs of the populations they serve and work amongst.

In current global environments the processes of individualization, therefore, increasingly function through practices of work and play that involve mediated environments and wireless technologies as well as the "free" inflow of consumer goods produced by multinational corporations. Online and offline, virtual and real are interweaved in these sorts of practices and processes. Thus, in talking about the interweaving and layering of online and offline contexts, in this book, I do not rehearse the tired binary of "virtual" vs. "real"—even when I raise the problematic in discussing specific contexts and cases—instead I engage the continuum. Focusing on that binary—either to contest or extend it—misses the point of the Internet and cyberculture in/as everyday life. Rather, I show how the virtual and real are intertwined and how we move in and out as well as live simultaneously in both. Thus, more specifically, in this book I try to understand how and why certain kinds of speaking positions from within historically marginalized (subaltern) populations emerge online. Using a notion of "technocultural agency" at the online/offline interface and IN the interface—developed by drawing on and extending work by scholars such as Linda Alcoff, Bruno Latour, Langdon Winner, Mark Meadows, Jennifer Slack and Greg Wise, Lucy Suchman, Donna Haraway and Katherine Hayles—I look at texts, images, performances and embodied "voicings" of subject positions in these online settings. A spectrum of methods, that range from observation to immersion have been used in the examination of various technocultural contexts and emerging technocultural agents.

Technocultural Agency

Identities produced within digital contexts, enabled by computer software and hardware, are made possible through the co-production of socio-cultural digital place and global networks involving time-space compression. Such socio-cultural platforms for identity stagings are co-produced by those who code, use and access them. The socio-cultural literacies of these inhabitants determine the kinds of free labor (Terranova, 2004) they contribute toward the building of these spaces. The continued inhabiting of these spaces leads to a reorganization of social space and everyday practice similar to that experienced by call center workers from India who are tuned in to time zones and cultural practices in the Western world as described by Ananda Mitra in his work on outsource call center workers (Gajjala, 2011). Therefore they experience a social, affective transformation that orients them toward life in global multicultural communities similar to those encountered by those in diaspora. Further, these online residents also experience displacement and disorientation similar to that produced in social encounters within diaspora. However, this is still not the same as that encountered by traveling bodies.

Further, rather than speak of identity through virtual community as has been argued in past literature about social formations online (and this includes some of my own past work), I conceptualize this online presence as networked identities (Enteen 2011) and placed bodies online/offline (expanding upon work by Mitra 2006 as well as by Boellstorff, 2008).[2] While networks function nodally, they are "instances"[3] that people travel through. When we labor in them or infuse them with enough relational and consumptive affect, we are placed in them—intensely and immersed—for short and longer periods of time. This results in a space/place overlap and a time "warp" of sorts as we are simultaneously still and transitioning through. This is what Enteen might call "the placement of bodies in dispersal in global locations both online and offline" (Enteen 2006).

Technocultural agency is produced in the interplay of layered literacies and nuanced identities as the user at the interface is forced into renegotiating his/her ability to act and define herself/himself at the online/offline and global/local interface. The process of unpacking how we become technocultural agents reveals to us how we are *placed* and in turn how we *place* ourselves within and in relation to "cyberspace." It reveals how we are clearly situated within unequal power relations manifested within the current continuum of local-global-local through hierarchies of literacies and connectivity.

This technocultural agency allows us to engage global cultures and negotiate heterogeneous complexities by affectively drawing the mind and body into an immersion that produces a split-ness that places the subject both inside and outside, here and there, locally and globally—in the screen world and the offline world. Thus, seemingly multiple yet firmly located and placed subjectivities are produced in such contexts and can be mapped through online signifiers of offline literacies, and offline practices of reaching for the global through digital and other wired and wireless technologies. In each specific performance and emergence of technocultural agents there is an interplay of knowledge and prax situated in specific socio-cultural and geographic configurations that plays out in a continuum of local-global-local.

For instance, in the Second Life environment described in chapter three, there were several avatars connected to bodies from various time zones and geographical locations. They were each quite firmly located in their offline contexts. Yet together, several bodies in virtuality were developing unique intersectional cultures in Second Life as they produced influenced by their inhabitation of the virtual world. Thus they also produced offline local cultures that emerged specifically through their online/offline social, cultural and economic engagement, adaptations and remixing of the simultaneous globality and locality of existence in Second Life. They translated and transitioned back to the local by routing through several online global contexts and intercultural encounters and settling back into their flesh embodied in particular offline local contexts.

During my immersion in Second Life as rad Zabibha, I encountered several instances of voluntary "migration" into Second Life worlds and people clearly chose how they wanted to appear and behave and which particular social group they wanted to interact with—all within the options available within the technological interface. However, each participant exhibited moments of displacement and replacement as their avataric bodies shifted their offline subjectivities into affective dispersals.

In a recent publication which draws on her production of self in Second Life, which was initiated when she participated in our group cyberethnographies of Second Life during a class she took with me as a graduate student, Samara Anarbaeva describes the assembling of intercultural identity through becoming and performing her Second Life identity. She writes of how Samarita Ibanez came into being, clearly indicating that she felt she made a choice of identity here. "I made the choice of being Samarita Ibanez, because I could be anyone I wanted," she writes and continues to explain as follows:

> After I registered I picked an avatar to represent me in Second Life as my face and body. I went with the fox shape. I did not identify with any of the basic avatars,

> which were Asian, White, and African-American avatars. A fox seemed like a neutral choice, because I thought I would avoid of the framing and stereotyping on Second Life. Once I got to know the islands and the rules on Second Life a bit more I started checking out clothes, different avatars, and places. . . My experience showed my decision-making process and the negotiation I entered into while finding an avatar identity based upon my own values and my awareness of what race means to me. When I could not identify with any of the choices presented to me I chose a neutral identity to avoid being stereotyped by others. I figured I could always change my identity after learning more about how to use Second Life. Although I could have chosen any name in the world, I chose to be "Samarita," an extension of my offline name. I decided that even though my avatar did not look like the offline me or not necessarily represented me, I at least wanted to keep my first name, and with it the markers that define my identity—my heritage, culture, ethnicity, and the ties to my family. (Anarbaeva 2012)

In another example of local-global-local technocultural subject formation, I observed a young lady from remote South India who came online and initially proclaimed that she had no real intention of getting immersed or absorbed. She just wanted learn the skills and possibly find a job and/or make money in other ways as suggested by the prevailing (in 2007) discourse about Second Life. During her initial forays into Second Life, she and I (aka rad Zabibha) met. We learned of our shared origins and linguistic commonalities based in South India. She started to type to me in a roman script version of my mother tongue—saying she felt more "at home" on Second Life now that she had found someone who understood the same vernacular Indian language as the one she spoke in her everyday offline. Later as she had inhabited the world for several months we experienced generational and socio-cultural based rifts and drifted apart. I came to know that she was no longer in Second Life as the avatar I had encountered, but had rebirthed herself as another avatar—very punk-like and westernized in appearance and practice. She had in fact "assimilated" and the only trace of her "origins" to those viewing her profile but not interacting with her or having any degree of familiarity of any of her particular situated regional, local, socio-cultural or linguistic-based local practices offline were what can be viewed in her group memberships. Thus, for instance, at least in this particular avatar of hers, she still revealed her membership to one particular group (visible upon examining her profile and groups she belonged to) that affiliated her to Telugu speaking users on Second Life.

In research examining online social networks of women's blogs and queer blogs, articulations such as constrained agency and networked agency have been put forth by those studying how socio-culturally marginalized women and men form coalitions and networks through online blogging. Thus Yahui Zhang contends "that blogging, as a form of self-writing and as artistry, reflects the gendered, embodied, and ethical subjectivities of Chinese mother bloggers as well as their constrained agency" (Mitra & Gajjala 2008). Rahul Mitra and I on the other hand, have argued that "queer 'desi' bloggers [are] more in tune with a network, rather than an imagined community, on two main counts: the absolute insistence on individualism, and the sheer heterogeneity of queer 'desi' blogs and comments, thus giving rise to a notion of networked agency."

There is an interesting simultaneity of, partialness of, and clearly assembled nature to technocultural agency. This leads to a perception that the individual has the ability to act as a unified individual that is at the same time "multiple" as s/he enacts individuality differently or similarly in each of the online environments. The ways in which power structures and hierarchies mediate, constrain and shape this ability to act are made invisible. Yet patterns are never consistent in their seeming individuality across platforms. Even in her own performance of mediated selves the shape-shifting nature of performativity within each network and virtual world that occurs according to how code functions in each place is taken for granted as a necessary and naturalized practice of being and becoming in present-day global modernity. It is noted as an advantage to be viewed as mobile rather than viewed as forced mobility/immobility or the constraining of agency since to move "westward" in any form—embodied or disembodied—signifies progress and the only desired trajectory of so-called democratic and upwardly mobile globalization of the individual. This leads to a perception of choice as the user of online and wireless technologies appears bricoleur—like as having the multiple options and choices noted by Herold, Minocha and Rybas (2012).

> To use the terms of Claude Levi-Strauss as discussed by Jacques Derrida (1993), individual humans are choosing from a bricolage of pieces of personal convictions, histories, impressions, opinions, and experiences to assemble different, but interconnected identities regardless of whether they are actively "creating" an identity online in the form of an avatar, or "living" one or more offline. (Herold, Minocha and Rybas, 2012)

Indeed this choice is real—it is not false—but the choices are based in the needs of particular logics of globalization of capital and labor that continue to unfold endlessly through hierarchies privileging particular kinds of bodies and affects.

In a sense then, it is true that technocultural agency permits, empowers and mobilizes the voicing of various thus far marginalized identities. Such identities materialize and enter the global stage "sideways" or crablike—but must shape-shift to globally coded norms in how they stage and reassemble their identities in order to maintain their presence. Simultaneously, however, this technocultural agent is placed/fixed within the structures and the invisible hierarchies of online and offline networks. Further, this leads to the formation of "media-spaces created by diverse global civil society actors to communicate issues of concern to them and to further their aims" (Clifford, Haynes, Pickard, Keenan, & Couldry, 2007).

It is this interesting partialness of agency and this ability to act as an individual while simultaneously being disciplined by the structure and invisible hierarchies of the network that permits the voicing of various thus far marginalized identities. In an attempt to reveal how this happens, methodologically, there is a need to engage a continuum of possibilities along key dialectics and continua. Such dialectics and continua include space/place, virtual/real, embodied/disembodied, membered/dismembered/re-membered and voice/voicelessness to talk about technocultural identity.

In this book, therefore, I signal the need to engage the continuum of possibilities along key dialectics of space/place, virtual/real, embodied/disembodied, membered/dismembered and voice/voicelessness to talk about technocultural identity. These identities are produced thus through linkings between desire and recognition (Anarbaeva, 2012) and a movement toward material and cultural capital. This process of Self and Other placement occurs through visual performance and discursive Self and Other representations and through dis- and multiply- embodied performativity and through layered socio-cultural, linguistic and technical literacies and access. Subjects are thus *placed* historically, contextually and in relation to one another and to layered contexts within online/offline networks. This placing leads to a reconfiguration of identity, labor, and literacies in sync with transnational capital flows. These placements, displacements, and re-placements simultaneously produce and disappear, shifting labor relations within the global economy as labor forces are retooled and reskilled to work in digital economies, while making invisible specific offline production processes and labor conditions.

Voice and Voicings

In attempting to look at how voice becomes possible through digital mediation, I examine how individuals act within communities as their subjectivities are shaped. I focus on the *how* of the production of voice and of individual subjects that "speak" in the global public sphere as they emerge as actors within interdependent global/local hierarchies. I not only ask who gets mapped out and why but seek to understand HOW this happens through structured and structuring processes of labor, consumption and capital flows. I seek to understand, therefore, how what I term "voicings" are produced in either offline development contexts or in diverse online contexts (including development projects using online venues to facilitate their work) and under what conditions "subaltern" speech gets heard. However, rather than stop at a euphoric celebration of this emergence of voice from thus far marginalized groups, I also try to investigate what implications the emergence of such voice—using the term "voicings" to note their performative and contextually staged nature—might have for the existing and emerging structures of power. Therefore I examine the "subaltern" as staged even as I note that there is in fact subaltern participation and agency involved in this (Self and Other) staging of the subaltern.

Thus rather than use an essentialized, static notion of "the subaltern" I draw on Gyanendra Pandey's (2010) description of the subaltern citizen which he mobilizes in order to "initiate a conversation on questions of marginality, citizenship and history" (Pandey, 2010, 1). The commonly circulated and used notion of "subaltern" only allows us to note subaltern participation in an either/or framework and carries with it the implication that there is an authentic subaltern out there that we will reveal to the world. For instance, in everyday articulations about the subaltern we mostly note that either the subaltern speaks or does not speak; either the subaltern is visible or is not visible; either the subaltern is represented or is not represented; either the subaltern is authentic or is inauthentic. This notion is problematic. Such binaries deflect focus from noting partial and structured participation that allows networked agency and participation in the public sphere albeit constrained. I wish to understand how voice emerges in any of the contexts I examine in order to understand where oppression shifts to when particular marginalized groups gain voice within structures of globalization.

On the other hand, even the ways in which the concept of "voice" is used when writing of empowerment of marginalized peoples invoke authenticity and immutability of voice across time and space. As Couldry (2010) contends, the notion of voice is often also reduced to just that of consumer voice. Further, in the context of global mediated platforms online, such articulations of voice are made in a consumerist, neoliberal framework and the "notion of freedom is purely individualist and makes no reference either to people's socially oriented goals or to the conditions of social cooperation necessary for any meaningful notion of freedom" (66). Therefore, I use "voicings" to suggest the shifting nature of voice as acts of speaking occur within various contexts. In this way I signal how "voice" is a construct based in situated, contingent speech acts shaped through existing power hierarchies, where the marginalized speaker emerges for a moment as a speaking agent as s/he speaks through the cracks and fissures that occasionally or accidentally seem to permit subaltern speech to be heard in the mainstream. After voice emerges in this manner and finds a way to carve a space for the agent, the speaker is subjected/disciplined into the existing power structure. Thus, for instance, while the Dalits (members of a historically ill-treated lower caste in Indian society) of India have voice online and in various activist venues offline and online, they are heard only when they voice their issues and concerns within frameworks recognizable within existing discursive logics shaped by current power hierarchies (see Chopra 2006).

Globalization processes include material and discursive hegemonies produced at the intersection of the economic, the cultural, and the social, and are mediated in multiple ways through old and new mediascapes. These processes feed into economic and cultural local formations. Global technospaces are produced through and are a consequence of economic globalization. For instance, digital diasporas from regions such as South Asia are a product of transnational commerce. Thus, the theoretical lenses for engaging these contexts continue to be developed as I immerse myself in various (trans)rural, (trans)urban, online, offline, first-world and third-world locations. These lenses serve to pose questions and to describe how seeming contradictions contribute to situated praxis within the global-local continuum of everyday economic and communicative practices.

Subaltern Empowerment, Socio-economic Globalization and Digital Divides

By following the image of the "subaltern" through the Internet-mediated contexts, this book also looks at how global/digital financial access is routed through the Internet and therefore shifts local hierarchies into forming socio-cultural and economic dependencies with "outside" locations. Thus the extending of relations or labor and capital that form the basis for present day global economic processes extend into practices of philanthropy, consumption, entertainment and subaltern empowerment based in a neoliberal growth at all costs paradigm driven by a logic of mass production and overconsumption. Notions of empowerment and the role of [wo]men's labor in the shaping of organizations online and offline also impact and shape the presence and absence of "the subaltern" online. This line of investigation then is a continuation of my journeys begun through my past research that asks that we view the notion of "cyberfeminism" through a critical and careful lens while also noting the "veiling of the subaltern" in online settings (Gajjala 2004). This current book also links with the question that repeatedly appears in my past work—about transnational women's labor and globalization (Gajjala 2002). Questions of affective labor, feminization of labor, location and place are also significant to this project and are touched upon and elaborated on as they emerge in the specific contexts I examine. It is therefore no surprise that most of my collaborators in this book are those who were either already on this journey through their nonprofit work and activism offline when I met them or those who joined the journey along the way and allowed me to supervise their doctoral work as dissertation chair and mentor.

This work draws on understandings that come from my research over the years examining Internet spaces in relation to offline community practice at the intersection of development and globalization, rural and urban, and how they are being impacted by multinational economic globalization drives. I suggest that these languages of (wo)men's emancipation in globalized media spaces are in fact recodings of familiar liberal feminist discourses interweaved with a capitalist, consumerist rhetoric of individual choice. I suggest that the celebratory discourse of women's empowerment through the Internet that prevails draws on a neoliberal notion of empowerment, which gets mobilized in the service of economic globalization. For instance, lexicons of women's empowerment and the "new" of media and feminism perform a multicultural, "inclusive" global village while routing around communities whose image and praxis cannot be easily appropriated into the rhetoric of individual choice in consumption. The communities thus made invisible are often communities that are part of hidden labor forces (migrant farm labor, sex workers, sweat shop labor, workers producing computer hardware and so on) on whose social and economic immobility and lack of access to resources rests the mobility, individual-appearing choices, and freedom of other layers of workforces that contribute to and benefit from multinational economic globalization.

Software design, like railway tracks and overpasses, allows the mapping of globalization through only certain routes and for only some populations of the world. It allows chosen mobility for the transnational elite, which is predicated on the immobility and forced mobility of others. Current manifestations of the global village have no real or virtual roads to places where there is no software, thus making it possible for us to indeed make the claim that all roads lead to software. In fact, roads are built for and toward software production and consumption, as we can see with the increasing urban encroachment and engulfing of the rural and related production communities. However, neither can we assume some exotic Other or subaltern who is sitting around unconnected and unliberated by the wonders of the information superhighway. The logics of global business and the necessity to connect to mass markets will certainly ensure that connection—of some sort—not only happens, but also becomes required.

However, unlike the physical architectural barriers that shape the ways in which this routing around occurs in the case of urban transportation, digital and wireless architectures function differently in the way they route around and marginalize. While exclusion and inclusion are based in skills, financial and cultural micro practices and global, transnational standardizations, cyberspace provides the users who live and perform in the interactive network a "spatial customization" that seduces the user into a productive and individualized form of self-expression (Andrejevic 2007). This allows the illusion of freedom from scrutiny and access to the global while leaving unquestioned the hierarchies of the global that necessitate this access for survival. Thus, as common Internet lore celebrates Twitter and Facebook "revolutions" as if they represent subaltern voice in global settings (when in actuality these were manifestations of long hours of planning and years of networking in offline global and local settings amongst people with the required cultural capital and skills for such intervention in such settings), authorities are able to track down protestors through sudden changes in privacy settings MacKinnon, 2012) (as well as sloppy and speedy recoding of new features. The connected and unconnected no longer represent the only kind of digital divide there is, and even when it appears to be the divide, it is more complex than that. What appears to be connectedness may be mere representation, what appears to be exoticization may be necessary marketing for survival. What appears as individual authentic voices are thus voicings that are produced performatively through an interaction of invisible interface design and political, economic and discursive hierarchies that have coded the subaltern as data. Thus, as Spivak noted in 2002, "the invasion of so-called cyberliteracy in the subaltern sphere is frightening" (285). The question in the context of what some might term as digital divide 2.0, of course, is how and when it is frightening. Within neoliberal frameworks even the notion of empowerment and the work of nonprofits and NGOs have become laced with a different sort of complexity. As noted by Ganesh and Barber, the use of ICTs for development comes at a cost to the subaltern. Implicit in many articulations of the problem of digital divides and access to technology is an assumption that capitalism automatically allows equitable distribution of resources and that neoliberal market forces foster universal access in the end with ICTs as tools of market capitalism. The framing of the digital divide as haves and have-nots within development models, according to Ganesh and Barber (2009), prevents us from understanding the economic dependence of the privileged on the have-nots.

We can no longer talk about the global as urban or as the city or as the developed world. The "rural" local in fact exists more in the romantic imagination of the urban elite than it does in actual geographical reality. We can no longer even point to the rural regions of the developing worlds as somehow outside modernity (if they ever were). Romanticizing the rural of the developing worlds through media, fiction, travel writing, and in nationalist or diasporic writings has been happening for a long time—and now we can add to it the production of the rural in online settings. This rural appears in icons, texts, dialogues, interactions, and even Wikkimappia markings and Facebook groups through the nostalgia of the urbanized worker. However—when examined offline—these rural sites have shifted and contain as much urban encroachment as any other place in the world. So what does the binary of rural and urban stand for in literal terms anymore? On my trips to the rural during my travels—partly as a tourist from the US, partly as someone looking for my own roots in rural South India, partly as an ethnographer examining current rural locations and practice—I have observed that nonprofits move in with humanitarian goals and development projects while the corporates move in to recruit labor and buy up real estate. Both these groups move in with some form of new technology as solution—sometimes implicitly, oftentimes explicitly. Both claim empowerment of the underprivileged as their prime agenda. Thus on my journeys to the villages in South India, I have often wondered where the boundaries between the rural and urban are. Is there a "real" rural? At times I thought that the temple in my father's ancestral village was where I would see this realness—and I found that the idols were adorned in "NRI" (nonresident Indian) wealth. So would that mean that the temple and idol are now "inauthentic"? The priest who remembers my father can potentially tell me stories about my own ancestry if I have time to wait and listen. But, where is the "real" village? Is it in the priest's retelling of stories? In the physicality of the fresh-water well outside the temple that I was told would soon be filled up with dirt and covered up to be prepared for some sort of construction? I have often wondered what sort of Escherian stairs I had set foot on upon entering the village of my parents' birth and childhood—where was the paradox?

Writers such as Nigel Thrift (2002) have pointed out that "wherever we go in modern cities, we are being directed by software . . . [and] these programs have come to run cities in very strong ways, and to direct human bodies around them" (323). A key factor to note in relation to software is that, while the ways in which software is prevalent in urban locations can perhaps be mapped through circuits of software use, the hidden ways in which software is routed around certain other (even rural) geographic, socio-cultural, and economic spaces is not as obvious. Therefore, the implications of software becoming a key technology of government and world economies continues a "modern" and colonial legacy of eliminating skills, communities and cultures based in modes of production and everyday life that are not connected to or find no entry point into the software networked "global" society. Subjectivities are reconfigured and appropriated through an interaction of economic and cultural factors and hierarchies are shifted and maintained in ways that work for the select few who have access and control over ownership and the cultural capital that shapes constructs of identity and ignorance and definitions of skilled and unskilled workforces.

Thus the interweaving of socio-cultural and economic activity in relation to ecommerce and various other types of cyberspaces invokes multiple connections and complicities within processes of globalization. Amitava Kumar (2001) points out that "it is precisely the Internet and computers, which were supposed to produce a borderless world, that have thrown up .... a racially marked sense of the local" (85).

The racial marking is perpetuated not only through labor and immigration patterns from the US and other Western regions, but also through education policies in relation to technological training in countries such as India. Mathews, Kamat, Mir, and Mathew (2004) have noted that while

> the growth of the IT labour sector was based on changes in the immigration policies of the US.... these policy changes reflect how nation-states alter their national policies to meet the demands of the global economy. ... [and] are indicative of the unique political context and culture of each country. In the case of India, the education policy changes relate to caste politics while immigration policy of the USA shares the legacy of US race politics. (5)

It appears then, that in relation to the Internet, the relationship between economic forms and cultural forms is indeed "complex and multi-directional" (Williams 1991). Taking a look at this complex multi-directional relationship between economic and cultural forms in the context of globalization leads me to ask various kinds of questions in relation to how social formations are manifested online and offline. How are "diversity" and "multiculturalism" defined within an increasingly "global" digital economy for instance? We have always been "global" and "local" in various ways through history, as people traveled, colonized and migrated—why is there such an emphasis in present times, on the "globality" of the world? Questioning the uneven power relations involved in the global circulation of literacies, material, labor and cultural capital, I reiterate a question asked by Gayatri Spivak (1998): "In what interest, to regulate what sort of relationships [material, social, political and cultural] is the globe evoked?" (329). Similarly, what sorts of relationships—material social, political, personal and cultural—are being regulated within current hegemonic definitions (whether implicit or explicit) of diversity and multiculturalism.

Online presences and absences are shaped by marketing and laboring needs of this emerging global digital economy. Current forms of online networks and communities are not only transitional but the transitional, shifting, updating nature of these networks, technologies, spaces and places in itself is the condition upon which this global marketing process relies. The continual production of newness generates continuous consumption. This too is not an altogether "new" phenomenon—car manufacturers and clothes industries have done this in various ways even in pre-internet times. Now, in the Internet era, it is all further speeded up. This observation about the continual production of newness is indeed not new either, and neither is globalization itself in any way "new." Colonialism openly set in motion a logical force that justified the global circulation of resources for consumption by the few. Soon enough the masters of industry realized they were producing more than the elite few could consume and learned they could sell more in the name of sharing and providing empowerment. Global circulation of raw material and labor was the basis for industrialization of the Western worlds. In current manifestations of globalization, neoliberal logics reframe this hidden logic in terms of increase in access and opportunity. Thus we are offered increased access and opportunity to consume and work to consume, while the management of labor, skills, literacies, modes of production as well as the circulation and flow of capital are still controlled through particular socio-economic hierarchies. We are told how empowered we are to consume and labor in Internet-mediated environments as we "flexibly" multi-task opening windows of shopping, coding, grading, instructing, learning, writing papers, banking, giving charity online, sharing hobbies, daily sweet nothings, and even providing sexual pleasure.

Further, in the Western world itself there are digital divides based in age and class. According to the US Department of Labor (2008), in 2007 nearly 47 percent of workers age 55, and older, were women. Furthermore, the US Census Bureau (2005) projects that by 2035 those 65 and older will represent 20 percent of the total population. This, coupled with the fact that people 55 and older are expected to make up 20.3 percent of the labor force in 2020, complicates how intersections of technology, gendered labor, and techno-literacies will influence labor markets and the positioning of aging female bodies within work/school spaces. Even so, while the issue of aging populations needing to reskill themselves in digital environments seems obvious to most, the digital and socio-cultural as well as technical divide among younger generations—so-called "digital natives" is not so obvious. I have been teaching within digital environments in blended classroom settings (using both online and offline contexts for teaching) since 1996. Over the years I have watched how the digital divide has shifted from issues of mere access to the technological device to issues of skills in sophisticated programming and in socio-cultural negotiation of these environments even amongst these younger generations. Thus, we have youth cultures that inhabit digital environments and access various technological gadgets merely as consumers and users. These groups of youngsters take social media and virtual worlds as well as wireless access for granted but are not always skilled and literate in terms of coding or even in terms of socio-culturally negotiating mixed generational spaces in CMC-based work and play environments. Thus this so-called "digital natives" generation appears technologically savvy but is in fact not literate in the modification of the design or the coding of software—neither are they comfortable in social environments that are not inhabited by others of their own generation. In short, the niche cultures that are possible in online spaces do not require them to intermingle socially or to learn intellectual or everyday skills that other generations—let alone other socio-cultural groups based in race, ethnicity, class, geography and gender—can teach them.

The digital, technological interface plays a crucial role in the transformation of the offline Other into a neoliberal democratic subject who labors to both empower herself and, in turn, her subaltern Other. Work examining the neoliberal conceptualization of the notion of empowerment of the subaltern such as that of Barbara Cruikshank and Aradhana Sharma allows us to make connections that enable us to see how the idea of empowerment gets mobilized in the service of economic globalization while keeping invisible the networks of power that dictate a particular kind of subject formation based in the continued absorption of risk (in the name of flexibility) by the individual. Sharma therefore notes that "[e]mpowerment has become a ubiquitous term and a buzzword in transnational development circles whose meanings, deployments, and consequences are anything but self-evident (Sharma 2008, 2).

The encounter with and continued dwelling within online environments produces such neoliberal "empowered" democratic subjects through layered cyber literacies. This newly empowered and cyber-literate neoliberal democratic global citizen then becomes trained to become part of a transnational labor force that functions through the implicit and explicit coalitions. These coalitions include state policies, international laws, as well as international and local NGOs that work together to meet multinational corporate labor needs. Thus technologies of citizenship and logics of empowerment produce the modern global individual who is able to participate in a global labor force.

Through interaction and participation these individuals and groups thus far on the margins also contribute to the shaping of organizational cultures, best practices, and work environments. Thus there is a shift in what the hegemonic culture looks like even though the dominant players controlling the capital flow and structures of power may still be drawn from pre-existing hierarchies in such structures. Previously subaltern praxis does indeed feed into the tacit modes of doing and being within such environments. Therefore, while I do demonstrate how neoliberal governmentality shapes identity, agency, and voice at the online/offline, global/local interface, I do not wish to paint an image of the subaltern with no agency or choices. I merely argue that the choices are constrained within hierarchies made invisible by the discourse of democracy, voice, and empowerment in online settings.

Notions of individual empowerment and voice play a key role in the transformation of the nonglobal Other into joining a neoliberal democratic global labor force. Historically, such technologies of liberation and citizenship have been instrumental in the drawing in of labor from women and other groups of people perceived to be socially marginalized to work for the prevailing hegemonic or dominant structure of power. Examining periods of transition in technologies of production such as the shift from handloom to power loom in the Western world, for instance, shows the processes by which young women were drawn into the labor force and worked to counter resistance from older workforces potentially resisting the changes in production technologies and related organizational processes (see Gail Fowler Mohanty and Janet Greenless for instance).

The production of the neoliberal democratic global laborer also happens through the uncovering of subaltern praxis and their tacit modes of production while in turn recoding and recording them into the mainstream either to be museumized for future reference or to be appropriated and absorbed into the global. The subaltern must translate her speech in order to be heard. This translation and transformation in turn leads to her newfound "voice" that empowers her to participate in the mainstream. Thus I seek to understand how what I term "voicings" is produced in either offline development contexts or in diverse online contexts (including development projects using online venues to facilitate their work) and under what conditions "subaltern" speech gets heard.

Subaltern in Internet Space

The backdrop for the book as a whole is an examination of the issue of the subaltern in relation to modernity and globalization with the Internet and related globalization as a backdrop for the discussion. I explore some implications of this way of looking at "the subaltern" and the issues that arise when we look for subaltern "voice" as opposed to subaltern praxis space and subalternized communities of production, offering up instead a notion of "voicing." Through ethnographic narrative, I problematize the framing of cyber literacy merely as access to existing online structures without consideration for subaltern communities of production that exist in parallel modernity (a topic that so far has only been touched upon by Spivak in her work on "Other Asias" and suggested in Butler and Spivak's "Who Sings the Nation-State"). Even though my past and ongoing work has addressed these issues through specific studies of online environments or in dialogue with nonprofit fieldworkers and officers such as Annapurna Mamidipudi, Seemanthini Niranjana, and B. Syamasundari in India, I take the opportunity in this book to foreground my past and continuing examinations with the theoretical discussions around the concepts of subalternity, affect, and cyber literacy. I do want to state however that this theoretical frame and any issues with it come solely from my perspective and that I do not speak for any of my current or past coauthors and collaborators. Even some of the coauthors, in this book, let alone those who have written with me in the past, may or may not agree with the way I have chosen to analyze and interpret our dialogues and collaborative data collection online and offline. Therefore I am solely responsible for any faults, mistakes, misrepresentation and interpretations of contexts and data in all the chapters that I have authored and/or co-authored in this book even when the co-authors have either dialogued with me or provided the contextual and visual data for the writing.

This book, in a sense, is about the modern/postmodern desire for the Subaltern. It is about the nostalgia for the subaltern and the data-ization (coding) of the subaltern. It is also about the modern collector's obsession over skills and literacies imagined/known to be in the subaltern sphere, which is imagined to be premodern. It is about the fear and anguish—angst of activists and nonprofit workers—that virtuality is continually disappearing the subaltern even as we continually reproduce the subaltern image to gaze upon. What forms this virtuality—just the "internet" as a set of technical tools? What technologies of power, literacy and culture play into these "internets" that weave online and offline through the rural and urban, through the private and the public, through the nation-state and scattered hegemonies?

This investigation is also about the fear of losing the very bodies we obsess over and desire in the name of the subaltern as they fade into the realm of the imagined and the virtual where the visual continually replaces tacit praxis from simultaneous pasts and presents as we repeatedly lay claims to decoding the Other's knowledges and literacies in order to make them available for appropriation and consumption in the Global. It is about how we freeze, mummify, and museumize even as we wish only to recover and empower the subaltern. To this end, I explore specific online/offline intersections for traces of subalternity. Could it be that subalternity can be heard, seen, and felt only through the affect and through rememorizing that touches us through the subconscious? Perhaps we only know the subaltern through our senses to see, feel, hear, taste, imagine and think through something other than the ever-present visual screening that persistently throws up the cognitively explainable in the present in front of us. But if so, what is the risk in constructing the subaltern as outside the rational as we implicitly reproduce the Cartesian binaries?

In trying to answer why only a few among countless local social movements succeed in making their voice heard and have real prospects for empowerment in the contemporary global arena, Clifford Bob (2005) discusses how the marketing model provides the motivations for the disparate levels of international success and support/activism for local *challengers/ insurgencies/ movements*. He argues that marketing concepts such as "demand and supply" and "marketing strategies" are applied to activities of local political movements, and that their ability to be heard and noticed is framed by an implicit global marketing logic. They are compelled to compete for entry into this global marketplace for support and popularity that transnational nongovernmental organizations in the developed world have been granted. The competitive market paradigm is veiled, however, in a discourse of empowerment and altruism. This veiling produces an "analytical blind spot." This blind spot perpetuates a deceivingly simple understanding/rationale for the growth of transnational NGO assistance while, in actuality, "winning NGO support is neither easy nor automatic but instead competitive and uncertain." Chapters 1 and 2 also take up the issue of the marketing paradigm and how it impacts the use of online networks and related financial tools for activist and social entrepreneurship ventures.

Notice that nowhere thus far have I noted that we must feel morally compelled to empower or give voice to the subaltern online. The perception of the oppressed subaltern is, after all, still part of a benevolent imaginary that has its roots in the desire I speak of—the desire to know the Other because the Other may know what we forgot about ourselves. Maybe. Who knows. But it is certainly a desire—this urge to uplift, empower, give voice to. The desire to own (possess) what the Other can teach us about the world. So the dilemma continues—what right have I or any other researcher to say that the subaltern cannot or should not be voiced online? Does that not presume the same romantic binary that I critique in chapters in this book?

We are indeed possessed in this quest for the Subaltern. The more global our economic and political environments become, the stronger the impulse. Is the desire productive or is it suspect? Perhaps a little of both. Given such an obsessive desire—productive or suspect—what's at stake in conceptualizing or producing "the subaltern" in online contexts? The completely offline and unconnected, as well as those uninitiated into cyber literacy, can only be produced by those who are online and cyber literate and also drawn into so-called self-production. Does that mean that I am calling the completely offline (if that is even possible these days) body the "subaltern"? Maybe, maybe not. Imagining the existence of such a completely offline body is itself an act of producing the subaltern. Yet it is only through a production of the subaltern that we can garner assistance and commitment for the actual material empowerment of the underprivileged of the world. This critique is meant to raise issues to suggest that those in the business of empowering be self-reflective—but not to paralyze them.

So my goal is not to argue that particular bodies are subaltern or to question who and what is a subaltern—but to look at how the subaltern is produced in multiple contexts and discourses and to speculate on the reasons for this production. The desires for the subaltern—the urge to empower and give voice—these can lead to an opening up of socio-political public space or a closing up of this space to unrecognized Others. The obsessive desire in itself is not suspect, for I would like to believe that we are all well-intentioned human beings. Nor are the efforts all for naught—some people on the margins do benefit materially and culturally. Empowerment of some sort is always a given—but what sorts of oppression and power hierarchies any particular moment of empowerment leads to—that is something time will tell in every person's life. So for now I would certainly like to believe that the desire for the subaltern on the part of the academic, the activist, the Nonprofit worker, the funder of NGOs and so on is well-intentioned.

Questions of Method/Methodology

My investigations in this book utilize a combination of methods based in offline ethnographies and in online ethnographies such as observation, conversation, interviews, action research, visual analysis, textual analysis and so on. Offline work involves a deep immersion and involvement for days and weeks at a time in South India—rural and urban—interrupted by gaps where I returned to my own place of work in the US where my offline engagement with these issues was mostly in pedagogic settings. Online work involves a deep immersion in various online environments over time that was blended into my offline pedagogy and other collaborations and investigations. Thus, ironically, more of my immersive inhabitation is online rather than offline even though embodied (being online is never disembodied). Overall, the understanding of craft in various contexts that this book relies on is drawn from critical participant ethnography drawing from Geertz's notion of hanging out as method—which Soyini Madison extends in her work on critical ethnography. This notion of hanging out as method allows for a soaking in of the context and affective aura and permits the researcher to pay attention to the minutest of details without discounting them as unimportant. Such details of interactions and context contribute to the wider examination of online craft networks and are based in my ongoing dialogues among offline U.S craft guilds, Nonprofit workers in non-western countries such as India and Indonesia in relation to the digital financialization of the globe.

My journeys to the rural South Indian weaving villages happened during my time working with members of a nongovernmental organization (NGO) named "Dastkar Andhra" located in Secunderabad, India. I also did a few visits while consulting for BASIX, a microfinance institution, and for the Byrraju Foundation, a nonprofit foundation connected with the IT company Satyam computer services. In my offline journeys through rural South India, ethnography is my main mode of investigation. However, while entering the field, I also work for the NGO Dastkar Andhra which works on behalf of handloom weavers in a variety of ways. Parallel to this, my offline ethnographies include traveling to various craft guilds, craft and fiber shows and expos, and the amateur practice of weaving, spinning, quilting, knitting, crocheting, and the dying of yarn. Therefore, my ethnographic method intersects with action research. In addition, whether I travel as a collaborator with the NGO workers and officers, as a participant of craft guilds or as shopper or ethnographer, I am continually marked. In India I am marked as a nonresident Indian tourist and consumer and collector of handloom fabric and crafted artifacts to be transported back to the US in order to be used/displayed in my home or given as gifts to friends living here. In the US among mostly rural northwest Ohio communities I am marked as outside (even though a citizen of the United States) in certain ways and included as inside through the practice and understanding of processes engaged in by these groups of individuals.

However, I must note that the marking as academic in itself neither places me hierarchically in a fully outside or inside position—nor does it in itself frame me as more or less powerful than those I work with. What frames me as possibly more powerful than those I work with is my academic location and the potential for me to mistranslate events onsite. Therefore the "with" must be considered as a very tenuous and delicate "with." The marking serves as a continual reminder to me as ethnographer that humility and uncertainty are an integral part of the learning process. Assumptions of intrinsic scholarly authority on the part of the researcher get her nowhere in the attempt to understand the contexts and motivations in any situation being investigated. The researcher's authority and power is not in the field per se—it is in how she represents the field, and how her work mobilizes the field toward specific power formations. Well-meaning ethnographers can by no means avoid falling into this trap—it is in the academic structure of persuasion.

Latour (1986) notes the power dynamics implicit in the process of translation from other contexts to academic circulation and describes how this happens through the formation of "immutable mobiles." He writes:

> knowing" is not a disinterested cognitive activity; harder facts about the other cultures have been produced in our societies, in exactly the same way as other facts about ballistics, taxonomy or surgery. One place gathers in all the others and presents them synoptically to the dissenter so as to modify the outcome of an agonistic encounter. To make a large number of competitors and compatriots depart from their usual ways, many ethnographers both had to go further and longer out of *their* usual ways, and then come *back*. The constraints imposed by convincing people, going out and coming back, are such that this can be achieved only if everything about the savage life is transformed into immutable mobiles that are easily readable and presentable. (p. 15)

Therefore, I am not suggesting or claiming that by emphasizing humility, participation, contribution or what I term "epistemologies and pedagogies of doing" (Gajjala, Rybas, & Zhang, 2010) are a way to extricate the researcher from such potential complicity and appropriation. But I am attempting to disrupt and turn topsy-turvy previously established binaries—"immutable mobiles"—through my writing, understanding fully well that these may interpreted as "native" information on faraway premodern lives regardless of all the disclaimers I make. The difficulty is not in the understanding through learning, traveling, and doing—the difficulty, struggle and dilemma is in the craft of writing. If as a researcher and academic I am to establish that I can write appropriately for the academic audience, then I must risk the flattening of what I have learned. If I am to break with tradition in academic writing, I must risk not doing it effectively, sounding uninformed or losing my own voice and location as "scholar." Within these stated constraints my methodology is a struggle that includes the process of crafting the academic text.

Online, the increasing availability and access to various synchronous and asynchronous interactive communication tools online have instigated much discussion and experimentation during this past decade regarding the potential for the use of these interactive tools within a variety of work and play activities. Subjectivities produced in the context of virtual/real interaction and within related techno-mediated environments cannot be understood unless the "observer" enters these spaces and tries living in them, working with them, doing things with them. In other words, academic analyses of techno-mediated subjectivities must self-reflectively engage and observe the self (and the Other within the self) "inside" technospaces. "At the momentary intersection of the human being and the machine," writes Munt, "there is spatial praxis: there is technospace." Through acts of building and inviting of participants as well as of inhabiting various online forums and communities, I have been immersed in studying such spatial praxis.

In cyberspace, the ethnographer does not always have to travel in the kind of physical space where the whole body encounters the field face to face. But the travel in time and cyberspace allows her/him to live in the field in a different way and to do concrete participant observation. In order to do so effectively, the ethnographer must first code herself into existing in these online worlds. The physicality of the body is expressed through everyday material practices, even when those practices involve online production of self. The practice of *engaging* such a technological environment produces the subject/agent. Meaning, therefore, is made through doing—doing in this case is coding, programming, typing oneself into existence and building objects.

For instance, Jenny Sunden's book *Material Virtuality* writes of the typing into existence that is a requirement for any sustained online identity. This act of *becoming* online creates a close relationship between the typist and the character she/he types into existence in the online world. This sort of relationship is no doubt the basis for the process of transformation described in the 3-D film "Avatar" released in 2009. It is, of course, no coincidence, I am sure, that the character, Mary, played by Sigourney Weaver, who heads the team that is providing intelligence (implicitly and explicitly) to the Military and to the Corporation is clearly modeled on popular images of the female anthropologist (in short, she seems very Margaret Mead-like).

Examining where we place our bodies, or where our bodies are placed (whether visually, textually or through architectural and city design and mapping) in time and space—in relation to technologies old and new—and how we interact with these environments leads to an understanding of the complexity of unequal power relations and structural formations and design within a global cyberspace.

Neither the cultural nor the economic routes into online worlds are mutually exclusive. The cultural entry point tends to precede the economic layer sometimes and the economic quest for jobs tends to precede cultural transformations. Thus digital places and global networks become potential transitional places (Naficy, 2001; Gajjala, 2011) and contact zones for the formation of transnational subjects able to work within the increasing digital global economy (Cooper, 1997) through socio-cultural processes facilitating the further intellectualization of labor (Bratich, 2008).

In a struggle to get multiple locational views, I have dialogued with multiple collaborators—the ones that emerged as co-authors of chapters in this book are only those who actually wrote with me. Each chapter deals with specific macro and specific micro contexts that are elaborated on from multiple viewpoints and in turn written—even when co-authored—as if in "one voice." This is the nature of traditional academic writing. Yet the stories remain in the telling and revealing of multiple voices and locations and histories—some visible, some untellable and even others even unknowable and unknown. Thus my "method" also involves inviting several people to co-author with me in a framework I suggest—waiting to see how their entry either turns the framework on its head or illustrates it differently. The responsibility—for the framing, conclusions, mistakes, misrepresentations, inclusions, exclusions and sloppiness—is all mine. Those that co-authored came to a stage I had arranged—they came either in agreement, tentatively, or in clear expressions of resistance to it—and in the process I have learned much from them. It is my hope that they have learned from me as well. Several of my co-authors are my doctoral advisees and with them it has been a deep bonding experience. With the others—as in my immersion and relationship building in the virtual world of Second Life—we had intense moments of inhabiting online or/and offline worlds. On field trips to villages in South India we got to know each other in intense moments of dialogue and affect, each experiencing our own angst and nostalgia over a lost (to us) rural India as we drove past the lush rich lands near Godavari river or we lamented the dry poverty in some other regions. We marveled at the aesthetic skill and business acumen of the weavers in Pochampalli, together felt the loss of sari designs of a past aesthetic embedded in our mothers' saris or our own collections from past decades, explored our caste and class locations in relation to the weavers; struggled over "Indian" vs. "NRI" or "American" perceived identities and barriers among us. We also worked through issues of academic/activist binaries—but certainly not to the satisfaction of any of those concerned. In writing together, then, relations are built, broken and/or realigned. These stories of how we wrote or fought each other do not come through in this book. The madness, the accusations, the intense connections, the feelings of alienation and loss, the loneliness and isolation after the return from the intense immersions whether in virtual or real environments—perhaps narrating those will form a personal memoir at a later time. Suffice it to say this is a project built with much love that overcomes all the misunderstandings and the mixed feelings around it—if any—on my part at least since it is entirely possible I have left a trail of collaborators and people I write about at various access points or gatekeeping vantage points who are very angry with me and will only be further angered by my writings in this book.

Finally, a note on the structure of the book. Each chapter can be read as an independent essay. What pulls the collection of essays together is the central theme of examining the notion of subaltern in relation to digital modernity and globalization. What all of the cases in this book reveal is how the production of the subaltern as well as the use, misuse, and circulation of digital and mobile technologies are part of neoliberal forms of globalization. The dual forces of NGOization and ITization produce the conditions for the existence of subaltern voicings online. What is written in this book will be expanding into a larger project as I am currently engaged in continuing auto-ethnographic investigations in that area. The issue of handloom and craft in modernity is not restricted to issues of third-world development, nor is the issue of weaving the virtual and real only about the so-called subaltern and related digital divides. Weaving of the virtual and real happens in layered and nuanced ways across class, generations and geography—therefore my continuing investigations also include a closer examination of labor and consumption in immersive environments across international "digital diasporas."

Chapter Outlines and Structure of this Book

In a sense this book is actually both a continuation and backdrop—written in retrospect, yet not—for my past publications, which were mostly about fully online settings with a backdrop of understanding drawn from my continuing offline journeys with nonprofit workers in rural and urban South India. Thus this book comes out of a necessary stepping back (for me) into a contextualization of a lot of what is happening on the online stage. Yet it is also a stepping forward—for much of what was visible online during the 1990s is feeding back into offline grassroots discourse as well as social entrepreneurship. Social entrepreneurship associated with the coexisting financial and social economies online and the proliferations of social networks with embedded micro-transactional practices through sites such as paypal, etsy.com, ebay and kiva.org have indeed become the latest web 2.0 mode of employment. Thus micro-credit loaning practices through web 2.0 tools have become facilitators for a prevailing discourse of modern (globalized) individual initiative and success.

Through the chapters in this book, I take up the issue of how individuals act within communities and of individuals reconfigured as networks spatially online. These networks are placed through interaction and imagined commonality as they inhabit websites and portals (through web urls, MOOs, MUDs and social networking sites), as well as three-dimensional estates (such as in SIMs or Second Life) and home regions (such as in games like WoW). Their subjectivities are thus shaped through affective engagement within such places where power hierarchies and notions of property and ownership emerge to shape subjectivities at the online/offline interface. Through such interactive networked yet constrained voicings, the users at the interface are produced as actors or subjects within interdependent global/local hierarchies. Thus in the chapters that follow, my collaborators and I not only question who gets mapped out and why, but seek to understand HOW the technocultural global (neoliberal) subject comes into being processually and structurally. In chapters 1 and 2, we do this through our visual analysis of microfinance website profiles of lenders and borrowers; in chapter 3 I look at Second Life contexts, while in chapter 4 my co-authors and I map out how a particular technology that is considered old and traditional is in fact placed in a modern context with modern socio-economic relations redefining the technology and its emerging uses. Chapter 5 is written by two of my doctoral advisees (now independent scholars in their own right) and lays out the context of Kente and Adinkra in relation to globalization in a way that works well with discussions in chapter 4 and the context of the handloom in India in relation to concepts such as modernity and tradition.

Each chapter provides entry into a certain context. Each context relates to issues that impact how technology shapes socio-cultural environments, which exist in a particular conjuncture of spatio-temporal local to global continuum or global to local continuum. Therefore I also do not pose the local and global as binaries—even if in specific cases and articulations in conversations with co-authors the binary sometimes emerges as a struggle. The binaries of virtual/real and global/local often emerge as discursive, conceptual struggles because the articulation of them as binaries shapes policy and theory formation in such a way as to frustrate and block particular possibilities for collaborations, coalitions, and negotiations. In a sense, these binaries can be said to produce and be produced through neoliberal politics, but I do not focus on mapping that binary in the present project. That is not the goal of this book because I wish to center the intersections that are written about in the chapters that follow this introduction.

Chapters 1 and 2 take up the issue of nonprofits and the production of subaltern presence online through the example of online microfinance. I co-author these two chapters with doctoral advisees and we examine three online social entrepreneurial networks for delivering micro-credit loans to financially disadvantaged individuals (several from the developing world) for setting up small businesses. The websites we look at are kiva.org, microplace.com, and lendwithcare.org. The context for these chapters is the Internet as technology and cultural interface for the production of subaltern identity visually. Individual workers at the interface of nonprofits and of the Internet labor to produce empowerment—drawing on IT skills, complex, layered understandings of tacit modes in multiple offline locales while investing emotional energy and commitment to the empowerment of the Other. Feminist discourse of empowerment and cyberfeminist praxis that deeply inform these logics of empowerment both set the stage for and become complicit in local and global transnational formations. The question of whether this is something to be hopeful about or to despair about is left as a contradiction that needs further exploration through in-depth examination of specific cases. These chapters are framed more along the lines of production of voice and agency online and makes a plea for future work that can take such examinations further into an examination of economic practices offline and a close examination of the online economic transactional tools to reveal how the voicings and placement of the so-called subaltern may provide opportunities for empowerment or further reproduce neocolonial oppression.

In an attempt to interweave these issues, chapters 3 and 4 are drawn from my work in relation to and with my nonprofit related offline collaborations. Investigating the global to local continuum, chapter 3 plunges the reader into an online/offline immersive ethnographic journey that splits my identity into Radhika Gajjala/rad Zabibha where I had to labor both online and offline to learn skills and literacies to build a business on Second Life. Thus it is a co-authoring between the academic writer "Radhika Gajjala" and the Second Life explorer and business owner "rad Zabibha." The chapter that follows rad's business (ad)ventures actually explains more about the offline context for her quest. In chapter 3, then, I draw upon an examination of two apparently opposed cyborg locations and technologies to show how, in specific instances, globalization, technology, economics, culture and diasporas intersect. Chapter 3 is a condensation of more than five years of immersed ethnographies and laboring in the virtual world of Second Life. The labor of production of self, various objects and the setting up of a business on Second Life can only be understood by the inmates of such an online world—be they novice or expert coders and digital artists.

Chapters 3 and 4 thus introduce different theoretical articulations, yet the common thread that strings them together is the exploration of identity in relation to globalization, digital market economies and technology. Chapter 4 is co-authored with my nonprofit collaborators. The essay takes the reader into thinking about a totally different technology—the handloom—but in relation to marketing issues, policy and globalization that overlap with concerns in the other chapters. This chapter is inserted in the book to show that the issues raised regarding the production of subaltern presence in online contexts cannot be adequately understood or investigated without a close look at issues faced by nonprofit workers offline while they attempt to link parallel and alternate producer communities to global markets as they negotiate national, international and transnational policies and production contexts. My co-authors in chapter 4 are from the nonprofit organization Dastkar Andhra. In this chapter we examine the handloom as technology, embedded in everyday life where the interplay between economics and culture is inseparable. It serves to provide an understanding of complexities involved in attempts to insert existing communities of production formed around older technologies such as the handloom in India into globalizing economic formations and markets. This is an examination of issues made visible in economic practices of consumption, production, and marketing at the site of handloom technology. The three of us reflect on the questions raised, not so much from an intervention angle, but from positioning what have been categorized as "traditional" knowledges in contemporary times while problematizing the very conceptual categories of "traditional" and "modern."

Chapter 5, on the other hand is a chapter co-authored by Precious Yamaguchi and Franklin Yartey (both of whom worked with me on their doctoral dissertations, neither of which was actually about Kente and Adinkra). It draws on their auto-ethnographies and journeys in relation to handloom and craft technology in Ghana and works well with the issues raised in chapter 4 by my co-authors from Dastkar Andhra.

Thus, in this book as in past work, I continue to ask how gender, race, sexuality, ethnicity, class, caste and nation are mediated in global/local technocultures, specifically at the online/offline interface of the computer. In looking at these mediations, I examine how subjectivities are produced. Identities produced within digital contexts enabled by computer software and hardware, are made possible through social networks formed online and offline as well as through the coproduction of socio-cultural digital place and global networks involving time-space compression. Social Network systems, MMORPGS, game consoles, locative media, emotion mapping and related ubiquitous, static and migratory technologies and their archives remap temporal and spatial relationships while producing specific modes of mobility and immobility based in a producer to consumer continuum. This continuum is hardly smooth and fluid—it is jagged and mediated by multiple hierarchies of labor, management, marketing, and finance. These socio-cultural contexts are coproduced by inhabitants who access these contexts.

The progress narrative embedded in the increasing financialization of the globe through digital technologies makes economic globalization and neoliberal governmentality appear to be seamless and logical routes to the empowerment of the underprivileged of the world. However, thinking about and closely examining subaltern subject positions that emerge online in relation to offline production communities allows us to see how so-called ruptures in the fabric of modern globalization are produced as seamless while simultaneously disallowing full access. Therefore, one of the chapters is based on conversations about handloom technology in modern India in an effort to problematize conceptual categories such as modern and traditional, and to suggest that perhaps the social relations of production around specific technologies do not always work along the modernist teleology presented in neoliberal readings of progress and modernity.

Notes

1. We acknowledge conversations and collaborations with Venkataramana (Vinnie) Gajjala and with Annapurna Mamidipudi during early examinations of microfinance in India. We also thank Samara Anarbaeva for assistance in collecting data during my early stages of the project. Anca Birzescu and I began investigating these issues as a follow-up to work I was doing in 2004 looking at women's empowerment and globalization, when Anca joined a team of doctoral advisees working on related topics and helped collect data for visual analysis. In 2005, during my faculty improvement leave, Annapurna introduced me to the microfinance organization BASIX in Hyderabad, India. Subsequently we recruited "Vinnie" who is a Development Economist to explain microfinance to us cultural studies researchers. Samara was a research assistant of mine around that time and she helped collect some data in previous publications from which some of the theoretical articulations in the first two chapters of this book are drawn from. Franklin Yartey joined our team after the Anca, Samara, Vinnie and I had finished working on various versions of what eventually came out in print as our co-authored article in 2011 and he added further insights based in his location and drew from this work to develop his own dissertation on a closely related topic.

2. Also see my continuing work related to placement of labor and coding of affect (Gajjala 2010)—developing through work such as that discussed in this book.
3. An instance variable is a variable in object-oriented programming and seems to be prevalent in iPhone app programming and in social network app programming. See www.blurtit.com/q691269.html for a quick explanation. Code variables such as "instances" are developed and used for coding efficiency. Such coding efficiency is practical and is part of the "DRY"—i.e. "Don't Repeat Yourself"—principle of software development that requires that things are defined once and only once. Such principles end up globalizing particular culturally specific standards in visual cultures and in practices of networking and gaming.

CHAPTER ONE

PRODUCING THE GLOBAL: MICROFINANCE ONLINE

Radhika Gajjala, Franklin Nii Yartey and Anca Birzescu

In a motivational speech given at Oxford, UK for TED Global[1] in July, 2010, the co-founder of the site Kiva.org, Jessica Jackley, recounts her pioneering journey into the world of online micro-lending. She talks about how her experience in Uganda and Tanzania, where she saw the effects of micro-lending first hand, led her to set up Kiva.org with Matt Flannery. She narrates her experience as follows:

> A few months later, I went back to Uganda with a digital camera and a basic website that my partner, Matthew, and I had kind of built, and took pictures of seven of my new friends, posted their stories, these stories of entrepreneurship, up on the website, spammed friends and family and said, "We think this is legal. Haven't heard back yet from SEC on all the details, but what do you say, do you want to help participate in this, provide the money that they need?" The money came in basically overnight. We sent it over to Uganda. And over the next six months, a beautiful thing happened; the entrepreneurs received the money, they were paid, and their businesses, in fact, grew, and they were able to support themselves and change the trajectory of their lives. (Jackley 2011)

Such a narration by the cofounder of Kiva.org already gives us an idea of the tone which is set for the whole venture. They invoke emotions of sentimentality and sympathy. The need to invoke such emotions through narration in their field reports and journals is a clear strategy for good advertising and is embedded in the training received by the kiva fellows. Shameem Black notes that this

> structure of feeling gesture[s] toward a recognizable emotion of other-directed concern is crucial to how such websites function and foster digital monetary transactions. Such expression of recognizable/transactable emotion implies a form of selfhood that takes shape through its immersion in the well-being of others, sentiment helps produce a fundamentally ecological subjectivity. (269)

Thus there is an interplay of affect and marketing in such field journals. Such interplays are based in the contradictory individual community impulses based in the push for global inclusivity.

In this chapter, we attempt to unravel contradictions apparent in how empowerment, agency and necessity play out in the connecting of the subaltern to the global. Thus we signal toward the processes of production and commodification of a globalizable, mobile subaltern commodity packaged in digital platforms based in staged interactivity. The present chapter explores mechanisms of producing voice, empowerment, and subjectivity as these materialize in online socio-financial networks. We focus here on the case of kiva.org. The next chapter continues this line of investigation by examining platforms for micro-lending provided by CARE international through lendwithcare.org and by Ebay through microplace.com. In both chapters, we draw on feminist frameworks in examining gender, race, ethnicity and development in the context of an ever pervasive globalization underpinned by economic integration, media convergence, and global expansion of the Internet. We do this in order to trace the implications of voicings from the margins of the global economy. Together these chapters serve to give an overview of how online microfinance globalizes the idea of micro-loaning to the poor while mobilizing the sentiments and philanthropy of a particular middle class across nations. This "middle" is mobilized in the project of drawing subaltern populations into a particular kind of global that is based in the production of individualized subjects. Such subjects become the desired labor forces and investors within transnational corporatized environments. The quote at the beginning of this chapter is an example of a discourse that shapes a majority of practices of empowerment and philanthropy that are mobilized from Western regions of the world via the Internet. In this chapter and the next, we examine some of these practices as they become apparent when we do a close textual analysis of microfinancial social networks such as kiva.org, microplace.com and lendwithcare.org.

Digital micro-transactional technologies have become salient tools for transnational financial exchange. At the same time, social media tools are being used in struggles for democracy and civic engagement, advocacy and empowerment. Thus, when networks such as kiva.org and lendwithcare.org adapt the use of such micro-transactional financial tools along with web 2.0-based social media tools in the delivery of microfinance, they emerge as socio-financial networks in global space. These instruments become global players—actors—in political and economic reconfigurations within the larger neoliberal framework of governance. Therefore, we examine how these global players produce and represent the needy and those that are invited to help the needy. We do this through a look at how combinations of online and offline practices play into the representation of third-world Others and of raced, gendered and classed bodies. We ask how such representations might have the potential to impact materiality even in offline locations. Our intention in undertaking such a critical examination is not to debunk the mission and any positive outcomes of microfinance in general. However, we reveal how the interplay of online and offline practices of microfinance networks formed in global Internet- mediated space reproduces tropes of colonization, and serves to exoticize and Other the third-world borrower through these global Internet-mediated social environments. Globalization of microfinance in this manner has far greater and broader implications than those addressed in this book. This investigation will be carried out in relation to other digital financial networks and transnational capital frameworks in continuing work by the first author of this chapter. Thus we make no claims as to the comprehensive nature of our investigation. Rather we open up these issues for examination and hope others will join in these conversations.

Internet and related wireless, digital technologies referred to in present times as "Social Media" are often considered to be tools for the empowerment of the marginalized people in our world (Best, 2005; Stengrim, 2005; Huesca, 2001; Owens & Palmer, 2003; Pickard, 2006). Indeed, social media tools are currently being mobilized for global activism and advocacy in various locations worldwide (for instance in the Occupy movements in the USA and in revolutions in Egypt, Tunisia and so on). But what is often missed in the characterizations of such movements is not only the amount of offline groundwork and negotiations that take place. Thus, MacKinnon points out that

> the digital activists who played a key role in bringing down the governments of Tunisia and Egypt did not spring immaculately from Facebook and Twitter. They started building interconnected online and offline movements well before either service was conceived, using a variety of platforms, services and software—some built by companies, some built by themselves or created noncommercially by others. They were also major contributors to—and beneficiaries of—the digital commons. (Mackinnon, 2012, 21)

Even in other contexts, NGOs and corporations have actually been working together in producing the global. They are not always in tension—as is sometimes assumed—for NGOs are not all resistant to the mainstream and even several corporations have corporate social responsibility wings that are administered through nonprofit foundations. NGOs have come to serve an intermediary, bridging function in globalizing local economies so that in fact transnational corporate logics have access to them. As Kamat suggests:

> The global phenomenon of NGOs reflects the new policy consensus that these groups are de facto agents of democracy rather than end-products of a thriving democratic culture. This is evident in the astonishing speed with which NGOs have emerged in countries on the verge of establishing democracies. The leading role ascribed to NGOs foretells a reworking of democracy in ways that coalesce with global capitalist interests. Global policy institutions are actively enlisting NGOs in the economic reform process, but in doing so, they undercut their popular role as forces of democraticization.

Thus, in offline contexts where nonprofit volunteers have engaged in attempts at reform and advocacy for a long period of time, we repeatedly encounter their angst. Aradhana Sharma effectively describes the dilemma of empowerment that the nonprofit worker faces in her work on neoliberalism and empowerment in grassroots organizations in India. Another complicating factor is that it is now considered "normal for the world's most powerful governments to consult with multinational corporations to shape a range of financial, trade and foreign policy objectives" (MacKinnon, 2012, 11).

Advocacy groups, Non-Governmental Organizations (NGOs) and philanthropic groups are using a variety of wireless and digital tools with great ease. Thus, the poor of the world have mediated access to the Internet and to global space through the efforts of activists and nonprofit volunteers and workers. These activists and volunteers, in turn, have assumed roles as advocates and representatives of the disempowered of the world. Social media and wireless technologies and devices serve as tools that help connect these advocates of the disempowered while also making it possible for them to showcase the concerns and issues of the marginalized populations in online global space. However, as Mackinnon once again cautions, most socially networked "public spheres" of this sort are backed by privately owned companies which are headquartered or have main stakeholders mostly in the Western nations.

> Google and Facebook are just two of the many companies whose products and services have created a new, globally networked public sphere that is largely shaped, built, owned, and operated by the private sector. Digital platforms, services, and devices now mediate human relationships of all kinds, including the relationship between citizens and government. Struggles to control and shape this sphere are intensifying around the world. These struggles will only escalate as the stakes continue to rise. (Mackinnon 2012, 9)

In such a context, the micro-transactional features that are provided by financial tools such as paypal have become important tools for fundraising for these groups of activists and volunteers. Local and offline development projects increasingly compel NGOs and nonprofits to access global audiences and benefactors by competing for online visibility. Thus digital micro-transactional technologies have become salient tools of consumption, production, representation and transnational financial exchange. Platforms such as kiva.org and lendwithcare.org for example have adapted the use of micro-transactional financial tools and social media tools to the delivery of microfinance. These instruments thus become players in political and economic reconfigurations within the larger neoliberal framework of governance. Such online microfinance portals are actors in an emerging global nonprofit staging of humanitarianism and philanthropy.

The importance of mapping the ways in which everyday practices and hierarchies shape online identities through processes of inclusion and exclusion (gendered, raced, classed online subjectivities) has been underscored in the introduction to this book. The effects of cyberspacial praxis are real and shape transnational labor models and patterns. Freedom online, like freedom offline, is always negotiated and defined by existing hierarchies of power. We should be cautious when asserting that the Internet provides liberated and fluid identities.

The growing presence and use of information communication technologies (ICTs) and in particular, Internet technology as virtual infrastructure of socio-economic globalization, is an undeniable fact. At the same time, cyberspace has become a site for marginalized voices to emerge in activism and protest as diverse populations gain access to the Internet and related literacies. ICT tools have increasingly become critical means for the advocacy of social change and justice in the global arena. A myriad of nongovernmental organizations (NGOs), international social actors, activists, and social movements are interlinked transnationally through ICT-based social networking systems. They work toward the shaping and the sustaining of a global civil society.

More often than not, the mechanisms and tools that make possible the existence of this global civil society are discussed in laudatory terms. However, such a celebratory approach to digital technologies "often excludes meaningful recognition of the vast technical, cultural, educational, and class divisions that exist among and between nations" (Custard 2008). It is important to recognize the value and types of hierarchies produced through these networks as they foster social change while not assuming that all social change is for the benefit of the downtrodden. It is equally important to understand the kinds of representation and re-presentation of local and global actors and the contexts that implicitly and explicitly privilege one over the other. Therefore, the analysis and discussion in this and the following two chapters examining online microfinance draw on transnational feminist and civic-driven change (CDC) approaches to development and empowerment to examine online microfinance.

Rather than stopping at a euphoric celebration of this emergence of voice from thus far marginalized groups, we try to investigate implications of these emerging voicings for existing and emerging configurations of power. Furthermore, by examining the emergence of voicings as a phenomenon within the larger structures of globalization, we want to understand how and where oppression shifts when particular marginalized groups gain voice in such structures. The portals that are used to deliver microfinance and to connect lenders and borrowers are adapted from certain prepackaged standardized formats and features that each nonprofit adapts for its own use. The expectation is that the officers, fieldworkers, activists and volunteers can focus on the business of advocacy and social justice through the Internet without having to be skilled at hardcore coding. The (in)visible online interface includes features for micro-transactions of various kinds—social and financial—that allow the staging of authenticity and "reality." The subaltern thus *seems* to be speaking online directly to us—unmediated. It therefore appears as if the subaltern now has global access and is no longer tucked away in the dark depths of the globally unheard "local."

As noted in the introduction of this book, we employ a particular understanding of "voicings" in this project. Namely, we identify the implications of the use of the concept of "voice" when writing of empowerment of marginalized peoples. Such use invokes the authenticity and immutability of voice across time and space. Therefore, we use the notion of "voicings" to suggest the shifting nature of voice. These voicings are performative—they are acts of speaking that are enabled by, and occur within, specific contexts. Our goal is to attempt to illustrate the ways in which the production of the subaltern subject position through cyberspatial discourse and practice serves to further disempower subaltern communities in relation to global spaces of speech and action. To this end, we examine specific instances where subalternity and subaltern causes are reproduced through events and representations in online spaces.

Transnational Feminist Approach to Development and Empowerment

Our analysis is framed through a transnational feminist approach to development and empowerment. Microfinance has been primarily acknowledged as a strategy to empower women in the global south. Our overarching goal is to critically address the obvious and not so obvious impacts on empowerment by the global restructuring that happens through the spread of digital finance. Governance is increasingly being delegated to private institutions and international actors primarily accountable to market rules, and the Internet and related wireless tools are being mobilized in these projects in the name of empowerment of the subaltern. Oftentimes, these rules are not ethical and democratic practices even as they claim to be so. Neoliberal marketization and its negative influence on already marginalized people could be more thoroughly understood if we include in its definition processes of social inclusion/exclusion and aspects of inequalities of power, production and distribution (Elliott, 2008).

Even though globalization allows projects of equality and empowerment to have transnational reach, we must be aware that one insidious outcome of global restructuring and of neoliberal economic policies is the reconfiguration and resurgence of imperial ambitions within current global hegemonies. What appears to be empowerment could be only a restricted notion of empowerment circumscribed to a neoliberal philosophy that emphasizes the individual but does not properly address structural inequalities that hinder more comprehensive processes of empowerment.

The same neoliberal understanding also tends to profess a one size fits all model of empowerment by disregarding the range of political, economic, and cultural contexts that lead the way to complex and sometimes contradictory possibilities for empowerment. This is why a transnational feminist perspective is also an analytical alternative to global feminism which is rather delineated by the same neoliberal stance, in that it has been criticized for propagating a Eurocentric, Western hegemonic and homogenizing feminism (Mohanty, 2003; Narayan, 1997, 2000; Parameswaran, 2008, etc.). It is a feminism that carries with it the marks of imperialism, professing a North-South/ top-down prescriptive model of feminism for the rest of the world, and not necessarily for the benefit of the rest of the world. More specifically, in this narrow view on empowerment, gender is defined as having a universal, monolithic character worldwide, without acknowledging the reality that gender is simultaneously embedded within much more complex power dynamics alongside other social markers such as race, class, religion, nation, ethnicity. It is, therefore, an expected conclusion of this narrow premise that oppression is being addressed partially and inadequately while empowerment has in reality limited prospects. Elliot (2008) points out to the co-option of empowerment as a neo-liberal strategy to fulfill other goals in the development realm: "too often development agencies see empowerment as only an instrument for reaching other goals, just as contraception can serve the goal of population control rather than women's choices. . . . Program goals may be achieved, but without individual transformation it is not empowerment" (8).

The approach guiding the current analysis therefore invites the researcher to always remain alert and always question the hype around global civil society as formed through global communication enabled by digital and wireless technologies. Although some may argue that in 2011 we do not have the same issues of digital divides and lack of literacy and access as we did in 1999, we would like to point out that the divides are not merely a result of access and technical and/or linguistic literacy. The issue is that even having access and literacy does not allow for active choices to be made by these Others. These are Others because the Center expands in the name of giving them access and allowing them voice through translation and transformation. Targeting her critique at the instrumentalization of global feminism toward ambiguous goals, at the erroneously homogenizing representational discourse by Westerners in regard with the Subaltern non-West, and therefore, implicitly, at mainstream, Western-based strategies of development and international human rights projects and social movements, Spivak (2001) identifies their main cause as the "absence of transnational literacy" and the "failure of translation," or "restricted permeability of cultural and linguistic translation":

> . . . the impatience of human rights interventions. . . too, is a failure of translation, after all. The patience and the respect required to weave the discourse of the subjectship of human rights on to the right-to-responsibility conflict-resolution systems historically available to the so-called beneficiary group, invariably stagnant under earlier regimes, is always lacking. In the absence of this particular brand of transnational literacy[...] human rights can become a nasty little weapon, working in the interest of the manifest destiny of the United States as the last best asylum for all. (16-17)

We argue thus that the ICTs employed in the global development activities, as in the case of the Web 2.0 tools used by the Kiva micro-lending organization, need to be examined in an analytical framework which emphasizes the importance of grasping the ways everyday practices and socio-cultural hierarchies circumscribe the production of online identities and processes of inclusion and exclusion (gendered, raced, classed online subjectivities) (e.g., Enteen, 2009; Gajjala & Altman, 2006; Nakamura, 2002).

Paradoxically, even feminist discourses of empowerment and cyberfeminist praxis that deeply inform logics of empowerment at the interface of nonprofits and of the Internet set the stage for, and become complicit in, local and global transnational formations. For instance, development websites online are susceptible to creating a monolithic, homogenizing imagery of third-world poverty, a poverty which is being marketed to and consumed by the Western gaze. Poverty, therefore, readily becomes instrumentalized in the service of globalizing economic goals, without attention to contextual complexities and hierarchies that might hinder the process of empowerment when not taken into account. Lingam (2008) contends, for instance, that "there are attempts to discipline women and communities and functionally cobble together "social cohesion" among the poor as a class without working on the deep-seated caste difference. This is a bigger challenge that is not amenable to solution by micro-credit programs" (135).

In this sense, fully aware that development models from the West can no longer be considered fully reproducible in third-world contexts, that universalizing categories disregarding context is a colonizing act in and of itself, Gajjala and Mamidipudi (2002) examine technological environments and community practices surrounding the situated design and use of technologies. They challenge the too often taken for granted, mere "transferring" of "so-called advanced technologies in the name of a notion of progress that is in itself situated in socio-economic, historical and political contexts not necessarily empowering to all communities of the world" (para. 8). Most importantly, they question whether "the bequeathed" are or are not empowered through the transfer of technologies produced and designed within socio-cultural environments situated in a Westernized and Masculinized world" (para. 2).

Gajjala and Mamidipudi (1999) bring forward a basic example, namely that of Venkatavva, a dark-brown, third-world woman from Adilabad, a community of weavers in rural Andhra Pradesh, India, for whom the measure of her empowerment, that is of choices accessible to her, is based as much on the failure of technology, not just its success: "Her children drink milk on the days that the bus doesn't run, because on those days the milk in the village can't be taken to the city and isn't worth money. On days the electricity fails she watches the traditionally performed storytelling enacted in the village square instead of the distant Santa Barbara on television" (14).

Globalization, through its emissary development projects and programs targeting the third-world cultures, turns out to be causing more harm rather than good to the livelihoods and well-being of third-world rural communities. Ghosh and Chandrasekhar (2004) trace the nefarious effects of neoliberal economic experiments implemented in the Indian state of Andhra Pradesh, such as the increasing rates of farmer's suicides and hunger deaths, in the massive shift toward "relying on incentives for private agents as opposed to state intervention and regulation of private activity." As they explain, it would be erroneous, as it is more than often presented, to contend that the dire situation is merely because the farmers and workers have been excluded from the process of globalization. The opposite, rather, is true: "they have been forced into market relations that are intrinsically loaded against them . . . , into market systems in which their lack of assets, poor protection through regulation and low bargaining power have operated to make their material conditions more adverse" (Ghosh and Chandrasekhar 2004).

The neoliberal paradigm of empowerment tends to disregard the range of political, economic, and cultural contexts that leave way to complex and sometimes contradictory possibilities for empowerment. In a critical ethnography engaging the financial activities among Sinhalese poor rural women in Sri Lanka, Chandrasekara (2009) reveals the ways local community socio-cultural aspects of finance practiced by these women produce social wealth beyond financial wealth and financial measurement. This outcome is in contrast with the current transnational financial system and its underlying principles. Sinhalese women observe a particular financial saving system, namely the *seettu*. This stands for household and group saving and is carried out and maintained through friendships, kin relationships and social relations:

> These community organizations develop *social wealth* through their thrifts, based on traditional practices of saving. Since transnational finance is driven by monetary values only, it overlays structures and that ignores local cultures, social networks and community identities necessary for the creation of social wealth. As a consequence, encounters with transnational finance inspire resistance . . . In an attempt to preserve their more traditional systems of exchange, such as *seettu*, communities find themselves working against finance. (300)

Along the same lines, Sharma (2008) explores the unintended results of empowerment as a technology of governance and development targeted at Indian subaltern women. One of the dangers of the neoliberal articulation of empowerment is the depoliticization of poverty and powerlessness, in that it has "quickly become a preferred tool with which to produce self-governing and self-caring social actors, orient them toward the free market, direct their behaviors toward entrepreneurial ends, and attach them to the project of rule" (xx). Exposing development as citizenship project in the case of Bolivia, Lazar (2004) suggestively describes the type of female citizens that development agencies and micro-credit NGOs strive to design in this country: "'empowered' individual, entrepreneurial, active citizens, who will take responsibility for their own and their families' welfare, and who are prepared for the market rather than the state to provide for their social rights" (301).

Online Nonprofits as Global

"Voice," marginalized or mainstream, does not emerge from the sheer need for the existence of a subject position. Rather the needs and pains of the unspoken of and unheard of populations the world over get voiced within contexts that make it possible for them to emerge and be recognized. Thus, as Spivak has suggested through her well-known work, "Can the Subaltern Speak," speech acts performed in resistance get rewritten, read, and voiced as subject positions that are slottable within an emerging mainstream logic. The making visible of the past and present practices of erasure of particular subject positions leads to the struggle for legitimization, which in turn leads to the formation of a subject position in future generations for which there is an acceptance (even if continually troubled and negotiated) within the mainstream.

There has been considerable celebration over how the Internet allows various marginalized voices to access the global and how empowering that is. Simultaneously, we see that there are many nongovernmental organizations (NGOs) springing up all over the world to champion some cause or the other. Among development NGOs representing the causes of underrepresented or marginalized populations, there is a particular type, namely the grassroots support organization, which functions as an intermediary, networking institution, fostering links between the beneficiaries (local disadvantaged rural or urban groups and individuals) and the otherwise inaccessible donors, financial institutions, and so on. This is the type of NGO that kiva.org, represents. Kiva is the sort of NGO that provides services indirectly to other organizations that support the poor or perform coordinating or networking functions" (Carrol, 1992). Nonprofits such as Kiva.org make use of the Web 2.0 social media tools to fulfill not only their networking function but also to permit actual financial exchange. In the process, the nonprofit's Internet-based interface provides a two-way access (albeit limited and mediated by various hierarchies of skills and technologies). Thus because of the offline groundwork performed by the nonprofit volunteers, the needy are brought to interface with people of comparative material privilege. However, in the process of being brought to interface with the global, the needy person is individualized in order that s/he can gain access to global systems. Thus we see that the nonprofit organization that creates access through its online platform becomes a key actor in bringing forth various economically marginalized voices into the global economic mainstream where the subaltern becomes a part of the neoliberal framework.

Such global nonprofit platforms are designed with the use of various persuasion formats and tactics not only to engage the mainstream but also to invite/lure the subaltern into the mainstream. In employing such tactics and formats for global networking, the NGOs attempt to give voice to marginalized populations and become advocates for particular causes. Kiva.org, for instance, is considered to be a very user-friendly platform for microfinance. As described in its own "About" section, Kiva "is the world's first person-to-person micro-lending website, empowering individuals to lend directly to unique entrepreneurs around the globe" (http://www.kiva.org/about). In this chapter, therefore, we look at how the interplay of online and offline connections and activities associated with this site impacts who speaks and how they speak in online microfinance sites such as kiva.org.

Social Media/Networks and Voice

Critical scholars focusing on voice have previously asked questions such as "who speaks" (Alcoff, 1993) and examined voice and silence in relation to material and discursive hierarchies, while liberal cyberfeminists and technophilic celebrators of the Internet make claims of the Internet's ability to allow voices from the margins to speak up (Landow, 1992; Rheingold, 1991). However, an examination of multiple and even chaotic voices as they emerge in these social networks allows us to highlight a different kind of disciplining role played by the technical interface and design. At the same time as the individual begins to feel empowered by the ability to speak up and to talk back to power in such networks, there is a quick and simultaneous appropriation occurring that quickly *places* this voice into a slottable position that can be located and categorized as known and knowable. However, it should also be noted that while appropriation occurs, there is also a certain kind of neoliberal empowerment occurring simultaneously.

In social networks—whether the explicitly leisure-oriented ones such as facebook and myspace or those formed to empower and finance individual groups from marginalized communities such as kiva—power plays out in nuanced, complex ways, and allows an emerging global capitalist status quo to reassert itself. Simultaneously, the structure does indeed allow for particular formations of marginalized voices to be centered and noted as empowered. Marina Levina describes the contradictory process and the appropriation of feminist notions of empowerment in her work on Health 2.0 websites. She writes:

> [E]mpowerment becomes part of an anticipatory regime that obscures the present interworking of network power in promising an empowered future self. I contend that Health 2.0 positions itself as a feminist apparatus ready to further the cause of women in cyberspace, while disguising its function as an anticipatory regime that appropriates feminist narratives of empowerment and then resells them to individual users. (Levina, 2012, 14)

In addition, we would argue that the way in which power plays out routes around these centered marginalized voices is by making them seem the exception to the rule who were able to lift themselves out of marginality by adopting values associated with the existing mainstream or, on the other hand, by exoticizing them (Gajjala,

Zhang and Dako-Gyeke, 2010).

Does this mean that the empowerment and voice gained by marginalized groups in such a setting—whether momentary or not—should be discounted as insignificant? No, that is not what we are arguing. We are signaling the process of emergence of multiple marginalized voices at the social network interface, while pointing to the simultaneous replacement of voice and identity in an emerging power structure. This process is tricky, in that it does not exactly replicate older hierarchies, but still rests on them nonetheless. We therefore urge that these shifts need to be scrutinized in order for us to understand what the paradigm and technical interface of "network society" might mean for us socially, culturally, and economically. Further, we are also interested in questioning whether just the fact of emerging voice in and of itself functions to empower. What expected and unexpected forms might this empowerment take and what paths, trajectories and networks are emerging to form current forms of globalization in digital platforms? Also what does this moment of empowerment mean for the various actors and contexts within and through which the voice emerges? Where does privilege and hierarchy shift, who and what does it oppress and why?

Online platforms are built through digital technologies that foster quick interactive moments through instant messaging, texting, frequent updating of status messages, continual blogging and tweeting. The technologies designed and the practices fostered necessitate and urge instant communication. This sort of instant and quick interactions may appear conducive to subversive and evasive one-on-one contact while in actuality they are simultaneously public and open to surveillance. As the case of the Egyptian Ahmed Hassan Bassouni, who was brought before a military tribunal and sentenced to six months in prison for setting up a page on facebook to advise people on issues related to joining the Egyptian military, demonstrates, the absolute insistence of Western-centric "democratic" rules regarding anonymity and free flow of information on the Internet actually backfire. In addition, the constant, almost whimsical, changes in privacy settings and guidelines in these online social networks exposes users to all sorts of legal hazards almost "accidentally." In the case of the subaltern on the margins of westernized democratic society—whatever her/his geographical location—the consequences could even be fatal. Thus the way power plays out in such contexts is nuanced and complex. A group of teenagers may produce "egocentric networks" on facebook and myspace as suggested by Boyd and Ellison (2007). But these same spaces also function panopticon-like to discipline subjectivities through uniform practices of work and play within such networks.

Production of Space and Identity through Digital Technologies of Knowledge Production

Kamari Maxine Clarke (2004) notes in her work on "Yoruba Networks" that travel and migration produce a shift from "spatial structure and organization to the process of producing space and identity with new technologies of knowledge" (p. 24). Such production of space and identity in offline materiality can be mapped through concrete following of bodies from particular locals to globals. Within online networks, however, the interplay of multiple locals at the site of the Internet-mediated global is more hidden and seemingly transient—thus making it difficult to capture and describe. Yet, the practices of producing networks and of socializing within these networks become multiply global and resituated and placed in various other different locals. This leads to replication and eventually standardization—a production of uniform social practice and norms through the use of the "third space" (Soja, 1996) of online networks based on practices that are assumed to be successful. Online networks can be viewed in this sense as allowing for the formulation of a "thirdspace," where third space represents—in Soja's reconceptualization of human interaction around the concept of space—"a product of a 'thirding' of the spatial imagination, the creation of another mode of thinking about space that draws upon material and mental spaces of the traditional dualism but extends well beyond them in scope, substance and meaning" (p. 11). This "third space" reinstates particular local hierarchies in different locales worldwide and names them as global. Clarke (2004) writes that

> shifts in capital, institutions, historical trajectories, and rules of citizenship resulted in the need to rethink not only the ways that agents in deterritorialized contexts reshape spaces to produce new meanings of place, but, most centrally, the relationship between particular places and . . . institutional "networks" that connect them. This shift from the local to the interplay between local and the global . . . is critical for understanding of how zones of interaction are not only imagined and shaped, but also aligned along domains of knowledge and power. (25)

While Kamari Maxine Clark is writing about deterritorialized space and territorialized subjects in offline networks, what she observes is relevant in online network contexts as well.

Networks, Social Network Sites, and Networking on Kiva.org

Among others, we draw on Kamari Maxine Clarke's (2004) conceptualization of networks in terms of territorialized subjects and deterritorialized spaces in order to critically explore microfinance online social networks. Tiziana Terranova's (2004) discussion of network culture, where she urges us to "think simultaneously the singular and the multiple, the common and the unique," is also useful to us as we draw from in-depth examinations of social network sites to point to the processes through which these social networks shape voice online. Differentiating between social network sites and the practice of social networking, Boyd and Ellison (2007) lay out what they see as the main features of social network sites. According to them, social network sites are Web-based services and

> allow individuals to:
> (1) construct a public or semi-public profile within a bounded system,
> (2) articulate a list of other users with whom they share a connection, and
> (3) view and traverse their list of connections and those made by others within the system. The nature and nomenclature of these connections may vary from site to site. (1)

They state that social *networking* does not necessarily happen on such social network sites. Thus even though social networking may sometimes happen on such social network sites, that is not the primary practice on such sites as those described by Boyd and Ellison. Thus they claim that social network sites are unique not because they allow meetings between strangers, "but rather that they enable users to articulate and make visible their social networks"; therefore, they claim that critical organizing features of these social network sites emphasize an "articulated social network" (Boyd & Ellison, 2007). However, they write about social network sites such as Friendster, myspace and facebook. In the case of kiva.org, the site we examine in the present chapter, the site is primarily about social *networking*. Users connect for economic reasons and the connections are mostly between borrowers and lenders for economic transactions focused on development and empowerment. Further, social relations are produced mostly online between groups of lenders with common lending interests and between borrower and field workers for kiva in mostly offline settings.

In what follows, in this chapter, we use specific instances of identity production and network interaction in kiva.org to develop the idea of emerging global networks by locating networks at online/offline intersections. These networks exist between virtual, imagined, anticipated social space and offline physical, material, socio-cultural and economic placement that includes practices of everyday life. Thus, we make a shift away from looking at representations of identities as stereotypes and essentialized identities across time and context. In other words we make a shift away from what Kamari Maxine Clarke (2004) calls the "geography of subjects within self-contained spaces" (2). Such a geography of subjects asks us to "relegate heterogeneity to homogeneity" while at the same time insisting on clear (yet artificial, even if political) boundaries between the named categories, and it is this geography of subjects that is mobilized in that service of contained and disciplined multiculturalism. Thus, while the examination of subjects within self-contained spaces provides important insights into stereotypes and the politics of representation within global media environments, and while we are not discounting the body of work that does this in relation to race and ethnicity in cyberspace, in this chapter we make a shift that allows us to look at the ways in which these networks legitimize dominant power hierarchies and how legitimation of membership in fields of power takes place. In order to examine the specific located intersections that produce specific identities and voices within networked environments online, we build on Clarke's conceptualization of "deterritorialized spaces" and "territorialized subjects."

Our conceptualization of "network" draws on Clarke's (2004) work and on Terranova's (2004) work. In what follows we draw on an examination of kiva.org to display the particularity of territorialized subjects located in layered online and offline networks and visible and invisible networks displayed in deterritorialized spatial networks. In order to get an understanding of how social networks contain territorialized subjects in seemingly deterritorialized space, we examine ways in which subaltern voice is placed in these socio-economic networks.

Kiva.org

Kiva.org is one widely noted case of microfinance online. It was founded in 2005 as a social entrepreneurship venture and is a not-for-profit, person-to-person, micro-lending website that acts as an intermediary that facilitates encounters between borrowers and potential lenders. The main objective of this site is to raise debt capital for microfinance institutions in developing countries directly from lenders. Its mission is to "connect people through lending for the sake of alleviating poverty," and it thus offers individuals the possibility to lend money to entrepreneurs/borrowers of their choice. The borrowers, mostly from developing countries but also from poorer populations in first-world countries, are cast as entrepreneurs who need funding for their small businesses. Traditionally, in the case of microfinance and its roots in rural South Asia, the borrowers were from populations that were not considered "bankable." However, in the case of online microfinance, it is not clear if the borrowers are all unbankable. The objective of online microfinance is to empower these small—scale entrepreneurs under the assumption that they will eventually be lifted out of poverty.

Compared to some other for-profit microfinance sites (such as microplace.com), Kiva.org's approach to the idea of poverty alleviation through micro-lending is slightly different, since its business manifesto subscribes to a not-for-profit micro-lending framework. To better understand its mision statement, we need to turn to the articulation of microfinance by the Nobel Laureate Muhammad Yunus, the promoter of not-for-profit micro-lending, founder and managing director of Grameen Bank, who "believes in the goodness of mankind, . . . calls us to rise above our baser instincts, . . . and warns that microfinance cannot return respectable financial returns and simultaneously remain responsive to the impoverished." However, Kiva's visual interface clearly negotiates the possibility of managing both practicality in relation to global financial processes as well as the ethics of micro-lending and philanthropy through such financial frameworks. The ethical dilemmas faced within the microfinance domain are manifested in the semiotic contradictions and negotiations visible in the ways kiva.org positions lenders and borrowers through its online public (inter)face.

Client impact transparency on the Internet underpins the intermediary role played by Kiva.org and is achieved through the work of Kiva's volunteering fellows who provide narrative descriptions of the borrowers' lives in their field journal online. This intimacy even as it is staged is nonetheless real, and relies on the affective pull at the interface. The intimacy fostered leads to relationship building between the middle-class lender and the subaltern through the weaving of online and offline and within a neoliberal framework of inclusion. This in turn produces a necessary condition of global altruism and cosmopolitanism. As Shameem Black notes, "Kiva's small-world sentiment offers a limited and limiting, but perhaps necessary, contribution to cosmopolitan practice"(Black 2009). This process of staging involves the use of social media, Web 2.0 tools. The diaries of Kiva volunteers document the impact of the microloans on the clients' businesses and lives, the pool of profiles of the clients/borrowers provide prospective lenders the possibility to make up their minds which individual/s to lend the money to, and, last but not least, the self-profiles of lenders or lending teams and groups make up the social network initiating the microloans. The networking practices fostered by Kiva help increase the chances of particular entrepreneurs in economically disadvantaged locations to get loans through exposing their needs to a much larger audience that, without the ICT solutions offered by Kiva, would be restricted to local contexts.

It is this logic and the impetus of globalization that compels NGO workers to reach out to global audiences and which necessitates the mobility of those who are geographically immobile such as indigenous peoples, immigrants and refugees who "become subjects of adjudication in human rights decisions, human rights and environmental activists." This is the logic that reduces them to the status of actors in global politics (Sassen 2004, p. 649). Sassen is quite optimistic about the constitution of new, empowered types of global subjectivities and politics, global domains and virtual public spheres. She traces two conditions that would make such a massive social transformation viable:

> One is the pre-existence of social networks, and it is here that the cross-border geographies connecting places, especially global cities, provide a conducive environment. The other qualifier is that it took a lot of organizing and work to develop adequate technical infrastructures and software to make this happen. Civil society organizations and individuals have played crucial roles. The result has been that particular instantiations of the local can actually be constituted at multiple scales and thereby construct global formations that tend toward lateralized and horizontal networks rather than the vertical and hierarchical forms typical of major global actors, such as the IMF and WTO. (650)

However, we take a more cautious stand regarding these conditions and their effects for the resource-poor actors. Manuel Castells (1996), for instance, warns about the socially and functionally selective diffusion of technology. He acknowledges that "large areas of the world, and considerable segments of population, switched-off from the new technological system" (32-33). Even when the issue is no longer that of lack of material access to technology, socio-economic and cultural power hierarchies and differentiated literacies lead to inequalities in participation. Close textual and visual analysis of Kiva interface shows instances where the Web 2.0 tools in fact reinscribe and reposition the Other within a spatial/territorial conception of the Internet. This territorial conception is in turn inscribed within a larger power structure that privileges particular literacies and cultural understandings. In this instance, there is no real possibility for lateralized, horizontal networks within the global formation of third-world micro-entrepreneurs. Moreover, the inclusion of third-world subjects into the mainstream global market, which at first sight appears as an act of benevolence toward the subaltern Others, is in actuality based in the logics of global business seeking to connect to mass markets. This is a context that leads to the commodification of Capital itself, and the digitalization of finance mobilizes transnational flows of Capital. Venture capitalists, businessmen, and more powerful investors worldwide can now sell packets of Capital to subaltern Others in exchange for real estate, equity and social capital—in the name of corporate social responsibility among other things (Deetz, 2007).

Within the polemics regarding the dominant space and place-oriented conceptions of the Internet, Enteen (2006) contends, contrary to the seemingly positive perspective of a network society, that hegemonic spatial conceptions of the World Wide Web extend and reiterate the contemporary geopolitical inequities in our offline world. In other words, they do not embody the transparency and "the connectivity and interdependence suggested by the term 'web'" (233). Territorial metaphors of the Internet have powerful ideological implications in that, like earlier colonial imagery employed to describe territorial incursion, they code social control, power of conquest, and hierarchical positioning into exploration and inhabitation, and thus might forcibly dislocate other discourses describing electronic communication (Enteen, 2006). As Enteen (2006) explains, "rather than recognizing the networks formed through online information exchange, the prevailing images of the Internet and world wide web locate individuals, not to mention data, within spatial coordinates" (229). Against an apparent deterritorialized condition made possible by cyberspace, Kaplan (2002) likewise argues that "a closer look reveals location and materiality in the mobility and disembodied discursive practices of new information technologies" (3).

Sometimes personal information is highlighted in the lenders' profiles while kiva fellows maintain blogs about borrowers' lives. Information in the lending team profiles also signals an understanding of the cooperative networking role of Kiva.org. Take for instance the following quotes by an American lender couple in the

"About" section of their profile page, "Cooperation is the key to making people feel less alone in this world" (Kiva Lender: Charles), or the info in a lending team's profile, "We loan because we care about the suffering of human beings," "Those of us who know we are one human family" (Kiva Lending Team). However, the principle of mass communication fueling this network site, that would ideally help transcend spatial metaphors and epistemes underlying hierarchical geopolitical sites in the name of globalization, is being hijacked by the ways in which the Web 2.0 networking tools are deployed within the economy of the Kiva.org site.

Kiva fellows' journaling about borrowers forms a keystone strategy that Kiva.org uses to build credibility within the global philanthropic system. Not only does this provide a platform for staging authenticity of the subaltern, the journaling serves to persuade prospective lenders of the reality (where the fellows from the U.S. provide evidence through acts of witnessing the subaltern sphere). This sense of reality also serves to convince the lender of the financial viability of person-to-person microloans, to assure the transparency of the impact of the loans on clients' livelihood, and to foster a degree of immediacy between lenders and borrowers, but it also produces specific subjectivities which are aligned with and informed by the general objectives of the organization. The profiles include biographical information about the borrowers and details about their businesses or business plans so that the overall content makes a strong case that facilitates website viewers' decision to start lending. In bringing the subaltern to the average middle-class lender's portal and empowering this middle-class lender to become a philanthropist through micro-loaning, the lenders get to build micro-networks along their preferred interests and causes. There are various groups formed by lenders aligning with particular group identity categories.

As a prospective lender, any Internet user can browse entrepreneurs' profiles uploaded on the website, and can choose someone to lend money to, using PayPal or credit cards. Any individual can join or create groups and recruit more lenders for specific types of borrowers. For instance, a prospective lender may choose to lend to a woman in Sierra Leone that needs the loan to buy peppers, cooking oil, fish, and onions in wholesale quantities for her small food market business. S/he may choose to loan $25, and s/he will be repaid within 6-12 months. The lender may then decide to relend once s/he is repaid.

Onsite, in the offline location, when the borrower is from a developing country, Kiva partners with local microfinance institutions (MFIs). These MFIs are responsible for selecting the qualified entrepreneurs as prospective borrowers. The MFIs have a process of their own that determines how they decide that entrepreneurs are qualified and how they are selected. Once the selection and vetting process that is locally done in the geopolitical location where the entrepreneur resides, the MFI teams in that location work with Kiva fellows to upload entrepreneurs' profiles onto the kiva.org online platform. The purpose of sharing these profiles is to ensure that future lenders can access their pictures and description and decide who they wish to microloan money to. As Sengupta and Aubuchon (2008) point out, in this process, "the lender does not receive any interest on their loan. Rather, journal updates and progress reports serve as interest, letting lenders know that their money has been put to good use" (p. 28). In 2009, more than half a million people had loaned over $76 million to 180,000 entrepreneurs in 45 countries through Kiva with a repayment rate of 98% ("Kiva launches Online Microfinance in the United States," 2009).

The total number of loans given out since the creation of Kiva until October 2011 was over $251 million dollars. This money was loaned out to over 648 thousand entrepreneurs around the world. In October 2011, there were a total of 1,004,334 Kiva users, out of whom more than half (633,008) had funded at least one loan. The average number of loans given by a Kiva lender is about 7 with each Kiva lender giving an average of about $250 dollars to a local entrepreneur. These lenders represent 216 countries worldwide, and 332,057 loans have been funded through Kiva since its inception. Out of the loans disbursed, 80.83% have gone to women with loans paid out to men representing just 19.17%. There was a high repayment rate of 98.90% with an average loan size of about $385.82 to individual entrepreneurs or groups. Kiva currently has over 143 field partners in 60 countries in the world.

In the rest of this chapter, we illustrate our arguments through examples and understandings drawn from a long-term collaborative research project that includes interdisciplinary participants and which was started in 2004 and 2005 when the first author of this chapter and her collaborator at that time, Annapurna Mamidipudi, worked on a project with the BASIX livelihood promotion institute (http://www.basixindia.com/) where they investigated the possibility of using online portals for the training of fieldworkers who worked in livelihood promotion. Financial inclusion services are provided by this institute, in addition to training and other livelihood promotion services. These financial services include rural microcredit lending. Later, the first and third authors of this chapter began to look at online networks for the empowerment of women along with a few other collaborators who had worked on projects resulting in the publication examining lexicons of women's empowerment and online nonprofits (Gajjala, Zhang and Dako-Gyeke 2010). The first and third authors of this chapter thus encountered kiva.org during that research project and proceeded to investigate. We drew in a development economist and a few other graduate student collaborators (see Gajjala, Gajjala, Birzescu and Anarbaeva, 2011) along the way, and the second author of this chapter then ended up taking up particular aspects related to the digitization of race in online microfinance and elaborating on this aspect in his dissertation. The first and third author still continue to examine digital financialization and nonprofits online through a transnational feminist lens in relation to offline nonprofits and movements to empower the subaltern in Romania and India. The second author of the current chapter proposes to look at issues of empowerment through the Internet in relation to the Ghana context.

Our analysis is based on continual examination of the site since it was first launched online in 2005 and specifically on detailed examination of over 35 lender profiles and over 35 borrower profiles along with membership in kiva teams and analysis of more kiva fellow journals for a period of two years. The kiva site managers keep making changes to the architecture of the site, in the name of improvements. Each example we use in this chapter is a freeze-frame of a particular time and particular relationships built through online/offline work and interaction based in the design and features offered through kiva.org at that particular time. In general, we approach this study through methods of textual analysis and visual analysis while critically engaging with the content and its seeming social implications. We use our knowledge and involvement in development contexts offline in first-world and third-world locations to assist in our examination. This study is thus a close look at the actual content of the website with a view to understanding the socio-economic transactions and processes that contribute to such Internet-mediated ways of micro-lending and borrowing.

While it is true that a majority of the borrowers came from developing nations, there were some profiles of borrowers who are based in the U.S. as well. The lenders targeted, however, are from the U.S. since Kiva is located in the U.S. and the transactions are listed in U.S. dollar amounts. The issue of foreign exchange through the paypal software and nation-state policies in countries such as India is often discussed in specific teams (especially team India) that want to lend to borrowers from those regions. However, we will not go into details of transactional problems and specific economic and political policy instances in this book. Suffice it to say that those are significant issues and do indeed affect access and the hierarchies produced just as the actual technical software conditions subaltern presence and absence in such space.

Meanwhile, the symbolic function of the visuals in the profiles themselves, whether of the lender or the borrower, is highly relevant to the understanding of hierarchies of globalization in these contexts. Various contrasts and binaries are produced through strategic absences and presences in the visual cultures of the Internet and they impact the everyday material conditions offline in the way they serve to distribute and redistribute cultural and material capital. In the case of most of the potential borrowers needing funding, subjects are positioned and framed as powerless and living in poverty. For instance, in the example of a profile of Lucila from Peru, in need of a loan from Kiva, the description of Lucila and her business is narrated through her personal, gendered life and situation (accompanied by images) as follows—where her role as mother and caretaking qualities are emphasized in a stereotypical manner and her business justified in terms of subsistence livelihood needs.

> Lucila is 40 years old and lives with her two children in the district of Olmos. It is an agricultural area with considerable trade and is known as the lemon capital . . . She has been raising and selling cattle for 10 years. She cares for her livestock in a location close to her home. Once they are fully grown she sells them to the general public or merchants who visit the area. She also is involved in farming. Her business provides an income for her children. Lucila wants to expand her business by buying

> more livestock so she can lower her prices and increase sales. She has requested a loan for 1000 PEN from Edpyme Alternativa. She is a responsible, active mother who wants to give her children the best quality of life (accessed at: http://www.kiva.org/lend/271951).

Lucila's description does not portray her in the same way as an entrepreneur in the Western world would be characterized. Nowhere do we see words and phrases that connect to popular ideas of entrepreneurship as dynamic, modern, aggressive. Rather she is a "responsible, active mother" trying to feed her children. Therefore the contradictory message here is that even though Kiva.org claims not to be giving charity—that it instead fosters and encourages entrepreneurialism and individual initiative—in actuality, the descriptions of borrowers like Lucila suggest the opposite. The lenders from backgrounds of comparative privilege are being given the opportunity to become philanthropists—not investors. In early versions of kiva.org borrower profiles—when two of the co-authors of this chapter began our study of Kiva—most of the borrower profiles contained snapshots that represented the borrowers with eyes cast downwards or not making direct eye contact with the camera. This is not just a simple coincidence. In fact this mode of representation continued even in 2011 (see http://www.kiva.org/lend/282533). The visual discourse does not allow Gaby, in this image, agency nor offer her the possibility to scrutinize potential borrowers. Gaby's loan of $375 was "to purchase ten units of woven cloth, two piglets, and "Chacachi" (regional animals)," and sure enough her value is implicitly equated with the rural and nontechnical nature of her needs. Gaby is seen sitting outdoors clutching a cloth bundle on her lap, hat behind her and a bag next to her. Rather than build social value for Gaby, the image invokes a homeless person to the lay person viewer from the more developed world. We do not see her in action with her skillfully woven cloth—we do not see her image contesting negative stereotypes of someone who is rural nor do we see her portrayed as an artist or as businesswoman. The camera here stands for the eyes of the prospective lenders since the photographic perspective substitutes the lenders' perspective. By contrast, in the lenders' profiles, the snapshots show them looking directly at the camera and their social value is elevated by the fact that they were able to help uplift the socially and materially backward Gaby.

The subject formation that is visible in these journals' content often relies on the highlighting of the contrast between third-world local knowledges and westernization and modernization (this sort of contrast is also visible in the struggles articulated by the co-authors and NGO officers who co-authored chapter 5 of this book). The borrowers' cultures are represented as a curious blend between primitive and modern. Emphasis is placed more on the unusualness of such hybrid subjectivities rather than on the circumstances underpinning their existence. This is demonstrable through the following testimony in one Kiva fellow's journal about her visit to a village in Guatemala:

> Someone asked me how it was that I seemed to have (almost) constant access to the Internet AND no indoor running water or heat. From an American perspective, it seems irrational and contradictory. But, Guatemala is filled with (seeming) contradictions and contrasts. I suspect that many of my "fellow" fellows have experienced the same in the countries where they are working. The family I live with has satellite TV, a wide screen television (and a television in every bedroom) but they have no indoor running water or heating. They still wash their laundry by hand in a lavadero, outside. They cook over a wood stove. The water for showers is heated by a fire lit under a big black drum, which they fill with water early, every morning (before the water runs out). They make their own masa from the corn that they grow. And they all have cell phones, MP3 players and their favorite "novellas" (soap operas) on television. (You Have Internet, but No Running Water? 2009)

You Are Fully Funded—Refreshing Content on Kiva.org

On Kiva, online social networking tools are used to create a global space for various local agencies and individuals to network and utilize the concept of microfinance. In order to observe the process of micro-loaning as it unfolds visually for the viewer of the website, we sat before a laptop and started to continually hit refresh while viewing a Kiva lender's page. What we saw was a visual "movement" of money—digitally adding on every time we refreshed the screen. We were examining the profile of Ana Maria Condore de Ramos, a married woman from Ica, Peru with two children. The profile was uploaded at 5:30pm ET on Kiva (at least that's when her profile first showed up for us as viewers). She had stated in her profile that she needed $725 for personal expenses. The loan indicator located on the right-hand side of her profile picture showed zero (0) %, indicating that she had not received any loans yet when we first saw her profile load. Within thirty-five minutes after the loan request had been posted online (as we repeatedly refreshed the website), she had raised 600 dollars (86%) of her total request. Thirteen lenders, most of whom had anonymous profiles, had loaned money to Ana. At 6:11pm ET (forty-one minutes later) Ana was fully funded by various lenders. Lenders were from the U.S. (Portland, OR, Salt Lake city, UT, Miami, FL, Austin, TX), from the Netherlands, and from Australia, among other countries. We examined other borrower profiles through this process of repeated refreshing. We noted that some of the loans posted by Kiva fellows got fully funded within five minutes of being uploaded.

While we did not examine the process and actual networks, online and/or offline, that facilitate the quicker funding of one loan over another, we know that there are various mechanisms of networking provided for lenders to cluster together in teams and to advertise, encourage and campaign for the funding of the particular borrower that sparks their interest. The speed with which the loan was funded could be attributed to the labor performed by some such lenders and others who wished to see their particular choice of borrower fully funded. Micro-transactional software such as paypal allows for ease of money transfer with no cost to the person transferring the money. They allow for the rapid transfer of money from individuals or groups in the United States to local entrepreneurs as far away as Kenya, Cambodia or Peru. Transnational lending networks such as Kiva contribute to the "dramatic levels of production and consumption" theorized by Andrejevic (2007).

The plethora of technological smart devices such as iphones, blackberries, androids, flip cameras, ipads and so on allow for various degrees of access for the materially privileged to engage in various forms of identity performances in cyberspace. These technologies offer "a virtual enclosure that allows individuals [or groups] to stay in constant contact with one another" (97). Such enclosures also function to produce "e-citizens" (Collin 2010), with thousands of young people being encouraged to participate politically in cyberspace. Similarly Kiva encourages people to civically engage in helping alleviate poverty around the world by lending to the poor. Andrejevic's (2007) notion of digital enclosure fits Appadurai's (1990) idea of the global configuration of technology (technoscapes) within which information is unleashed onto different technological trajectories. However, the speed varies depending on modes of access in the digital enclosure. For the global consumer from urban environments the ease of access requires as little as a tap on an iphone screen. However, for those who are being staged as the borrowers from lesser economically privileged locations, this process may take longer. Individual access to Web 2.0 technologies may entail physical travel to a local or distant Internet café and assistance from someone else with the skills and literacy required to be a participant in this global civic sphere.

For instance, the way in which Abena, a Kiva borrower (retrieved February 12, 2011 from http://www.kiva.org/lend/272022) from Ghana is portrayed shows no evidence of her possible access to digital technologies. Whether she has access or not, it is clear that her presence on kiva is made possible through a kiva fellow's representation of her. Structurally, as well, regardless of her own level of literacy or access, if she wishes to present herself as a borrower in need of funds, she must adhere to the structure rules and hierarchies set up to standardize how borrowers and lenders are portrayed. The first-world lender then is free to imagine that she may not have access. Because this visual representation is linked with stories that invoke premodernity, often narrated through the kiva fellows' journals, the lender envisions a person who is premodern. The ability to lend small amounts ($25) rather than larger donations to charity in a sense empowers the lender and builds social value to lenders even when they are unable to donate large sums of money, yet the social value of the borrower remains static. Implicitly, the first-world, modern citizen recovers her place in the global hierarchy as superior. Examining the image of Abena, one can see that this young entrepreneur is surrounded by basic technologies such as the two aluminum cooking pots, two three-prong clay potholders for cooking, long wooden ladles that allows her to reach into her pot to stir her fermented corn and cassava dough (banku—a staple food in Ghana). We also see a few pots and pans scattered around her. What we don't see are other technologies such as an iphone or any other devices that may be described as "smart devices" in the Western setting. Are we to assume that she is without agency because she is not portrayed as having ownership of digital and portable technologies? Whether she is or is not actually an active member of the digital enclosure and actually uses digital and/or mobile technologies, her image suggests that she is not and suggests that she is subaltern to the lender who lives among such techno-social ensembles. Whatever actual literacy and skills Abena possesses offline, the way her presence is showcased in the digital enclosure robs her of agency. Her identity is mediated and staged through Web 2.0 technologies that are culturally and ideologically associated with empowerment in the global sphere. Somehow this staging and so-called access—as objectified individual—allows the producers of the portal to imply that this subaltern can be rescued from her poverty through the Internet.

Digital Expressions

Kiva's peer-to-peer model of lending to the poor provides a "spatial customization" (Andrejevic, 2007, 102) that seduces the lender into a productive form of self-expression. We consider the lender to be the user of the online portal rather than the borrower in this case. The reason we say this is because the borrower avails of the services—micro-credit—but she or he is not the direct user of the online portal. Lenders on Kiva are given the opportunity to create profiles and images of themselves and also to choose to remain anonymous if they wish to. Johan and Esther (http://www.kiva.org/lender/esther2392), for instance, were amongst the lenders for Ana Maria Condore de Ramos whose profile we discussed earlier in this chapter. They created their Kiva profile page on January 29th, 2008, according to the information recorded on the profile site. At the time that we examined their profile they had made 53 loans to individuals and groups around the world and 77.4% of their loans went to females and 22.6% went to males (Kiva: Johan & Esther, 2011). Their profile photograph showed a happy couple with broad smiles on their faces, looking directly into the lens of the camera—their digital self-made identities (kiva avatars).

The description beside their photo states, "We want to help people who aren't able to start their own business to make a living. With only a small amount we can help them change their lives. It feels good to give!" (Kiva Lender: Johan & Esther, 2008). Johan and Esther are global citizens, empowered agents in the digital enclosure who seem to derive pleasure from the ability to donate. Entering this philanthropic digital enclosure did not require Johan and Esther to cross physical boundaries; they did not have to travel to Peru to physically lend money to Ana. All they had to do was to equip themselves with the appropriate technologies to provide information about themselves and to communicate with those on Kiva's network. They actually did not even have to establish direct communication with the borrower, nor did they have to build a long-term relationship with this woman from a distant culture. In short there was no real interpersonal or intercultural involvement needed. The task of relationship building in this instance could be outsourced to the kiva fellows who were young men and women from mostly first-world locations that travelled and blogged about potential borrowers and their native cultures. Not only did they need very little actual relational engagement, they also needed very basic everyday technological literacy. Andrejevic explained that entering into this digital enclosure means embracing interactive technology. The microfinance platform, however, protects the user from having to actually be interactive and involved. Kiva provides lenders like Johan and Esther with interactive tools such as the facebook's like icon (which links kiva effectively to the "like economy"), message boards, and the option to embed external links onto their customized spaces on Kiva, thus emulating the customizable myspace interface without actually requiring even the quite basic skills that used to be needed to customize a myspace profile. The interactive relationship building that occurs through these modes of networking is more with fellow lenders from similar socio-economic backgrounds than it is with the borrowers who continue to be conveniently at a distance, while appearing very close-by. Further, the kiva portal is designed so that no user can deviate too significantly in the customizing—the format is very standard and controlled. The tools that allow identity creation/modification/enhancement and circulation in cyberspace do not only provide people like Johan and Esther opportunities to help the poor without actually having to be with the poor, but they also allow them to feel digitally empowered as users of technology for connecting globally. They become global citizens through these fairly limited and constrained acts of profiling the self. Yet there is an intrinsic satisfaction exemplified by the expression "It feels good to give!" The product that Kiva is selling is this *feeling*.

Lenders, borrowers, Kiva fellows, and local microfinance institutions represent layers of dynamic digital webs in cyberspace. These webs have been woven through particular located practices of lending, relending, paying back of loans, postings of digital images of lenders, borrowers, and field partners through the virtual and social connections that are socially located. Both borrowers and lenders are being firmly pegged and put in their place with their roles in digital globalization easily carved out for them through the technological interface. Their technocultural agency is contained, networked and negotiated through two entirely different processes. The architecture within the platform as well as the offline steps and screenings (in degrees—for the lenders are implicitly "screened" upon entering the paypal system or when using a credit card) shapes the agency of users based on how it permits interaction. Both borrowers and lenders are actually subject to monitoring by Kiva and other authorities and technicians that control or access the digital interface. Further, for the borrowers, this relationship comes with rewards and punishments; they are rewarded with financial assistance in the form of loans and are punished if they fail to pay back their loans in full. For some borrowers it is a relationship in which they find themselves trapped.

Consuming the Digital

The interactive tools that Kiva offers to users present various possibilities for these technocultural agents to become global citizens. Kiva.org among others has introduced new ways of engaging lenders on their website by providing them with Web 2.0 tools that enable them to effectively browse and interact with thousands of images of third-world individuals. The process of lending to someone on Kiva has some similarities to buying an item online. For example, when a lender decides to lend to a borrower all she/he has to do is click on the lend icon, a copy of the borrower's photo floats from the original photo and makes its way into the lender's shopping basket, and the user is then notified that there is one item in the basket. The process of lending to the poor online, then, is similar to buying commodities online. You select your items and the items go straight to your basket, then you pay using paypal or your credit card. These digital representations of borrowers are thus commodities to be consumed. Kiva created an interface that closely resembles an online store where books, clothing, appliances and so on can be bought. The digital images of these borrowers, most of whom reside in developing countries, are treated like commodities for sale on Kiva.

When we go in and attempt this process of lending, it is possible to see that Kiva is also trying to replicate the process of shopping on sites such as Amazon.com where one has a cart to place selected items. Western and urban users of the Internet are already well trained in the use of such shopping tools online. Kiva reinforces these practices and the intrinsic and extrinsic rewards that come with them. The only difference is that everyday commodities like shoes, cell phones, books, clothes or groceries have been replaced by digital images of the poor for similar forms of consumption. Image economies on the World Wide Web thus posit new challenges and issues.

Visual and Social Impact

In order to better understand the implications of these representations for global social relationships, one should carefully consider several discursive formations contoured in these profiles. On the one hand, there is a resilient paternalistic rhetoric underpinned by the Western prescriptive ideology of progress and development with regard to "third-world" societies, and, on the other hand, a rhetoric of identity construction engaging a westernized multicultural middle-class. This takes shape through the establishment of categories of difference at the intersection of class, race, gender, and nation precisely through a sustained representation of the borrower as vulnerable. At work here is a practice of unidirectional cross-cultural encounters which encourages and reinforces a westernized gaze at the "third-world," but implicitly—and even unintentionally—denies respect and empowerment for the borrower within this online global space. Through the visuals and representations on Kiva, and advertisements we see that a modern global middle class seems to be undertaking the charitable mission of assisting and saving the poor in the underdeveloped world. As noted in a comment posted on a blog about Kiva, "what Kiva captured so well was the immediacy our culture thrives on, seen in countless ways and now through charitable giving—instant-gratification (give, be connected, see the instant results)" (Chang, n.d.). This renewed version of the image of the philanthropist from affluent countries becomes appealing to modern citizens, since it is strongly anchored in a global framework. Thus, for the sake of persuading other prospective lenders, a Kiva fellow argues that "you're a venture capitalist when you're on Kiva . . . you are financing somebody who is an entrepreneur in the developing world" (The Internet Archive, n.d.). Likewise, the founder of Kiva, Matthew Flannery, states that "the real solutions to poverty alleviation hinge on bringing capitalism and business to areas where there wasn't business or where it wasn't efficient . . . This doesn't have to be charity. You can partner with someone who's halfway around the world" (Kristof, N. D., 2007a).

Bringing Global Business Practices to the Subaltern?

To the extent that Kiva expands the debt capital for regional MFIs, its networking practices help increase the chances of entrepreneurs in economically weaker locations (those who have been screened and approved for loan disbursal by the MFIs) to get loans via the exposure of their cases to a much larger audience. Without the platform offered by Kiva, this would be restricted to local contexts. Kristof (2007b) further notes that, when we compare Kiva to other kinds of aid groups whose structure involves more paperwork and bureaucracy, Kiva appears to avoid those layers of bureaucracy. However, it is entirely possible that the hierarchies of authentication have shifted elsewhere, and that the layers have been moved into an offshore MFI location so that Kiva itself looks like a hassle-free interface. Therefore, the fact that Kiva avoids expensive aid groups by lending "directly to people who are screened only by groups with an all-local staff" (Kristof 2007b) does not necessarily constitute a step forward. Although, prima facie, it may seem as if Kiva has succeeded in lowering one component of the transaction cost—represented by multiple layers of bureaucracy and the huge amount of paperwork—a more detailed investigation is required to determine if staff costs incurred by MFIs (partnering with Kiva) for identification of borrowers (since the poor do not have access to the Internet), loan appraisal, disbursement and follow-up for monitoring repayment has indeed been reduced.

One the one hand, Kiva aims to bring Western (implicitly progressive) business practices to developing world contexts through the digital platform, yet on the other the organization admits to facing "an extremely unusual challenge of maintaining a supply and demand equilibrium (Walker, 2008), where borrowers must be supplied to lenders. A *New York Times* journalist quotes Kiva's public-relations director, Fiona Ramsey who states: "We don't want people coming to the Web site who want to make a loan and there's no one to loan to" (Walker, 2008). Thus there is a dual function performed by the platform and team of workers involved with the production and maintenance of the organization that bases its existence on this online platform. This dual function includes the commodification of the subaltern—the object to be consumed by the Western self—on the one hand and the production of a subaltern consumer and laborer for emerging virtual/global business.

Even then, there is a scarcity of potential borrowers. The reason for the scarcity of such micro-entrepreneurs is due to the lengthy process of vetting for prospective borrowers that is carried out by the local MFIs. Thus in fact the groups of networks that feed into the portal that is kiva are separated as haves and have-nots where the have-nots are more rigorously screened in order to be included in the community that is kiva. They have different rules of engagement and prospective borrowers are screened with the use of various kinds of criteria that involve both online and offline processes. The gatekeeping and screening processes are not easily understood unless one actually uses the online interface and also interacts offline with and through multiple online and other channels within the borrower locations. Even given the local bottlenecks, the unusual dynamic of Kiva's outreach to the lenders leads some users to get "so caught up in helping that they behave like collectors, looking to add new countries and new kinds of businesses to their portfolios (Entrepreneurs in Iraq and Afghanistan are particularly popular)" (Walker, 2008).

Do kiva loans really bring sustainable helpful economic transformations to potential borrowers? A *New York Times* article in 2009 suggested that there is also some confusion over where money lent really goes (Strom, 2009). Strom uses a blog post by David Roodman, a research fellow at the Center for Global Development in asserting that loans that are submitted on Kiva's website to be given to borrowers in poor countries do not really go to these borrowers. Rather, before the pictures and descriptions of potential borrowers are posted online, they would have already received the loans, and the local microfinance institutions will cover loan repayments so they can keep their high repayment ratings.

So are these borrowers really receiving the loans that have been pledged to them, or are the loans being diverted elsewhere? Some local microfinance institutions like Compartamos in Mexico charge their borrowers interest rates higher than 110 percent which supersedes the interest rates set by their lenders. This apparently allows local MFIs to achieve and maintain high ratings so they are able to attract more money (Hudon, 2008). In India borrowers have been rebelling against high interest rates imposed on them by local microfinance institutions by refusing to make payments on their loans, claiming that they were being exploited (Hudon 2008).

Producing Westernized and Global Subjectivities

In pursuing its mission to "connect people through lending for the sake of alleviating poverty," the online microfinance site offers individuals the possibility to lend money to entrepreneurs/borrowers of their choice. The apparently "unmediated" relationship facilitated through this portal is created through the online journals and videos about individual borrowers and the impact of the loans they received on their livelihoods. These are uploaded and updated regularly by Kiva volunteers termed as "Kiva fellows," who report from the offline site where the borrower lives. These diaries, written by such Kiva fellows and the online profiles of the lenders, each contain an inventory of all the borrowers that have received loans from the respective lender. Together, this visual cluster produces a westernized subject position that seems to have the ability to directly supervise and manage the process of empowering the impoverished Other from the other side of the computer screen. The lenders get to survey the borrowers, panopticon-like. The borrower and lender are thus produced as powerful imperial agents with the ability to manage the lives of the Others through their direct monetary contributions. Thus they are invited to become part of a mission to change the world into a better, more westernized (even implicitly Christian) place. The persistent recurrence of several terms on the website is intended to further advance the idea of a networked, horizontal agency/empowerment process, which goes beyond the traditional top-bottom empowerment paradigm. Words like *entrepreneur*, *lender*, *borrower*, and *(small) business* are thus a discursive confirmation for lenders on kiva.org that their actions are not just simple charity or donation, but rather investments in what is going to yield social return. For instance, James, a restaurant manager from Oregon, U.S., explains the reasons he loans on kiva.org:

> I'm not a wealthy person, but I get a great feeling by being able to help the Kiva entrepreneurs a little bit at a time. It's nice lending money to people in need and watching their progress and then helping someone else!

On the other hand, these same terms are pivotal in revamping the older version of the philanthropic image of the Westerner into an image of investor, which is at present far more appealing for the Western lenders since it is strongly anchored in a neoliberal capitalist ideology/mindset. Furthermore, one can also decode this as a discursive repackaging of the older image of the colonizer carrying out violent interventions to civilize the "uncivilized." Rather, this has been now replaced by the more palatable figure of the Western entrepreneur who, driven by capitalist ideals of progress and development, contributes to the alleviation of poverty in the third world. This is the figure adapted to contemporary globalization that Spivak (1999) describes as "an impersonal 'Economic Citizen,' site of authority and legitimation, lodged in finance capital markets and transnational companies" (276). A Kiva fellow notes "you're a venture capitalist when you're on Kiva . . . you are financing somebody who is an entrepreneur in the developing world." Nevertheless, the visual inventory of borrowers' locations in the lending history of each lender acquires a particular semiotic value recalling and suggesting imperial conquering and colonizing desires. The Google map view option one can find in the lenders' profiles makes possible a mapping of the receivers' geographical locations for all the loans made by a lender. The seemingly empowering network attributes of the Internet, which would ideally help transcend spatial metaphors and epistemes underlying hierarchical geopolitical sites, are being reinscribed into the hegemonic space and place-oriented conceptions of the World Wide Web. Originally intended to help network people in seemingly global deterritorialized online spaces, Web 2.0-based platforms can therefore easily reposition the Other within a territorial conception of the Internet.

Referring to the novel development paradigm promoted by kiva.org, co-founder Jessica Jackley emphasized that the "Others" on kiva.org have an active voice in the process of gaining their own empowerment. They actively take part in this process and they therefore cease to signify a remote, monolithic "Other." However, a more cautious reading of the textual and visual content on kiva.org highlights that, even though they are not silent and frozen in time and space as "Others," these emergent voices turn into monophonic third-world markets for the Western venture capitalists/investors. The Subaltern Other, a composite of economic class as well as racial, ethnic, geographical Otherness, is indeed allowed a space to emerge into global space through kiva.org. Nevertheless, the visibility of the Others is being constructed as an exception to the rule. The technical design and interface produces their voices as mainstreamed, and thus their possibly initial subversive nature is neutralized. This discursive strategy at play on the Kiva website reminds us of the Barthian concept of inoculation, a rhetorical form attributed to the bourgeois representation of the world. As Barthes (1972) explains, "one immunizes the contents of the collective imagination by means of a small inoculation of acknowledged evil; one thus protects it against the risk of a generalized subversion" (150).

The exposure of the Western subjects to the Subaltern Others at the website interface makes the Western, capitalist imaginary come to terms with their difference but only to the extent that that difference can be framed by the Western context as nonthreatening. Juxtaposed with numerous images of the third-world Other as terrorist or the raced and classed Other as criminal, the framing of this Other within such philanthropic contexts allows the Western and/or global Internet-using bourgeois self to feel in control. Furthermore, this process of exposure which prompts the third world Other to become known and knowable to the Western Self in a relationship of subordination may be attributed historically to the experience of imperialism and colonialism.

The partnership relations fostered on kiva.org can also be exposed when considering the mediated representation of the borrowers. The individual in need of a loan is first chosen to be represented as an adequate borrower by a local MFI—that is, the appropriate and token native informant with correct business practices. Next s/he is represented in the Kiva fellows' diaries, and the Web 2.0 tools themselves are filters which shape the final representation of the borrower. Thus the borrower image is managed at multiple levels so that the borrower appears deserving of the loan. By comparison, the lenders are far more in control when negotiating their representation on the site, having direct access to the website and related digital technologies. The knowledge and representations implied by the profiles' discourse can be further understood when taking into consideration their implications in real social power relationships. In this sense, there are particular discursive formations contoured in the Kiva profiles. At work here is a practice of unidirectional cross-cultural encounters which encourages and reinforces the Western gaze at the "third world," but denies the backtalking or the Other's gaze at Western subject positions. However, in the context of Web 2.0 technologies, the claim of interactivity is made as evidence of willing participation and choice on the part of the subaltern Other. "Third world" and racialized subjects are thus produced as empty/floating signifiers always ready to hold the meanings dictated by a neo-imperialist worldview and, implicitly, to reinforce a particular westernized subject location. The symbolic function of the visuals is highly relevant to the degree to which the contrast between absence and presence in the discourse produces othered subjectivities characterized by powerlessness, poverty, and piteousness. In comparison to the lenders' profiles, there are borrowers' profiles where the fact that the snapshots represent the borrowers looking down or in any event not making direct eye contact with the camera is not just a simple coincidence. The photographic discourse thus refuses agency and the possibility of scrutiny to the borrowers, objectifying them and eclipsing any real opportunity of "looking back" in a dialogic encounter with the camera. The camera stands here for the eyes of the prospective lenders since the photographic perspective substitutes the lenders' perspective. By contrast, in the lenders' profiles, the snapshots show these looking directly to the camera eye in an individualized, uncensored process of knowing and scrutinizing.

Entering New Frontiers: Kiva's 3D Virtual Presence

Kiva also developed a presence in the virtual world, Second Life. Immersive virtual worlds like Second Life are creating new opportunities for organizations like Kiva to raise money for their cause. In 2006 and 2007, there was much hype about Second Life and the ability to make money there working for and setting up corporations and/or advertising for them in new ways. This was a time when there was a surge of information about how virtual artifacts from games such as World of Warcraft were being auctioned on Ebay and how gold farmers in these worlds were making profits. In an attempt to cash in on the wave of commercial demand for virtual artifacts in games such as World of Warcraft and the formation of virtual economies in such game worlds, social virtual worlds such as Second Life attempted to build their own versions. While the corporatizations did not take off as successfully as expected or desired, it is possible to see, in 2010 and 2011, that many nonprofits are using Second Life in various ways. Second Life and the 2006-2007 boom in Second Life activity is discussed in more detail through rad Zabibha's experience later in this book, but for now it is enough that we note that nonprofits and activists are exploring options for the use of such virtual worlds for advocacy and community building—perhaps because a large portion of the world's middle-class younger generations are considered to be "there."

Thus Kiva has also set up a presence there. Kiva is giving away free virtual jackets, shirts and other virtual artifacts in order to invite more people to donate in Second Life, and communication networks are being established with thousands of avatars to help spread the word of kiva—that is, helping the poorest of the poor in developing countries. Nonprofits like kiva must find ways to sustain their efforts, and to basically survive in the competitive world we live in today. So we find them on Second Life employing various strategies to raise more money for their cause.

This chapter began with a description of kiva.org from a motivational speech given by its co-founder, Jessica Jackley. Her presentation and her online micro-lending endeavor can be indeed viewed as a feminist effort within the global development projects and actions. Further in this public talk, Jessica Jackley explains the range of personal experience, feelings, and reasoning that progressively lead to the launching of kiva.org. There are two instances in the text of her talk that are of particular relevance to our discussion guided by a transnational feminist approach. Jessica Jackley wishes to emphasize specifically the distinction between two empowerment paradigms, namely charity/donation versus transnational investing/micro-lending. In the following excerpt, she talks about the weaknesses of the former and the strengths of the latter, making use of powerful rhetorical appeals in her argument:

> I began to fear this group of people and to feel negative emotion towards a whole group of people. I imagined in my head a kind of long line of individuals that were never going away, that would always be with us. . . I gave when I was cornered, when it was difficult to avoid, and I gave, in general, when the negative emotions built up enough that I gave to relieve my own suffering, not someone else's. The truth be told, I was giving out of that place, not out of a genuine place of hope and excitement to help and of generosity. It became a transaction for me, became sort of a trade. I was purchasing something. I was buying my right to go on with my day and not necessarily be bothered by this bad news. And I think the way that we go through that sometimes can, first of all, disembody a group of people, individuals out there in the world. And it can also turn into a commodity, which is a very scary thing. So as I did this, and as I think many of us do this, we kind of buy our distance, we kind of buy our right to go on with our day. I think that exchange can ac-

> tually get in the way of the very thing that we want most. It can get in the way of our desire to really be meaningful and useful in another person's life. (Jackley, 2011)

Kiva.org co-founder's reading of the ambiguous discursive effects of the charity paradigm connects with transnational feminist conversations about the framing of the Other within this specific empowerment approach. The challenging aspects concerning the monolithic representation of the Other, the hidden motivations and desire one has when searching for/knowing the Other as well as issues of appropriation, commodification, and consumption of the Other, resonate well with the problematization of processes of empowering the Subaltern.

In contrast to the charity framework, which presupposes a top-bottom linear perspective, Jessica effectively argues in her talk for a more participative approach to empowerment, namely transnational investing/micro-lending, which envisages the active involvement of the Others in the process of empowerment. This approach is represented by kiva.org:

> It's about retelling the story of the poor, and it's about giving ourselves an opportunity to engage that validates their dignity, validates a partnership relationship, not a relationship that's based on the traditional sort of donor beneficiary weirdness that can happen. But instead a relationship that can promote respect and hope and this optimism that together we can move forward. So what I hope is that, not only can the money keep flowing forth through Kiva—that's a very positive and meaningful thing—but I hope Kiva can blur those lines, like I said, between the traditional rich and poor categories that we're taught to see in the world, this false dichotomy of us and them, have and have not. I hope that Kiva can blur those lines. Because , as that happens, I think we can feel free to interact in a way that's more open, more just and more creative, to engage with each other and to help each other . . . Second thing that I've learned is that loans are a very interesting tool for connectivity. So they're not a donation . . . And then third, from what I've heard from the entrepreneurs I've gotten to know, when all else is equal, given the option to have just money to do what you need to do, or money plus the support and encouragement of a global community, people choose the community plus the money. That's a much more meaningful combination, a more powerful combination. (Jackley, 2011)

The personal take on kiva.org in the excerpt above becomes a persuading set of arguments which acknowledges kiva.org's approach to empowerment and development. This approach appears to answer some of the key objectives discussed/addressed by critical feminists in reference to more traditional development perspectives that failed to fulfill them: the discursive debunking of the dichotomy of us versus them, a top-bottom perspective to development, community versus individualistic perspective to empowerment.

The well-intended presenter announces here a courageous undertaking likely to become subversive of the traditional dominant theory and praxis of development.

However, as discussed throughout this chapter and addressed in our analysis, the technical interface and paradigm of network society helps maintain and reaffirm, in complex and insidious modes, the global capitalist status quo. They allow at the same time for particular formations of marginalized voices of the Subaltern Other—a composite of economic class as well as racial, ethnic, geographical Otherness—to surface as exceptions to the rule, thus attenuating and even neutralizing their initial subversive nature.

Even more dangerously, the optimistic vision of poverty reduction by means of microloans and micro-entrepreneurship entirely disregards a crucial element that would otherwise radically change the perception by the audience of the development pattern so energetically promoted by the kiva.org co-founder. Equally, as shown in the visual discourse on the kiva.org micro-lending site, there is a total erasure of the historical, economic, and social circumstances as direct sequels of colonialism that produced modern poverty in third-world locations through displacements of local socio-economic systems. Through a process of decontextualization through online representations, poverty is depoliticized, and becomes an expression of these individuals' mere economic backwardness or incompetence. This erasure is all the more outrageous, in the cases of for-profit micro-lending NGOs. Profiting from micro-lending continues, in a vicious circle, the legacy of the colonial circumstances that had caused in the first place the economic inequalities upon which these institutions now depend, and, at the same time, it is "universalized as socially responsible" (Nadesan, 2010, 17). Nadesan (2010) further argues in this sense that

> microenterprise and microlending subtly appeal to Western audiences and business interests because they erase Western complicity in producing vast impoverishment in the developing world. Simultaneously these appeals absolve Western audiences of any responsibility for the failure of their governments and corporations to adopt economic and political policies that position the countries of the developing world as global equals.

The kiva.org co-founder contends that the Others acquire on kiva.org an active voice in the process of their own empowerment, that they actively and responsively take part in this development process, and that they cease to signify a remote, immobile "Other"; nevertheless, our analysis highlighted the risk for these emerging voices/voicing to transition from silent "Others" to a monophonic third-world market for the Western venture capitalists/investors.

It would be not entirely preposterous thus to argue that online social network sites like kiva.org, precisely because they advocate for development and poverty alleviation through a model of "transnational investing," and not simply by charity, might have the tendency to display a homogenized market of third-world micro-entrepreneurs for foreign investors from developed countries. Indeed, microfinance has become increasingly a job market niche promoted by international social actors and entrepreneurs from the Western hemisphere. Recruiters within the microfinance sector also acknowledge the important influence of ICTs on microfinance activities; hence their growing focus to promote and raise awareness about microfinance/social entrepreneurship job opportunities among college students/graduates—a population segment that possesses a comparatively higher ICT literacy than older generations.

Microfinance training efforts are being already made by learning institutions. For instance, University of California's Haas School of Business, has been offering introductory courses in microfinance, simulcast to more than 50 other business schools around the country[2]. Themes usually covered by such classes include microfinance and the history of informal savings; the major components of microfinance's ecosystem; an overview of issues in microfinance: gender, impact, alternatives; rates of return and cost of money; individual versus group lending; management challenges of MFIs; scale issues, strategy drift, and sustainability; applicability of entrepreneurship; gaining liquidity for investors; introduction to products in addition to loans, for example savings, insurance, and education; selecting an investment vehicle and process; assessing sustainability, and so forth. We argue that such normative discourse about microfinance and social entrepreneurship, which mainly emphasizes a profitmaking objective and, at the same, downplays the initial goal of poverty alleviation prophesized by microfinance projects, exposes development as pretext for further access to new resources and entry into new markets.

Nadesan (2010) critically articulates the underpinning motivations for the increasing promotion of micro-lending prompting the West to embark on such social entrepreneurship endeavors:

> As the opportunities for expropriating value from Western consumers decline with ongoing Western debt deflation, the institutions and agents of Western financial capital are looking for new terrain to colonize. The untapped populations of the developing world have emerged as a new focal point for the extension of credit and the creation of debt. Since Western forms of debt instruments such as credit cards and mortgages cannot easily be deployed among the world's most impoverished and unbanked populations, financial capitalism has developed a new strategy, microlending. (20-21)

In this chapter, our goal was to problematize the discursive processes of production, consumption and representation at play in transnational online microfinance lending sites formed through socio-economic Web 2.0-based software and also to show how development projects are being globalized through digital and wireless tools. Kiva.org is a very prominent and successful example of an online global microfinance site and continues to be a leader in the development of online/offline practices for the administering of Development 2.0 and Philanthropy 2.0. Other sites such as Lendingwithcare.org and Microplace.com will be discussed in the next chapter.

Notes

1. TED (Technology, Entertainment, Design) is owned by The Sapling Foundation, a private nonprofit foundation devoted to "ideas worth spreading. TED traces back its beginnings in 1984 as a conference "bringing together people from three worlds: Technology, Entertainment, Design." The owning Sapling Foundation has sustained in the past projects that "use these tools to leverage every dollar spent and create sustainable change in areas such as global public health, poverty alleviation, and biodiversity." TED, in particular, "aims to provide a platform for the world's smartest thinkers, greatest visionaries and most inspiring teachers, so that millions of people can gain a better understanding of the biggest issues faced by the world, and a desire to help create a better future" (retrieved from TED website: www.ted.com/pages/view/id/42).
2. "The course explores why and how microfinance operations have grown to provide financial services to poor and low-income people on a sustainable basis. The course brings together advice and best practices from successful practitioners and institutions around the world as well as new technology startups targeting the industry." (www.mficonnect.com/group/berkeleymicrofinancesimulcastgroup)

CHAPTER TWO

PHILANTHROPIST OR INVESTOR? MICRO-LENDING TO THE OTHER

Radhika Gajjala, Anca Birzescu and Franklin Yartey

Global (Online) Microfinance

This chapter continues the line of investigation regarding the staging of the subaltern on microfinance online platforms that the previous chapter was engaged in. We draw on the same methodologies of visual and textual analysis, from the same critical frameworks as in the last chapter. In addition to elaborating on implications of themes that emerge from the examination of kiva.org, we look at how two more global micro-lending platforms—lendwithcare.org and microplace.com—produce a discourse of neoliberal modernity. As we noted in the previous chapter, kiva.org emerged as a leader in online microfinance and showed how online microfinance portals could become global microfinance organizations. Lendwithcare.org and microplace.com are two more online microfinance models that are global but function slightly differently. While one is produced by a well-known international nonprofit, CARE, which is an organization that is already global, and sustained by an offline organization that existed prior to the online microfinance site's existence, the other is produced by the commercial venture, Ebay that had built a global reputation prior to and independent of its acquisition of microplace.com. CARE International is based in the UK—a country that is one of the world's leading trading powers and financial centers, and that has the third-biggest economy in Europe after Germany and France (Central Intelligence Agency, 2011). CARE International works in more than 70 countries worldwide, and due to their long history of providing relief to people around the world, the lendwithcare.org site is therefore culturally and financially located within CARE International's powerful network.

Sure enough, while CARE explicitly fosters the discourse of philanthropy, Ebay produces a discourse of the micro-lender as investor. In this chapter, we describe some examples from these two platforms to show how this happens. For instance, unlike Kiva.org that started in the U.S. and continues to be located mostly in the U.S. but becomes global in its services and networks, lendwithcare.org was developed by a global nonprofit organization that was already an established global NGO. Microplace.com, on the other hand, was founded, like kiva, by a woman entrepreneur in the United States (Tracey Pettengill Turner) and is actually considered to be the first (and only) broker-dealer that specializes in microfinance securities for retail investors. But soon after, it was bought out by Ebay Inc., which had been started in 1995 and already had a global presence as a leading online auctioning and shopping platform where collectors' items (actual offline material objects) and antiques as well as virtual goods such as World of Warcraft artifacts and such were being sold and bought globally. Advertisements for this microfinance platform appear to users of Paypal as we go about our buying and selling of consumer goods online. Images flash across the screen to show us how, with a click of the mouse, we can be global modern citizens who empower backward and exotic "others" in rural Asian settings to become "individualized and global" producers and laborers. The reality of the loans on borrowers' lives is authenticated by means of virtual Web 2.0 tools. Thus, the goal of such a social-media-based visualization of the actual impact of the loans through online text and imaging is to show lenders that these loans are "real."

The two online microfinance sites we discuss in this chapter are different from Kiva in that they are sustained by online and offline organizations that already have global presence. In what follows, we describe the differences between kiva, lendwithcare and microplace. Finally, we discuss some implications of the marketing model of development that emerges from how these platforms function.

Globalization & Web 2.0 Technologies

In April 2010, the World Bank launched a competition that challenged software developers to create software applications related to one or more of the Millennium Development Goals (MDGs) using World Bank data. Several software developers from World Bank member countries were invited to participate in this contest (Apps for Development, 2011). These applications were supposed to assist in lifting people out of poverty, make people healthier, help people educate themselves, and improve the general wellbeing of people around the world by bringing technology and development together. Prizes to winners ranged up to $45,000 dollars. Some of these Web 2.0 technologies and smart phone applications will now be used for various development projects around the world. Web 2.0 and smart phone technologies have contributed to the redefinition of globalization and digital finance in the ways that allow for mobile consumers and investors. For example, nonprofit volunteers working for online microfinance platforms travel around the world and interview borrowers in developing countries. They use this information in the production of profiles for kiva. They also report out from these locations and write field journals online. The discourse being disseminated by Kiva, however, tells just one side of the globalization narrative, which is the happy side or the desirable story (Hay & Rosamond, 2002). Advocates of current-day modernity who celebrate globalization unproblematically (e.g., Friedman, 2005), paint a picture that shows globalization as beneficial and uplifting to everyone around the world. But what Friedman fails to communicate is that although globalization has brought certain modern benefits to society, a majority of poor people continue to struggle for the bare necessities of life (Parameswaran, 2008).

Drawing parallels to kiva, we see a one-sided story being told; we see advocates disseminating only one part of the globalization discourse. The discourse describes people in the developing world as needy, and the people who lend money to the poor as materially privileged. People in third world countries are thus positioned as weaklings by default. Even if this is a strategic articulation on the part of low-resourced nonprofits from within developing world contexts meant to gain access to very much needed material and other resources for underprivileged populations, the impact of the discourse produced feeds into an overall cultural imperialist framework. The discourse represents technologies as enabling the bringing together of the "good people" in the developing countries to help the poor and disadvantaged of the third world. This discourse does not tell the other side of globalization. In her work examining discourses of globalization in the media, Parameswaran (2008) notes how the local conditions and disruptions that make the success of outsourcing possible (in India for example), are left out of the global discourses surrounding the success stories of outsourcing. The fact that women are stigmatized by their family due to the long hours they work at call centers and the fact that many outsource workers are prone to panic attacks and other stress-related illnesses because of the nature of the work and the kinds of hours they put in, for example, are left out in the globalization narrative.

Similarly, the globalization discourse that Kiva represents shows a space where third world bodies are showcased, and empowered through loans from people of the West. There is no requirement that the prospective lenders on such sites actually become familiar with the local contexts and complexities of the borrowers' lives. There is an illusion of relationship building through hyperlinking and staged narratives with the only actual transaction that occurs being financial through platforms such as paypal. Digital money transactions form the only actual evidence of the relationship between the lender and borrower—and even that is mediated through online software, banking systems, the organizational platform of Kiva and the local microfinance institutions onsite. The question here is not just whether these narratives and digital representations of third world bodies are fair to the offline bodies they represent. It is not just about visual representation even though our analysis is of the visual. The visual produces an interactive (im)possibility and configures—guides and even dictates—the kinds of relationships that develop between the materially more well-off lender and the borrower from materially underprivileged parts of the world. Further, the online platform—the technological interface—also serves as a silent gatekeeper for both the development workers and the well-meaning philanthropists.

Globalization is not smooth and calm in its effects, but rather, it can be rough, unpredictable, and disempowering in its workings and impact on society.

Not only is the inequitable access to technology in low-income regional contexts (whether in remote underresourced Africa, Indonesia or the low-income areas in Cleveland and Detroit) at issue, but the fact that the control of information posted on online development platforms such as Kiva.org is mainly in the hands of mediators—who themselves have partial control in designing the interface—compounds issues of unevenness of access and representation in global public space. Financial transactions are "publicly" privatized and increased layers of literacies and skills become necessary for the individual to actually gain access to self-determination and choice in information sharing and financial control. This discourse ends up being monologic and is furthered through online socio-financial platforms for philanthropy and development work as well.

In the current chapter, we continue to examine global, online microfinance portals to try and understand the role of online discursive and visual interface mediation in the production of two kinds of roles allowed to the lender on these platforms that in turn shape the materially and socio-culturally more privileged self "relationship" with the subaltern Other. The two frameworks visible, we claim, are that of the philanthropist and the investor. The examples used here are lendwithcare.org and microplace.com.

Lendwithcare.org

An interesting phenomenon is the influence of kiva.org's micro-lending project on internationally well-established development organizations. A particular example is that of CARE International UK, part of the CARE International confederation, that stands for "one of the world's leading aid and development organizations." CARE has embarked on microfinance projects and launched the lendwithcare.org micro-lending website which replicates the online microfinance social network pioneered by kiva.org. Within the lending model visible on lendwithcare.org, an entrepreneur in a developing country may get a loan from a local microfinance institution (MFI) if the MFI deems her/his business plan to be worthy of funding. The local MFI then assists the entrepreneur to create and upload a profile on lendwithcare.org. The information thus placed online can be accessed by prospective lenders through the online platform. Lenders are provided a supply of borrowers—staged in a way that is intended to catch their interest. Lenders are also offered a menu of optional amounts they can lend, starting with the minimum amount of £15. Once an entrepreneur is fully funded online, the money is transferred to the local MFI. The MFI conducts the remaining transactions offline with the borrower. Details of these local transactions are invisible to the lender. Once the entrepreneur/borrower pays back the loan, lenders can withdraw their money from the lendwithcare.org platform online with no interest accrued. A small percentage of the amount of money is held back for reinvestment. Lenders are then given the option of relending to someone else or to donate the remaining money to lendwithcare.org. Thus the steps involved in lending via this site are mostly the same as the steps in lending through kiva. In the spirit of "epistemologies of doing," the first author (Gajjala) of this chapter did become a lender on at least one of the online microfinance portals discussed in this book to learn about this process.

The adoption of microfinance by development and charity institutions such as CARE is significant, however, in several ways: it reveals a paradigm shift within international development strategies proposed and implemented by developed nations. For instance, on the lendwithcare.org website, a critical eye might find striking the juxtaposition of two different conceptualizations of the poor. This can be noted on the "About Us" page, within the subsection presenting the current achievements and mission statement of CARE. Specifically, as can be seen in the excerpt quoted below, there is a shift in how economically disadvantaged individuals in need of help are labeled. The economically disadvantaged are described in a way that implies they are helpless while being referred to as "entrepreneurs":

> Today, we work in more than 70 countries across five continents. Although our efforts have expanded, our mission remains the same—helping poor families to change their lives for the better. At the heart of our global reach is a local focus. Ninety pence in every £1 we receive goes directly towards our poverty-fighting work. And over 90% of our staff are locally hired, which gives us invaluable access to poor communities and a profound understanding of their difficulties. To find out more about how we are helping to transform lives right now, click here. Lendwithcare is currently active in Togo, Benin and Indonesia, we will bring you entrepreneurs from The Philippines very soon, followed by Guatemala and India. (lendwithcare.org)

By offering microfinance services to the poor—suddenly labeled as entrepreneurs, CARE acknowledges the crucial importance of including the poor in westernized global market structures by giving them mediated access to digital financial systems. There is a suggestion that such systems provide the most efficient way for the poor to lift themselves out of poverty, regardless of the extra layers of mystification that this sort of online financial system adds. Even as extra layers of skilling and access are added on, the idea sold to the westernized lenders is that this online financial portal makes access simpler and easier. Herein lies a major contradiction in digital financialization moves currently underway through structures of multinational corporatization that heavily influence present-day modes of globalization.

Meanwhile, CARE continues to make promises such as "we will bring you entrepreneurs from The Philippines very soon, followed by Guatemala and India," in what looks like a direct appeal to the enlightened people of the First World. This helps produce and reaffirm two types of subjectivities. CARE seems to assume the role of a supplier of commodities through its lendwithcare platform. The commodities come in the shape of entrepreneurs/borrowers. As retailer, CARE appeals to prospective lenders from the Western audiences and facilitates their investing activities in the Third World countries mentioned earlier. Moneylending thus gives them access and entry into third-world lives and lands. The economically disadvantaged bodies and their lives are offered up as opportunities for investment in businesses. The borrower becomes entrepreneur by entering into a contract with the lender. Her/his success as entrepreneur is implicitly dictated through the cultural logics within which the lender resides. The Western audiences emerge discursively as prospective investors.

Here we see a new framework of development, all the more attractive for the Western lenders, in contrast to the older version of the philanthropic image of the Westerner. It is strongly anchored in a neoliberal capitalist framework. Also, the older image of the colonizer carrying out violent interventions to civilize the "uncivilized" now seems to have been replaced by the more palatable figure of the Western investor who (driven by capitalist, neoliberal ideals of progress and development) contributes to the alleviation of poverty in the Third World. This figure adapted to contemporary globalization represents what Spivak (1999) describes as "an impersonal 'Economic Citizen,' site of authority and legitimation, lodged in finance capital markets and transnational companies" (276). Such a discursive strategy further illustrates a new form of imperialism, namely digital, that circumscribes the formation of the new Subaltern in the current international division of labor. This particular form of imperialism was described by Spivak (1999) as "a displacement of the divided field of nineteenth-century territorial imperialism" (274). It is easier to grasp the reconfiguration of empire digitally, if we see the "Third World" as a "displacement of the old colonies," and if we understand that colonialism "displaces itself into neocolonialism," while recognizing that neocolonialism stands for "the largely economic rather than the largely territorial enterprise of imperialism"—all these interconnected with the dynamics of the financialization of the globe (3).

Furthermore, in taking on a microfinance approach to development and thus poverty alleviation, CARE acknowledges its partnership with and support from the private sector:

> Barclays, CARE International and Plan have joined together in an initiative to improve the quality of life for poor people by extending and developing access to basic financial services [...] In addition, CARE and Bajaj Allianz—the Indian arm of large insurance company Allianz—are working together to provide insurance for people in southern India, that were affected by the tsunami in 2005. The investment firm JP Morgan Chase supports a microfinance disaster loan fund project that CARE is implementing in the tsunami-affected counties of India, Indonesia, Sri Lanka and Thailand. [...] Furthermore, CARE International and the computing giant IBM are planning to jointly build the Africa Financial Grid, a centralized management information system designed specifically for microfinance institutions in Africa. (lendwithcare.org)

There is a continuing trend in the global context of development projects and activities that connect global capitalism to the grassroots through the Internet by adopting a corporate approach to sustainable development and empowerment of people and livelihoods in the Third World. This also resonates with the concept of corporate social responsibility. The result is an awkward coexistence of participatory development with the profit motive of capitalism. Sosale (2007) therefore asks whether there is "a possibility for the 'public good' and private enterprise to meet (without collision and casualties) in virtual space or does juxtaposing the two ideas continue to signify a contradiction in terms?" (5).

Yet in the early days of the World Wide Web when amateur html websites and listprocs were tools that required basic literacies and skills, there were no standardized global formats for such global presences of located nonprofits. The Zapatista movement, for instance, emerged online in such an html-based "crude" ethos and revealed the Internet's potential for activism and the potential of local activists reaching out for global exposure and support that is engaged when these nonprofits go global through opening up online presences independently outside of organized pre-existing formats. However, now we have platforms and are also developing smart phone and tablet "apps" that serve as global formats with built-in functions and templates that can only be tweaked in very minor ways.

Sosale's frame analysis of the website of Greenstar, a "development corporation," describes how global capitalist control and local empowerment play out on the Internet. She points to the "empirical condition marking globalization, where technology, culture, and capital constitute recurring and convergent themes" (11). In this sense, Sosale suggests that Greenstar supports sustainable development (which is also environmentally friendly) for partner communities in rural areas of developing regions through new information and solar energy technologies. In exchange, the company markets local cultural products such as crafts, music, poetry, folk tales, and oral histories—many in digital formats—from these communities. By its function, Greenstar represents "a constituent of a new global cultural economy" (2). This presents a paradox where "a for-profit company plans its pricing and distribution of profits in such a way as to benefit both itself and its partner communities of developing regions" (7). In Greenstar's vision, the empowerment of the rural communities partnering with it becomes self-sufficient and self-managing through global capitalist intervention. Thus equality is supposedly achieved through the inclusion of rural communities in a global marketplace as consumers and vendors through the Internet. This elides the question of addressing structural inequalities in society. However, Sosale's study reveals that a corporate approach to development privileges the hierarchies of global capitalist structures over indigenous economies.

The dismissive attitude toward fundamental changes in the social structure of developing regions has been discussed by other feminist scholarship as well (Sterne & Stabile, 2003; Elliott, 2008; Cooks & Isgro, 2003; Kurian & Munshi, 2003, etc.). Referring to the role of international development agencies, Sterne and Stabile (2003) criticize the USAID's refusal to consider structural issues, its "unsavory history" of lobbying for private, corporate interests internationally, and its problematic discourse of female "empowerment" considering "feminist challenges to female entrepreneurialism" and the assumption that technology alone could eradicate global poverty (364). Kurian & Munshi (2003) critique the promotion of "ICT for development" by the World Bank and United Nations Development Programme (UNDP), which are driven by "'experts,' whose knowledge and understanding of local contexts is minimal and whose agenda is often antithetical to local needs" (353).

Beyond the optimistic tone with which CARE describes the important development goals set and made possible through its partnership with the private sector, the fact of such partnership has to be seen, in the current context of market rule and financialization of the globe, as a necessity rather than a mere choice made by CARE. We must be critically aware of the ways global financialization reshapes the functioning of civil society, not always for the better. The case of CARE transformation reveals the growing authority of transnational corporate elites and of the corporatization and privatization of governments on the business decision making, which implicitly has consequences on public policy making. Fawcett (2009) provides a critical analysis of private sector partnerships at UNESCO (the United Nations Educational, Scientific and Cultural Organization) and points out how these contribute to extending the neoliberal project. Fawcett argues that a market orientation influences the institutional autonomy given to projects that are partnered with UNESCO.

Visual Content on Lendwithcare.org

In this section, we draw on a continuing project where we critically examine several profiles of lenders and borrowers on the lendwithcare.org website highlighting countries where lenders provide support. Here we focus on how differentiation of class and Westernization is made on this website. For instance, the profile photo of Yawa Akakpo, a prospective borrower who runs a stall located at the side of one of the main roads leading to Atakpamé in Central Togo, presents her sitting on a side of a cereal basket, probably in a storeroom, looking at the camera in what, from a Western viewpoint, might look like a submissive/docile manner. In the context of the World Wide Web in this sort of staging, it actually does not matter whether there can be another reading of her posture from another cultural context since the intended audience for this sort of aid-seeking website would share the semiotic meaning-making cultures of the Western viewer. We find out from the description in her profile that she sells pulses and basic grains including maize, as well as salt, tomatoes and various condiments including dried okra. She is portrayed as a hardworking person:

> She has been doing this for more than 30 years. She started when she was just 12 and is now 45 years old. She is married with seven children. Each of her four daughters helps her out from time to time, particularly if she has to be away from the stall or is ill. Nevertheless, she still works six days a week from eight in the morning to six in the evening, resting only on Sundays. (http://www.lendwithcare.org/entrepreneurs/index/269)

The text next to this profile image further notes that this entrepreneur needs a loan because she will then be able to pay in cash and buy in bulk from suppliers so that she can negotiate a better price and better quality. As a consequence, her profit margin will increase even if she sells the same amount at the same price as before. Here once again we see the contradictory juxtaposition of the local contextual practice within a global framing of her need. The local contextual practice of negotiation requires her to have cash in hand—she cannot negotiate using credit cards or digital money of any sort. Yet the lender from the West can conveniently loan through the digital financial interface. The local MFIs will do the necessary translation. In fact, if local contextual social conditions are the same as social conditions in the lender's world—this works just fine. Except the juxtaposition of two contradictory practices and the seeming compatibility of translation from one to the other does not take into account the offline social realities of the borrower and the power dynamics of negotiations between the MFI workers and the global NGO as well as the social dynamics between the MFI workers and the borrower. These negotiations are still interpersonal and context-specific and require case-by-case strategies, tactics and negotiations on the part of the MFI worker as well as on the part of the borrower. As one of the nonprofit workers that the first author of this chapter conversed with in Indonesia while she was conducting field research noted, global NGOs situated in the West often offer up funding proposals and plans without sufficient understanding of unique local contexts and the responsibility and power to make it work or to corrupt it lies in the hands of the local nonprofit volunteers and officials. The transactions and translations are not quite as direct and transparent as suggested.

Continuing our visual analysis of Yawa Akakpo's portal-based virtual network, we looked closely at one of the lenders who had loaned money to her profile. This lender, Paul, is a 23-year-old from Haywards Heath, Sussex, England. In contrast to the highly structured photographic portrait of the borrower which confines her to a local socio-economic space circumscribed by conditions beyond her immediate control, the lender clearly possesses more agency when negotiating the online expression of his identity. He stages his own presence—even though this too is structured by the design of the portal—and has more flexibility in how he does so. He has posted a photo that represents him, in all probability, as a tourist/explorer—he wears casual cloths and carries a backpack, stands on a bridge over a river, and smiles uninhibitedly at the camera. Several inferences can be made from the photo, which, we presume (based on ease of access in the Western nations), was uploaded to the website by Paul himself. He likes to travel and discover new places, and through his self-representation, he gives the appearance of having the financial ability to do this. The fact that the lender's online identity expression connotes touristlike attributes should not be discarded without a closer consideration of its role at the intersection of cultures facilitated by globalization processes. Indeed, a particular sort of cultural convergence takes place when the global cyberspace (i.e. lendwithcare.org interface) makes local, pre-modern appearing identities and cultures (i.e. the identities of borrowers along with their remote/exotic cultures connoted photographically and textually in the uploaded profiles) accessible for scrutiny and discursive consumption by cosmopolitan cyber-tourists. Tourists like Paul do not need to travel offline to the remotes places of borrowers in order to experience exotic places and cultures.

Cyberspace thus provides a "spatial customization" (Andrejevic 2007) that seduces the user into a productive form of self-expression. Lenders can create and negotiate profiles of themselves and, at the same time, can peruse and operate with Third World profiles/identities/cultures. On the other hand, the local/premodern digital representation of borrowers enters the global space of the Internet as a product, and is thus framed discursively as a commodity to be consumed. Sosale (2007) defines this space as "the global consumer culture, a culture frequently identified with a postmodern global economy." This is a space where the cosmopolitan global consumer "seeks new aesthetic forms as a mode of self-expression and a declaration of identity." While some might be critical of the erasure of the local in its cooptation into the global, others may praise the online network interface for facilitating "various localities to enter the global market" (11).

Visually, then, we see a power hierarchy within this staging of the borrower's network on this portal. The hierarchy privileges a particular notion of global as westernized. There is a dichotomy produced in the representation of Global North versus Global South, even in philanthropic websites. This staging perpetuates a neocolonial rhetoric of Othering. For instance, the text that Paul posted in his profile manifestly makes for a neoliberal approach to development and empowerment. Thus, the "Why I lend" section in his online profile may read: "I really think that the most successful and sustainable forms of development and improvement of public services comes from community-based enterprises, not from handouts or aid donations. Lendwithcare is an excellent opportunity to invest in the skills and enthusiasm of individuals seeking to improve the lives of themselves and their communities." Sterne and Stabile (2003) take an ironical stand vis-à-vis the neoliberal focus on entrepreneurship which comes at the expense of structural and contextually relevant solutions to poverty:

> Neoliberals focus on the poor as a giant aggregate of freewheeling individuals who can use ICTs to pull themselves up by their bootstraps. Neoliberal policy constructs people in poor countries as "entrepreneurs" who simply need to bring their wares to

> "the global market"—often via the Internet . . . people are poor because they fail to take advantage of the bounties of the global economy." (365)

Another borrower, 34-year-old Dodji Assogba,[1] is a shoe businessman from Togo who also sells general health products. We are told that obtaining a loan will help him invest the money in buying more health products and shoes for his two businesses. Dodji's profile was listed on January 14, and he had managed to raise 30 pounds as of Febuary 13 out of 188.54 pounds needed to improve his businesses. Dodji stands in his health products store and looks directly into the camera lens. He is surrounded by his health products communicating to prospective lenders that he has a sustainable business and he may be also credit worthy. In looking at two of the lenders in Dodji's network, we noted that the lender from the United Kingdom, Mallory, invokes biblical narratives to provide reasons for lending: she states on her profile that she lends because "I am a #KindaAngel !!" (Lender profile: Mallory, 2011). She lends because it makes her feel like an angel. Unlike Kiva, lendwithcare.org—at least at the time of the writing of this chapter—lends just to people in Benin, Togo, and the Philippines, setting this raced lending interface apart from other lending sites like Microplace.com, Kiva, and ACCION.org. Lendwithcare.org lending model reinforces the binary between the powerful and the powerless, the Global North against the South, and the rich handing down money to the poor. The British are thus adopting and taking care of new postcolonial subjects in developing countries such as Benin and Togo. Lenders on sites such as Kiva and lendwithcare.org represent the new postcolonial activist within the neoliberal framework of governance.

Microplace.com: Producing the Socially Conscious Global Capitalist Investor

If the kiva.org interface stands for a milder discursive output of the neoliberal ideology of development, and lendwithcare.org implicitly offers up a new development model by giving the poor access to global marketspaces, microplace.com seems to openly embrace the capitalist ideology and its neoliberal principles of progress in yet another style. In this third model of online microfinance, one subject position above all acquires a particular symbolical weight at the interface. The westernized capitalist entrepreneur (with variations such as "venture capitalist," and "investor") is assigned savior-like attributes, along with the power to fight poverty in the (mostly Third) world. The identity of the entrepreneur is being produced in line with the attributes and purposes of the for-profit, interest-charging Microplace company. The image of the global tech-savvy entrepreneur takes precedence in the signifying practices at work on microplace.com. A subsidiary of eBay Inc. and a registered brokerage firm, microplace.com is a microfinance investment website. Unlike kiva.org, it offers prospective lenders returns on their loans and codes them as "investments." The returns range from 1.25% to 3%. Thus lenders can enjoy a dual return: financial and social. As an investor/lender on microplace.com, you can open an investment account of $20 and up. Unlike on kiva.org, the lenders cannot choose individual micro-entrepreneurs but they can choose microfinance projects to invest in.

The fact that Microplace is an affiliate of the giant e-commerce company Paypal should not be neglected in a larger discussion addressing the increased presence of global financial services in the development sector. This is further suggestive of the significant ways in which financialization shapes and impacts development policies and practices. The website acknowledges the creative ways in which e-financial services can be harmoniously combined with micro-lending investment activities:

> We want to unleash the capital in people's investment portfolios and harness it to make a difference in the fight against poverty. Imagine the possibilities if Paypal's 70 million users were to each commit $500 to Microplace—making $35 billion of financial services funding available to the world's working poor. By engaging with you and its community of partners, merchants, and consumers, PayPal believes it's possible to realize that kind of radical, positive contribution. Similarly, microfinance is about creating ways for the world's poor to access the same financial tools that we enjoy in order to help them cope with the unpredictability of their incomes and life circumstances. (https://www.microplace.com/about_us/paypal_family)

One of the short introductory videos embedded in the Microplace home page, provides a condensed overview of the way this online micro-lending platform functions in relation to its promised outcomes. It also clearly underlines the harmonious cohabitation of profit-making business and social responsibility in the context of digitalization of finance and the globalization of neoliberal economic practices:

> Once you invest, your money is bundled with other investors by U.S. based groups, then directed to local Microfinance projects in the region you selected, whether in the U.S. or around the world. As with any investment, there is some risk, but these U.S. based groups work hard to manage that risk, and make sure your money gets to those in need. Investing in microfinance projects lets you compound your money and the social good. Here is a glimpse at the difference your investment can make: . . . Your investment might help Pablo. He's a fisherman on the Amazon River. Your investment could help support a Microfinance project that enables Pablo to buy insurance for his boat. With Microfinance, you now have a sustainable way to invest in people and the world you want to help create. (https://www.microplace.com/ accessed April 14, 2011)

The sense of newness in the online presentation of the profiles of Microplace investors, when compared to lenders' profiles on kiva.org, is brought about by a more contoured sense of business ability and "entrepreneurial" world view. These qualities are made apparent through both their photographic and textual representations. This is in keeping with an entrepreneurial, "self-made-man" philosophy of individualized progress. In such a view, the investors need to be able to clearly appreciate the entrepreneurial creativity of the prospective borrowers, rather than attending exclusively to the altruistic aspect of poverty alleviation in their decision to invest money. For instance, Kalyani, who is an investor interviewed in a promotional clip about Microplace, shares her individual success and progress ideology:

> I believe in people. I believe in people who have drive, who have motivation, who have passion, who are hard workers. And I've met a lot of people in developing countries who, with very little, could do so much. My family is from India originally . . . I know personally where I've been successful has not been just when somebody has given me the answer. They've given me the tools to find the answer . . . I love clicking on the stories on the Microplace website to see some of the women, for example, who've been able to take the investment, and are able to do something to provide for their families . . . I would love to see more people go to Microplace and invest. (Overview—Buzz" Microplace, https://www.microplace.com/buzz, accessed January 20, 2011)

The clip presents an investor whose family is originally from India. This speaks for the company purpose to promote a more inclusive, multicultural image of the global savvy investor, who is westernized but not visually white or of European descent.

While the diasporic subject position is shaped to form a particular segment of investors, the located third-world subject is drawn in to become a global consumer/borrow through the web interface. Through digitalized financial services and microfinance projects, they seem to become active participants in the capitalist market processes. In contrast to borrowers' profiles on kiva.org, the borrowers on microplace.com are featured as happy looking, independent, enthusiastic individuals, always smiling in their profile photos.

Kiva.org versus Microplace.com

Kiva.org and Microplace.com are apparently similar (just as lendwithcare.org seems similar) but upon close inspection we can see difference in their approaches to the idea of poverty alleviation through micro-lending. Each visual interface clearly negotiates the possibility of juggling both practicality in relation to global financial processes as well as the ethics of micro-lending and philanthropy through such financial frameworks. The ethical dilemmas faced within the microfinance domain are manifested in the semiotic contradictions and negotiations visible in the ways that each of them positions lenders and borrowers through their online public (inter)face. Their business manifestos subscribe to two opposing views on micro-lending, namely interest-making micro-lending versus nonprofit micro-lending.

To better understand the difference, these two views are best articulated by two prominent figures in the world of microfinance. Promoter of nonprofit micro-lending, the Nobel Laureate Muhammad Yunus, founder and managing director of Grameen Bank, "believes in the goodness of mankind, . . . calls us to rise above our baser instincts, . . . and warns that microfinance cannot return respectable financial returns and simultaneously remain responsive to the impoverished." Vikram Akula, founder and chairperson of interest-making SKS Microfinance Ltd, on the other hand, believes that "the goodness of market forces[...]channels our greed into economic opportunity for the downtrodden," and therefore "questions a microfinance system which, crimped and corralled by limited philanthropic capital, is powerless to serve the next creditworthy poor person in line" (Lewis 2011).

Upon examining the web presence of each of the two online micro-lending enterprises, we see that each conveys one of these two ideologies more clearly than the other to the prospective lender. While in actuality both sites can be said to be negotiating the two views and even sometimes simultaneously representing both views, we see that one (Kiva) privileges altruism while the other (Microplace) privileges the financial returns motive. It is possible to see how this is portrayed visually in the screenshot where we have juxtaposed an image of a lender from Kiva and an investor from Microplace. There is a difference in the way that each site represents the person who is contributing the money for the loan. The Kiva lender image is a straight frontal shot, taken in a conventional manner, with the lender looking fairly "no-nonsense." The image seems like it is meant to draw the attention of the serious philanthropist and activist. In other lender images on Kiva, there are images of couples in what are culturally viewed as "honest" and "clean" looking postures in the Western world. Through a close look at several such images in our larger project, where we examined up to 35 lender profiles and 35 borrower profiles, we began to understand that Kiva works through a visual and textual (through Kiva fellow journals) appeal to the altruism of the potential lenders (lender as philanthropist, do-gooder, etc).

Microplace, on the other hand, seems to be representing the lender as a go-getter, an investor who is making a profit—the young smart investor and global citizen who can do philanthropy and profit all at once. The discursive mechanisms apparent in both textual and visual content of the websites produce specific subjectivities, suggestive of both lenders/investors and borrowers, informed by the general objectives of the two organizations. While the two micro-lending websites discursively cater for the humanitarian aspiration of global poverty alleviation and sustainable development, they help shape and reinforce somewhat distinct subject positions along the lines of particular needs and desires. The subaltern Others and the Western Subjects are simultaneously constructed, and sometimes one subject position is implied in the other's discursive design, as is the case of the visuals (both photographic texts and videos) on the websites.

What is suggested here is a form of digitally-enabled development as the new form of the civilizing/modernizing mission of the West in the Third World. Some would argue that this is merely a form of technological benevolence that conceals newly reconstituted imperial tendencies in the digital age. For, as Spivak (1999) explains, "the great narrative of development is not dead . . . the well-meaning raps upon raps upon the global electronic future that we often hear is to provide the narrative of development (globalization)—democratization (U.S. mission) an alibi" (371).

Marketing Model of Development Movements/Efforts

In this chapter we have also attempted to answer the urgent call for critical scholars to examine the intersections/interplay of local and global practices, which have been continuously disciplining marginalized people in both local and global contexts, in order to make a step forward in the process of revealing the agency oppressing insidious mechanisms of hegemonic ideologies. We particularly focus on online-offline contexts relevant for processes of agency and voice emergence and negotiation in the case of online development social network systems and their offline/local partnering development social actors in the particular development sector of microfinance.

In our research enterprise, we also took from political science scholarship, namely the marketing paradigm advanced by Clifford Bob (2005). He explores the reasons why only a small number of local social movements manage to make their voices heard internationally and have real chances for empowerment in the contemporary global arena. "How and why do a handful of local challengers become global *causes celebres* while scores of others remain isolated and obscure? What inspires powerful transnational networks to spring up around particular movements? Most basically, which of the world's myriad oppressed groups benefit from contemporary globalization?" (p. 2). Bob employs a marketing model to critically examine the underpinning motivations for the disparate levels of international success and support/activism for local *challengers*. By *challengers* (as well as *insurgencies* or *movements*), he describes local political movements in particular. This constitutes a down-to-earth organizational perspective to the activities of local political movements in connection with the support and popularity gained from transnational nongovernmental organizations in the developed world. Most importantly, Bob's analysis involves marketing concepts such as "demand and supply" and "marketing strategies."

Our analysis of kiva.org has sought to further the questioning of the generally optimistic view of the emergence of "global civil society." It has applied the marketing paradigm in conjunction with a transnational feminist approach in order to critically explore development movements/social actors in developing countries, and transnational social networks geared toward development goals—an increasingly popular phenomenon circumscribed by globalization.

Bob's main argument is that transnational success and increasing assistance to local political movements is directly proportional to the framing strategies operated by local challengers to match key characteristics of potential international supporters. They attempt to tap the media for international awareness, and employ promotional strategies so that their "parochial demands, provincial conflicts, and particularistic identities" equate interests, expectations and agendas of prospective international supporters (p. 4). Instances of such framing strategies impact the tactical, cultural, ethical, and organizational attributes of the movements and may include tactics to universalize their conflicts, or the promotion of a rhetoric which easily resonates abroad. This process proves to be problematic: Though framing is dynamic and mutual for local challengers and transnational NGOs, the power differences between the two remains unchallenged and local groups are most likely to undergo a process of reinvention and alteration.

Last but not least, the marketing model analysis cautions about the politics and agendas of international NGOs, which involve careful calculation of mutual interests and concerns, and which, eventually, do not necessarily answer the real needs of local movements. In an acerb competition for members and funding, NGOs often select less needy local groups, seemingly more capable to use the aid successfully. A transnational political space is thus created that is marked by self-interest and competition rather than by altruism and cooperation.

Similarly to the marketing perspective on social movements, a transnational feminist approach to development within the context of globalization is specifically prompted by a critical view on the current neoliberal economic policy that prophesizes markets as the main mechanisms producing economic development. This approach seeks to articulate the intricacies regarding the realization and negotiation of empowerment and agency among underprivileged populations. Within a particular development frame of microfinance, the concept of networked agency heralded and advocated by global actors such as transnational advocacy networks or NGOs, and which materializes by means of Internet social network systems (as is the case of kiva.org), begs for a research framework which has the potential to map the problematical intersections of local and global that are circumscribed by current international politics.

Likewise, the analysis in this chapter attempted to advance a thorough consideration of empowerment and the complex ways (and consequences thereof) in which it is being conceptualized, used, and assessed by hegemonic as well as genuinely transformative agendas. In undertaking this task, we do not overlook mainstream analysis, which emphasizes the achievements of micro-lending, and we do not deny that the Internet might exert an empowering influence for marginalized populations in very specific global/local intersections, or that online micro-lending communities such as kiva.org can provide potential strategies against poverty and towards empowerment. But we want to bring a broader focus when assessing these programs' outcomes: efficiency as well as ethics takes into consideration multiple social stratifiers/markers such as technological literacy, language, race, gender, class, caste, geographical location, and cultural context.

Communicating Likeness

NGOs and people who need foreign assistance have to market themselves internationally (Bob, 2005). To draw attention to a cause in a developing country, for instance, advocates must attract the attention of rich international agencies, by communicating to NGOs like Kiva that they deserve assistance for various reasons. There are hundreds of activist websites that have sprouted within the last few years (Bob, 2005), and kiva.org is no exception.

Kiva.org and its partners seem to be no different from the plethora of NGO activist websites who have been accused as the base soldiers of Western power and influence (Bob, 2005). Bob asserts that many NGOs have developed and died out due to competition and their inability to attract foreign aid from the West. It is a matter of the survival of the fittest for most local NGOs in developing countries, and in Africa alone almost half of the Kiva partner NGOs have been closed down. For example, one such partner in Kenya called the Rural Agency for Development was closed down for reasons describe by kiva below:

> Development (RAFODE) in Kenya, Kiva discovered that some entrepreneurs were not receiving the full amount of their loans. This violates Kiva's policies and we have terminated our relationship with Rural Agency for Development (RAFODE). All of the loans made to entrepreneurs served by this Field Partner have been refunded. We hope you realize that our audit uncovered a true exception to the norm; the vast majority of our Field Partners administer your loans with the highest integrity. (Kiva: Kenya Rural Agency for Development, 2011)

What we read above is obviously Kiva making sure that their field partners are administering the loans effectively. Though kiva explained that borrowers were not receiving the full amounts of their loans, kiva does not provide further clarification on why their partners in Kenya were not disbursing out full loan amounts to borrowers. In Ghana, some microfinance institutions that are partners with kiva have been closed down. Part of the reasons why Women's Trust, Inc., one of the local microfinance institutions in Ghana, was closed down is described by kiva with the following statement:

> "We have come to learn that credit alone is not enough to help a woman sustain herself and her family above the threshold of poverty. Three components play a vital role: access to credit and, equally important, access to education and healthcare" (Kiva: Ghana Women's Trust, Inc., 2012).With regards to another microfinance institution, Kraban Support Foundation (KSF) in Ghana, kiva posted this statement giving reasons for closing this institution. The partnership was closed in mid-2007 after Kiva discovered

> irregularities in the application of its policies by Kraban Support Foundation. Over the course of the partnership, Kraban Support Foundation raised approximately $500,000 in loans. All loans were marked as repaid from the entrepreneurs and Kiva repaid lenders to Kraban entrepreneurs. (Kiva: Ghana, Kraban Support Foundation, 2011). Subsequently, Kraban did not send all the funds to Kiva, and a repayment plan between Kraban Support Foundation and Kiva was agreed upon. The repayment plan spanned from September 2007 to March 2009, through monthly installments. Since November 2008, Kraban Support Foundation has been delinquent in its payments to Kiva in an amount close to $100,000. Kiva continues to pursue legal remedies with regard to collection of funds owed from Kraban Support Foundation. (Kiva: Ghana, Kraban Support Foundation, 2011)

From these statements, one can see that some of these microfinance institutions are struggling to survive: 50% of kiva partners in Ghana have been closed down, so it will be interesting to investigate more into why some of these kiva microfinance partner institutions failed, and why the Kraban Support foundation was delinquent in its payments.

Balancing Expectations

NGOs have to frame themselves to match the leading ideologies of the donor NGOs in the Global North (Bob, 2005). Bob describes these processes as *Substantive Matching*. Other processes include Cultural Matching, Tactical Matching, Ethical Matching and Organizational Matching. Bob (2005) noted that local NGOs, for example kiva partners in developing countries, adopt the cultural patterns of their home countries, and this can have its advantages and disadvantages. A local NGO that does not subscribe to certain ideologies will not be able to attract the necessary support that it needs; thus it will not survive. So lenders who see themselves as "good people" are more likely to provide funds to local microfinance institutions whose mission is to "do good" and help alleviate poverty in their country.

African countries around the world marketing themselves or attracting the much needed foreign aid and investment from developed countries package themselves to match the prevailing cultural patterns and ideologies, which to many countries is a necessary evil (Fürsich & Robins, 2002). In doing so their citizens are "othered" on websites that seek to help attract foreign investment. The images and texts used on most of these websites endorse the "Western gaze" (Fürsich & Robins, 2002) and allow their citizens to be "othered" by their potential investors. On Kiva for example, the profiles of borrowers are crafted in a way that may help them raise money. The profile of Naomi Turkson from Abura, Ghana on Kiva's website reads as follows:

> Naomi Turkson is married and has four children. She has been through senior high school. Naomi has been selling provisions, cooking utensils and earthenware pots at Abbrem Agona near Abura, Cape Coast, for 10 years. Her husband is a teacher. Her income helps pay for their children's school fees and utility bills. Naomi will use the loan to purchase additional utensils and earthenware pots to sell. She plans to build another shop at a different locality. (Kiva: Naomi Turkson, 2011)

Naomi is portrayed here as someone who has a family with four children, thus culturally matching her and framing her as someone who has family values. We are told that she is educated and has had a business for 10 years, showing that there is stability in her life and she has been able to sustain her business for 10 years. This will be an appropriate person to lend to because she seems to have a sustainable business. We are also told that her husband is a teacher. Kiva is painting a particular picture for prospective lenders. Here is a lender who may be credit worthy due to her sustainable business and who comes from a family that values education, most likely Western education. Naomi is marketed in a fashion that may attract funding.

The process of attracting foreign investment complicates the identities of inhabitants of a country when they are represented on the World Wide Web as a means to attract investment rather than being represented as the co-authors of achieving economic stability and progress for their countries. So long as the Global North dominates cyberspace, Web content creators will always craft their messages to appeal to these audiences. Third world bodies are branded as goods that are consumed through the Western gaze (Fürsich & Robins, 2002).

Globalization and the competition for scarce resources have led many developing nations to create new ways of reconstructing or repackaging their cultural identities to match the expectations of affluent donor countries at the intersection of various cultural ideologies. Kraidy (1999) describes these processes as the creation of hybrid cultures, and he explains that in doing so, local cultures are able to assimilate with global cultures without being damaged. Kiva partners in developing countries like Ghana and Kenya follow the same processes in attracting investment.

NGOs are more likely to support groups that employ methods that are deemed appropriate by donors (Bob, 2005). Drawing parallels to some of the microfinance institutions that have been closed down by kiva, we deduce that some of these institutions may not have been appropriately or ethically matching themselves with Kiva. Kiva uses words like "violates," "integrity," "irregularities," "delinquent" in describing why relationships with particular partners were terminated, showing that those partners were not appropriately matching themselves to Kiva, resulting in the withdrawal of funding (Kiva: Ghana, Kraban Support Foundation, 2009).

Globalization, Empowerment, and ICTs

Globalization, through the instrumental role of global communication, claims to have brought forward transnational projects of equality and empowerment. However, we must be aware that one possible insidious outcome of global restructuring and of neoliberal economic policies is the reconfiguration and resurgence of imperial ambitions within current global hegemonies. In this sense, for instance, what appears to be empowerment could only be a restricted notion of empowerment, circumscribed to a neoliberal philosophy that emphasizes the individual but does not properly address structural inequalities that hinder a more comprehensive process of empowerment. The same neoliberal understanding also tends to foster a one-size-fits-all model of empowerment that disregards the range of political, economic, and cultural contexts that might provide complex and sometimes contradictory possibilities for empowerment. Along these lines, ICTs employed in the global development activities, such as the Web 2.0 tools used by the Kiva micro-lending organization, need to be examined in an analytical framework which emphasizes the importance of scrutinizing how everyday practices and socio-cultural hierarchies contribute to the shaping of online identities, hierarchies, and processes of inclusion and exclusion (gendered, raced, classed online subjectivities) (e.g., Enteen, 2006; Gajjala & Altman, 2006; Kolko, Nakamura & Rodman, 2000; Nakamura, 2002).

In contrast to the seemingly positive perspective of a network society, hegemonic spatial conceptions of the World Wide Web extend and reiterate the contemporary geopolitical inequities in our offline world, rather than echoing "the connectivity and interdependence suggested by the term 'web'" (Enteen 2006 , 233). Enteen further explains that "rather than recognizing the networks formed through online information exchange, the prevailing images of the Internet and world wide web locate individuals, not to mention data, within spatial coordinates" (229). Against an apparent deterritorialized condition made possible by cyberspace, Kaplan (2002) argues likewise that "a closer look reveals location and materiality in the mobility and disembodied discursive practices of new information technologies" (3). It would be sensible to argue that such online sites, precisely because they advocate for development and poverty alleviation through a model of "transnational investing" and not simply by charity, display a homogenized market of Third World micro-entrepreneurs for foreign investors from developed countries to invest in. Such representations displace political subjectivities of these micro-entrepreneurs, or other economic and cultural factors. These are not required for successful fulfillment of the specific objective of micro-lending efforts. Unfortunately, they reinstate the discourse of Otherness globally, while drastically limiting a process of empowerment locally. Lingam (2008), for instance, warns about the erroneously homogenous image of poor people: "there are attempts to discipline women and communities and functionally cobble together "social cohesion" among the poor as a class without working on the deep-seated caste difference. This is a bigger challenge that is not amenable to solution by micro-credit programs" (135).

Civic-Driven Change (CDC) Approach to Social Change and Development

Our critical scrutiny of the place and role of ICT within a development framework contextualized by social networking also resonates with the civic-driven change (CDC) initiative whose efforts are geared toward the exploration and communication of "a perspective of change in societies that stems from citizens rather than states or markets" (Biekart & Fowler, 2009, 2). This distinct approach to social change and development is seen as an important component of a much needed solution in a global context where the poverty gap is widening and where the current mainstream-aided development policies have more often proved to be counterproductive. It further helps to draw a critical distinction between development and transformative change, both of which imply in turn different agencies. Whereas the former paradigm foregrounds the agency of institutions promoting the top-down development model and communication, the latter is about civic agency (people's action in shaping society) acquired through civic participation and active citizenship fundamentally based on the participatory process of communication (Gumucio-Dagron, 2008, 2009; Schultz et al., 2009). The civic-driven change initiative points to the lack of communication as a participatory process as being one of the main reasons for the shortcomings of the classic meaning of development. Most importantly, it views citizens as "subjects of change, and not just objects for the trial of experimental economic and social policies"(Gumucio-Dagron, 2008, 2).

The same awareness of the distinction between top-down/vertical and horizontal communication, which the civic-driven change approach emphasizes when comparing classic understanding of development versus transformative change, has prompted us to set forth on a critical exploration of the ICT role for development communication and, in particular, of the use of Web 2.0 social networking tools in the case of the kiva.org micro-lending enterprise. Even as we acknowledge that Internet technology may foster the promotion of networked agency through what Castells (2007) termed *self mass communication*, it behooves us, as critical researchers of communication, to move beyond the ecstatic view of the Internet as vanguard for participatory communication and civic engagement. We must examine unintended social outcomes for global and local polity of the ways ICTs are being used for development purposes. Agreeing with Gumucio-Dagron's (2009) emphasis on the acute need of instruments for monitoring and evaluating the "quality of the processes of communication for social change" (461), we acknowledge the need to make social actors involved in development projects accountable for their approaches to communication. Our critical exploration is therefore in line with the call for a "panoptic view on communication approaches to development needed at all levels of organizations intervening in the process of transformative change" (Gumucio-Dagron, 2008, 8). An analogue distinction highlighted by civic-driven change approach between access to information and participation in the communication process (Gumucio-Dagron, 2008, 2009) has also been a premise for our study, since it is important to examine how Web 2.0 tools fulfill the objectives of a process entailing a communal engagement with media where decision making and information production is ideally carried out by citizens themselves.

In order to get a better understanding of how this plays out, it will be important to know what the unfiltered stories of some of these third world bodies featured on the Kiva website are. What are some of the struggles they go through in securing and repaying these loans? This is worth investigating and it is our plan to explore these in future works.

Notes

1. See www.lendwithcare.org/entrepreneurs/index/363

CHAPTER THREE

SNAPSHOTS FROM SARI TRAILS: CYBORGS OLD AND NEW

Radhika Gajjala with rad Zabibha

In this chapter, I draw upon an examination of two apparently opposed cyborg locations and technologies to show how, in specific instances, globalization, technology, economics, culture and diasporas intersect. Such intersections produce very specific, situated contexts for productive labor forces to emerge at the interface of technologies "old" and "new." Through these situated contexts, the individual is *placed* in relation to market forces and community production logics through which labor and affect are placed in hierarchies of digital globalization. I examine this local/global relational placement of productive labor online and offline by looking at how the "sari"—an implicit and explicit signifier of "Indian" identity in current times—is produced, marketed and worn in two "cyborg" contexts. Thus the two cyborg locations that I look at are that of the handloom sari and the Second Life (SL) sari. Both these locations would be equally "exotic" and unfamiliar to most readers in the Western academy. Through these explorations in two very different *places*, I critically engage two main frameworks that have been used to talk about Indians online and in relation to globalization—the concept of *digital diaspora* and the *global/local* binary. To this end, I frame the notion of place along the lines of cultural geographers' articulation of place as relational.

Throughout this article there is a distinction made between place and space. I use space to mean social space. Most of the places also contain multiple social spaces and several of the social spaces are multiply placed. The question will then be raised—why is Second Life being described as a place rather than a space? A virtual world such as Second Life can be viewed simultaneously as a mediated social space online as well as a place inhabited through the human-machine continuum of the avatar. In addition, both Second Life and the offline rural handloom villas where the cloth sari is produced exist in relation to the global-local continuum. Through an examination of how labor and capital flows circulate in these contexts we can see the contingencies that produce each place as global sometimes and local other times. Observing the ways in which the actual practices of production take place at the interface of each technology—the computer in one instance and the handloom in the other—allows us see that global social space is produced through multiple located practices drawn from local and global places. Thus both these locations can be viewed as global and local.

Before I proceed, I must explain some key terms and concepts being mobilized and also provide brief background and context for each of the sites. Thus I begin with quick descriptions of the sari and the pit loom. I then proceed to discuss concepts such as digital diaspora, avatar as technology and weaver as technology. Next I explain my methodology and go on to describe issues that arise out of my journeys to South Indian weaving villages and my journeys as a Second Life avatar ("rZ") trying to build sari business there. My journeys to the rural South Indian weaving villages happened during my time working with members of a nongovernmental organization (NGO) named "Dastkar Andhra" located in Secunderabad, India. My continuing collaborations with members of that organization, my continuing work with online craft networks, and my offline practice of amateur weaving and spinning in northwest Ohio inform my research in offline contexts, processes and practices of production of handloom saris. This means more than six years of immersive ethnography, based in what I previously termed as "epistemologies of doing" (Gajjala, Rybas, & Altman 2007), within the online three-dimensional world called Secondlife.com. Several graduate and undergraduate students were (and are) a part of my ongoing ethnographies and my method of investigation includes perceptions and dialogues from my continuing pedagogies at the online/offline interface (Gajjala, Rybas, & Zhang, 2010). All these interactions inform my understanding of production in that environment.

The Sari

The sari is apparel worn by Indian women through history and associated culturally with Indianness in present times. In Western worlds, it is used as a signifier of Indian tradition.[1] For an image of a sari as worn by a Second Life avatar browse http://cyberdiva.org/blog/category/rad-zabibha/[2]

The Handloom

A handloom is an implement used to weave cloth that is operated manually by weavers using their hands and feet. There are two kinds of handlooms relevant to the weaving context that I discuss: the pit loom and the frame loom, both of which operate broadly on the same principle. The loom is placed in such a way that the weaver can sit comfortably and work. With the pit loom, literally translated from the Telugu term *gunta maggam*, the weaver sits on the loom and his/her legs are in a pit, dug in the ground. The warp of the loom is stretched just above the pit vertically toward the weaver, and parallel to the ground. Thus the weaver is on an even level with the loom. The shafts/harnesses of the loom are controlled by a series of foot pedals called treadles.

The weaver is able to operate these treadles with his legs comfortably. This ensures that the weaver's hands are free to handle the shuttle. The warp is separated into two layers and the weft threads in the shuttle are thrown from one end of the warp to the other end. The inserted weft is pushed into place by a suspended reed known as *acchu* in Telugu. Such pit looms are used for weaving finer and lighter fabrics like saris, dhotis and fine dress materials.

Digital Diaspora

The term *"digital diaspora"* is easily used to talk about how diasporic populations the world over use the Internet to connect to each other. Scholars such as Anna Everett (2009) and Jeniffer Brinkerhoff (2009) have each used the phrase in relation to very specific situated histories of forced migrations (African American histories of slavery) and transnational travel respectively. The link to labor flows and hierarchies of colonialisms and digital globalization is clear in both. In most general usage, however, the phrase "digital diaspora" is used to describe migrant populations without attention to the specific conditions of subjectivity that produces diasporas. Further, it is interesting[3] that international NGOs (specifically the United Nations) and transnational corporations as well as national businesses have mobilized the notion of digital diaspora in "reverse brain-drain" efforts (Gajjala, 2008), where successful transnationals and migrants with moneys to invest actually get to return home (Mallapragada, 2006).

The global/local binary that is used in conjunction with such uses of the notion of digital diaspora positions specific placed "locals" outside of a repeatedly unnamed global. However, as cultural geographers have pointed out, the separation of global and local into mutually discrete concepts is problematic. In such an articulation and coupling of digital diaspora and global/local, it appears as though digital diasporas are what make us global, while the local is somewhere out there in "subaltern" space. This sort of articulation is not only "a denial of a fundamental ontological fact of our time: namely, that the global is *in* the local," (Castree, 2004, 135), but also ignores the fact that the global is made up of multiple locals.

So what is at stake in conceptualizing the users of online communication tools from various offline locations as "digital diasporas"? Various scholars have examined how terms such as *diaspora*, *postcolonial,* and *multiculturalism* tend to get deployed academically at a time when free-market ideologies need nations to open up to transnational flows of capital, consumer goods and labor (see, for instance, Dirlik, 2006).

Further, why do we now use the term digital diaspora to describe these users of communication media when we have not used conceptualizations such as "radio wave diaspora" or "television diaspora" or "telephone diaspora" or "telegraph diaspora." Part of the answer of course is that the digital media used for digital diaspora formations are interactive and potentially allow people from all over the world to feel that they are sharing a global "place" without actually having to get physically or socially displaced in their offline contexts through a drastic change in the material environment.

This particular kind of "diaspora" occurs through affective transformations and acquisition of multiple, layered, technical, cultural and other literacies. At the same time users are also under the illusion of being in global social space, with a perceived choice in where and how they engage this space. In addition, while the commonly invisible labor and structure of hardware manufacturing and complex software coding is what makes this platform for access to globality possible, actual users get to feel as though they are in fact "empowered" to produce their particularities within this global space. This allows the formations of various niche local places online *within* global places such as World of Warcraft, Eve online, Second Life, Farmville, smartphone applications, blog rings, and so on. People with very particular similar interests and specific collaborative missions—even if the logic of similarity and collaboration is produced and based wholly in the particularity of the software-driven social and technical interface—can gather in common space. Thus online networks formed through digitally mediated communicative media—whether accessed via desktop computers, X-boxes or iPhones—permit local place to exist within the global and vice versa.

When print media became mass media, Anderson wrote about imagined communities around the act of reading a newspaper. He argued that it allowed the imagining of common place through what Anderson called the "convergence of capitalism and print technology on the fatal diversity of human language creat[ing] the possibility of a new form of imagined community which in its basic morphology set the stage for the modern nation" (46). Thus print media being made accessible—actually or potentially—to "the masses" went hand in hand with the growth of modern capitalism and of internationalism as modern nations emerged.

Anderson's work has also formed the basis of a lot of the arguments being made as we talk about digital diasporas and virtual communities, but very few of the works that celebrate imagined community online make a clear political economy connection. In the case of interactive digital and wireless technologies—they go hand in hand with transnationalism based on global flows of capital and labor. The interactivity of the online technologies in current forms—as it is made possible through the World Wide Web—is a logical extension for digital finance. In Dan Schiller's words:

> The architects of digital capitalism have pursued one major objective: to develop an economy-wide network that can support an ever-growing range of intra-corporate and inter-corporate business processes. This objective encompasses everything from production scheduling and product engineering to accounting, advertising, banking and training. Only a network capable of flinging signals—including voices, images, videos, and data—to the far ends of the earth would be adequate to sustain this open-ended migration into electronic commerce. (Schiller, 2000, 1)

The unique features and processes involving intra- and inter- exchanges through multiple media parallel with transnational business networks are the backdrop against which digital diasporas form.

So we see that there are very specific circumstances that allow a political-economic moment for mobilizing the notion of digital diaspora. Globalized markets as well as the interactive nature of online technologies are unique features allowing this to happen. In such a context, we also need to take into account the layered and nuanced ways in which such diasporic subjectivities are produced if we are to understand how the global/local continuum plays out in specific situations in present-day cultures and economies.

At the same time as the physical material conditions of the digital user, consumer, and producer may not drastically change, it can be argued that in the digital time-space continuum, and in the ability to record practices that leave behind histories and actual archives, there is something unique. The texts thereby resulting can in turn be viewed as diasporic agents/actors in and of themselves. It can also be argued that in the formation of online representations there is a certain situatedness. There is a sense of "landing" some*place*. There is a simultaneous affective reproduction of travel from place to place. There is also a sense of disorientation and displacement through encounters and placement in relation to other cultures that simulates culture shock. Thus, it can be argued that the quality of digital existence contributes to the use of phrases like "digital diaspora" and "virtual community."

However, in order to understand how globalization and technology play out in transnational economies, we must take the argument further. Attempting to understand what power hierarchies may be permitting the articulation of these online existences as digitally diasporic is necessary if we are to understand global and local placements and interlinked online/offline hierarchies.

Basing my investigations mainly at online/offline intersections traveling to and from India and the U.S as the point at which to enter 3D South Asian digital diasporas, I explore how this plays out. Of course, this results in a struggle on the part of the academic trying to articulate these layers and nuances through specific contexts as we try not to universalize in harmful ways. But it is at these intersections where struggles over meaning, cultural practices and economic processes take place that globalization plays out in the everyday.

Therefore, those of us who want to look to see where and how spaces of articulation and resistance can be found must look at seemingly unusual intersections and juxtapose seemingly contradictory situations to try and grasp what may be happening. Thus it is my hope that this work begins a mapping of global virtual-real markets which opens up ways of seeing globalization and technology in relation to specific contextual transnational capital and cultural flows that shows how intertwined economics and culture are in the everyday practices of living online and offline.

Method: Epistemologies of Doing and Ethnography

Anthropologists and archeologists travel thousands of miles to faraway places in the world and live there for extended periods of time in order to represent the people and culture there. Their legacy has left us with one of the most important qualitative research methods: ethnography. It is important not to forget that colonial legacy left to us by the implicit projects of nineteenth century anthropology. Those of us who are feminists and critical researchers using ethnographic methods continually encounter points of complicity with those epistemologies.

Offline

In my offline journeys through rural South India ethnography is my main mode of investigation. However, while entering the field, I also work for the NGO Dastkar Andhra which works on behalf of handloom weavers in a variety of ways. Parallel to this, my offline ethnographies include traveling to various craft guilds, craft and fiber shows and expos, and the amateur practice of weaving, spinning, quilting, knitting, crocheting and the dying of yarn.

Therefore, my ethnographic method intersects with action research. In addition, whether I travel as a collaborator with the NGO workers and officers, as a participant of craft guilds or I travel as shopper or ethnographer, I am continually marked. In India I am marked as a non-resident Indian tourist and consumer and collector of handloom fabric and crafted artifacts to be transported back to the U.S in order to be used/displayed in my home or given as gifts to friends living here. In the U.S. among mostly rural northwest Ohio communities I am marked as outside (even though a citizen of the United States) in certain ways and included as inside through the practice and understanding of processes engaged in by these groups of individuals.

However, I must note that the marking in itself neither places me hierarchically in a fully outside or inside position nor does it in itself frame me as more or less powerful than those I work with. What frames me as possibly more powerful than those I work with is my academic location and the potential for me to mistranslate events onsite. Therefore the "with" must be considered as a very tenuous and delicate "with." The marking serves as a continual reminder to me as ethnographer that humility and uncertainty are an integral part of the learning process. Assumptions of intrinsic scholarly authority on the part of the researcher get her nowhere in the attempt to understand the contexts and motivations in any situation being investigated. The researcher's authority and power is not in the field per se—it is in how she represents the field, and how her work mobilizes the field toward specific power formations. Well-meaning ethnographers can by no means avoid falling into this trap—it is in the academic structure of persuasion.

Latour (1986) notes the power dynamics implicit in the process of translation from other contexts to academic circulation and describes how this happens through the formation of "immutable mobiles." He writes:

> "knowing" is not a disinterested cognitive activity; harder facts about the other cultures have been produced in our societies, in exactly the same way as other facts about ballistics, taxonomy or surgery. One place gathers in all the others and presents them synoptically to the dissenter so as to modify the outcome of an agonistic encounter. To make a large number of competitors and compatriots depart from their usual ways, many ethnographers both had to go further and longer out of *their* usual ways, and then come *back*. The constraints imposed by convincing people, going out and coming back, are such that this can be achieved only if everything about the savage life is transformed into immutable mobiles that are easily readable and presentable." (15)

Therefore I am not suggesting or claiming that emphasizing humility, participation, contribution or what I term "epistemologies and pedagogies of doing" (Gajjala et al., 2010) is a way to extricate the researcher from such potential complicity and appropriation. But I am attempting to disrupt and topsy-turvy previously established binaries—"immutable mobiles"—through the snapshots I produce, understanding fully well that these may be interpreted as "native" information on faraway premodern lives regardless of all the disclaimers I make. The difficulty is not in the understanding through learning, traveling and doing—the difficulty, struggle and dilemma is in the craft of writing. If as a researcher and academic I am to establish that I can write appropriately for the academic audience, then I must risk the flattening of what I have learned. If I am to break with tradition in academic writing, I must risk not doing it effectively, sounding uninformed or losing my own voice and location as "scholar." Within these stated constraints my methodology is a struggle that includes the process of crafting the academic text.

Online

In cyberspace the ethnographer does not always have to travel in the kind of physical space where the whole body encounters the field face to face. But the travel in time and cyberspace allows her/him to live in the field in a different way and to do concrete participant observation. In order to do so effectively the ethnographer must first code herself into existing in these online worlds.

For instance, Jenny Sunden's book *Material Virtuality* writes of the typing into existence that is a requirement for any sustained online identity. This act of *becoming* online creates a close relationship between the typist and the character she/he types into existence in the online world. This sort of relationship is no doubt the basis for the process of transformation described in the 3-D film *Avatar* released in 2009. It is, of course, no coincidence I am sure that the character, Mary, played by Sigourney Weaver, who heads the team that is providing intelligence (implicitly and explicitly) to the military and to the corporation is clearly modeled on popular images of the female anthropologist (in short, she seems very Margaret Mead-like).

The online avatar/identity is curiously the production of both the offline and online world. Gonzalez (2000) critiques the naïve assumption that there is the virtual/real binary separating the reality from the virtuality (43). Actually, the closer one observes and participates in an online community, the more she/he would agree that the interplay of real and virtual is always present. No one can transcend the social categories and the repertoire of experiences, skills, and literacies that define who they are in the offline world even as they connect to online worlds. Likewise, the learning and understanding produced through online living definitely exerts influence on the perception of the offline world.

Methodological approaches informed by "epistemologies of doing" in conjunction with visual and textual readings and ethnographic investigations lead to an actual examination of subjects in process. The production of layered, situated subjectivities in techno-mediated environments—online and offline—allows an understanding of situated Agency within spectrums of choices and constraints. Examining where we place our bodies, or where our bodies are placed (whether visually, textually or through architectural and city design and mapping) in time and space—in relation to technologies old and new—and how we interact with these environments leads to an understanding of the complexity of unequal power relations and structural formations and design within a global cyberspace.

Thus I adopt critical ethnographic methodologies—whether under the heading of "cyberethnography" and "epistemologies of doing"—for research and pedagogy at these online/offline and global/local intersections and nodes. These ethnographies, interspersed with personal experience of being in communicative spaces of diaspora through my personal life, inform my analysis in thischapter.

Saris in Second Life

Saris are produced, marketed, bought, collected, gifted, worn in the online world of Second Life. They have meaning within particular cultural contexts based on what rituals and fashions are salient in those contexts. Thus, Gor rituals may determine how a particular kind of sari bought and scripted by a member of the Gorean community on Second Life is used, just as age-old Hindu rituals may determine how a particular kind of sari is bought and prepared by a member of the Hindu community anywhere in the world. They simultaneously shape and are shaped by global cultural practices and discourse as well as by local socio-economic and cultural practices in consumers' everyday lives.

What happens when a signifier such as a sari attached offline to processes of production that are viewed in common vocabulary as "premodern" travels into a digital space such as Second Life that is sometimes equated with "post-modern" science-fiction narratives? Is there more demand created for the actual fabric produced offline or does the mutated digital form that is named as a sari become objectified and decontextualized traveling into spaces where the labor to produce it comes from differently situated circumstances? In fact, is the sari the same kind of object when it is worn by an online avatar, be it a Sims character or a Second Life avatar, as when worn by a human being offline? For that matter, is the sari the same when worn by Michaele Salahi when she is gate-crashing Obama's reception for the Indian Prime Minister and when it is worn by my eighty-five-year-old mother while she is supervising the gardener in her everyday life?

In this layered traveling of the signifier online and offline, then, will the sari as signifier reinforce offline demand for the product made by the handloom weavers in India through the production of cultures that become aesthetically familiarized with the colors and textures?

In actuality, both the process of digital sari making and handloom sari making are distinctly different. Yet they are both situated in modernity and each is practiced and experienced as simultaneously local and global. Each context and place exists along a relational global-local continuum that is situated in modern practices of marketing, communication and consumption, which in turn shape the product and the process of production through local and global feedback loops. Neither of the saris are used/consumed in any sort of so-called authentic traditional way.

But does the articulation of sari as signifier in itself not virtualize the products—both the digital sari and the handloom sari? Is it not a fact that traditions for wearing and using the sari are produced and reproduced through interacting with daily social practices, aesthetics, convenience and expectation? For instance, what of the seemingly bizarre play on the modern and traditional as well-known sari retailers in Chennai announce their new line of "zippered saris," "pocket saris" and "reversible saris." Zippered saris thus can literally be zipped on as a skirt—this would be heresy for the older generations that believe that saris must be nine yards and worn in specific ways. For such older generations even the move from the nine-yard sari to the six-yard sari (or the nylon sari that emerged in the late sixties and stays and the cheap and light daily wear alternative to handloom cotton and silk) might initially have been heresy.

However, it is not only older generations of women who talk of sari traditions in daily wear. For instance, a blogger writes a post about "saris with a twist" in her blog on "Rediscovering Chennai":

> Sri Kumaran Silks introduced the saree with a pocket! yes, a pocket!! For the woman who needs to put her cell phone/keys/wallet somewhere quickly. Now they show a pretty, slim girl wearing it—but what about the fat ones? Does it then become like jeans where the pocket slings to the back? Hmm . . . I wonder how you sit down with a cell phone sticking out of a - ahem - back pocket? (Arundathi, 2007)

Shifts have indeed occurred through time. Innovations in sari designs are nothing new. And yet the shifts are hidden in the coding of the sari as "traditional" garb of Indian women. What's at stake in articulating this as tradition and for who? The answer to this question lies in modern identity formations and the dialectical relationship between global and local and the histories of formation of local identities in opposition to Western colonization that date back to the early years of the British East India Company's entry into the region we now name as India.

Thus it is an unreal and static viewpoint that allows us to freeze each instance visually and artificially as traditional, modern or postmodern. In the case of offline handloom production surrounded by brown bodies and non-Western scenery and practices, discourses that locate the processes of production and technologies as traditional and pre-industrial are invoked.

In the case of the digital world of Second Life, discourses of science fiction and of cyberspace as a "consensual hallucination" are invoked which suggest that such a world is post modern. In actuality both of them exist under similar conditions of modernity and globalization in relation to issues of labor, livelihood, and commerce.

There is much written on what happens to the newer technologies such as televisions, computers and cell phones when they enter these apparently non-modern places. Such writing often equates empowerment and material well-being with modernity. This discourse locates the process of modernizing in the introduction of artifacts and processes that come out of westernized urbanity (implicitly viewed as "global" and "cosmopolitan") into mostly non-Western rural space.

However, there is hardly any recognition or discussion about socio-cultural, political, and economic changes that might happen when and if a technology from this Other space is introduced into contexts of westernized urbanity. NGOs such as Dastkar Andhra have been working to reintroduce older technologies such as natural dyeing for yarn and handloom fabric. In actuality, what such an NGO does is to reintroduce such technologies and processes into urban space through their attempts to link existing rural communities of weavers to urban, transnational and global markets. The mainstream often views what they are doing as acts of preservation of "tradition" and authenticity rather than as "innovation" of technologies and of production and marketing processes.

Such "reverse" technology adoption is not totally unheard of, even if the logic of mainstream development and modernity still does not allow it to be taken seriously. It is, after all, what environmentally conscious farmers even in the rural United States are attempting in the name of organic farming practices. There is no real "return" to a pre-chemical fertilized, authentic land. Therefore, the re-introduction of practices of organic farming is, in itself, an innovation in farming and technologies. Thus, these farmers are (re) learning processes associated with "old" technologies.

Further, as economic setups in a post dotcom, post Enron, increasingly green thinking elites in society become more prevalent in westernized urbanity, it is likely that there will be more concerted and strategic attempts made to re-investigate the potential of so-called older, possibly more environmentally-friendly, labor-intensive technologies and production processes. Thus, for instance, what might be the impetus for the introduction of cycle rickshaws in a location such as San Diego while, at the same time, these very cycle rickshaws are being legally banned from the roadways for Indian cities like Hyderabad in the name of modernity?

In the case of saris on Second Life, we can hardly say that an old technology has entered a westernized urban context. All we can say is that a certain signifier of the product of what is viewed as "traditional technology" has traveled into what is perceived as the postmodern world, and transmutated into something else.

Does such a transmutation hold potential for making connections or is it just another way to broaden the chasm between the developing world's rural economies and emerging digital economies? Globalization processes include material and discursive hegemonies produced at the intersection of the economic, the cultural, and the social, and are mediated in multiple ways through old and new mediascapes. These processes feed into economic and cultural local formations. Global technospaces are produced through and are a consequence of economic globalization.

Avatar as Technology, Weaver as Avatar

On Second Life, the fashioning of avatars and their profiles become identifiers of particular traveling cultural practices that are situated both within specific geographical locales as well as within global virtual-real markets simultaneously. Thus, I view the crafting of avatar selves as *situated* practice—at radically varying contextual disjunctural and conjunctural online-offline intersections. The avatar is a technological artifact as is the apparel designed for it. Without the avatar, the sari on Second Life cannot exist. However, an avatar also exerts agency. The avatar forms an identity and takes on roles in the communities that it participates in. Without value in Linden dollars or value in terms of contributing social and cultural meanings within at least some Second Life communities, the Avatar identity will cease to exist.

In the case of the weaver too, he is at a human-technology continuum in another way. The weaver's function in relation to the loom and the loom's function in producing handloom textiles are clearly intertwined. The human being must become the cyborg weaver if he is to produce a good product. Both visually, aesthetically and affectively the weaver is immersed and appears as "one with the machine." The two must function together within a whole community that creates value for the weaver's product through continued marketing, consumption, and use in cultural rituals. This is the only way to produce handloom material—or there is no "handloom" cloth in existence at all. Any piece of cloth that is not produced with this intense exchange between weaver, loom, the community of consumers, the dyers and spinners, and so on, would not carry the label of handloom, obviously.

Thus, saris in both these contexts are produced through the use of multiple technologies. All the technologies concerned exist and are shaped through human-technology interaction. When there is a human being interacting with them the avatar selves/technological artifacts come to life and get *placed* in virtual worlds just as the human being also enters the virtual world seated at the computer interface. The computer as artifact exists as a medium, a translator. The handloom as artifact exists as medium and translator as well.

The handloom, however, has become a signifier of premodernity on the one hand and of exotic craft on the other. This technological artifact is made virtual to the frameworks of modernity in a different way from the way in which the economies of Second Life seem virtual to these same frameworks of modernity. The contradiction of trying to "modernize" handloom weaving in itself highlights the problems of process and ideology in relation to what is expected by mainstream globalization. Thus, when technophiles try to suggest that handloom weavers can indeed benefit from "new" technologies, they are stumped when asked how. They can only point to e-commerce as a form of salvation. However, e-commerce targets mostly export markets. In reality, the export market is not a reliable source of sustainable livelihood for the weaver, since it is dependent on fleeting fashion and fancy of the distant consumer who has not sufficiently incorporated it into their everyday. Thus, socio-economic activity within a community that would necessitate the use of the product repeatedly, over and over again, would necessitate the continued consumption of the product. This would generate demand that would sustain the weaver communities. Therefore, unlike the days when the Madras kerchief (rumal) was exported to Nigeria, modern-day exports of handloom products do not sustain weaver communities in the long run because they are separated ideologically from the everyday of the common consumer.

However, this was not always the case. Handloom products from South India were globally marketed even until the early 1900s. The case of handloom exports from South India serves as only one example of several historical situations that demonstrate that globalization and international trade are by no means an invention of modernity made possible by modern technologies of transportation and communication. The case of the Madras kerchief is thus a particular example of global trade that happened 400 years ago. According to Guru Prasad Puttu (2009), the "Real Madras Hand Kerchiefs" (RMHK) were produced by weavers in the South Indian weaving village of Chirala and exported to West Africa even as recently as the 1900s.

The earliest of these kerchiefs, it appears, were woven in plaids and checks without borders. The designs began to incorporate striped borders a little later. These kerchiefs ("rumals"), notes Puttu, acquired ritualist importance in the community practices of the Kalabari tribe in Africa. A British officer, Talbot, is said to have noted the use of this cloth and recognized/named it as "real Indian" cloth when he was in Southern Nigeria.

What is also interesting about the Madras kerchief is how its use as a sacred ritual cloth traveled through different places and religions. In the Medieval period, this cloth was used in Masulipatnam of South India in religious rituals currently associated with Hinduism. It was used to wipe the face of the deity. This cloth caught the attention of Persians and Arabs who had settled in the port town of Masulipatnam. They, in turn, exported this fabric to the Middle East and to Africa, as well as to a few European regions. These woven and embroidered cloth pieces (rumals/kerchiefs) were also imported into Mecca where they became associated with religious ritual as well. It is said that Hajjis (pilgrims journeying to Mecca) would wear these rumals on their shoulders to indicate their pilgrim status.

In fact, upon reading the history of the RMHK, it is possible to see how signifiers of authenticity and of religious rituals such as the Madras kerchief traveled globally and how this traveling blurred boundaries of authenticity and tradition by becoming embedded in various local community practices. Weavers weave for a livelihood, and their products must travel and circulate if this mode of production is to successfully provide for the weaver and his family. In examining such stories, we also see that the disruptions in these marketing links are partly the result of colonization and modern globalization, and form part of the foundation for the outdating of particular modes of production.

In current times when the handloom is associated with authenticity and with the premodern even as live communities thrive in parts of the world, the product can indeed be placed in a modern national or international market. The issue then is that, in struggling for space in such markets, there is little flexibility for equal or fair bargains for traditional technology because of the ways in which the handloom technology has been Othered.

Journeying to the Where the Loom Resides

It was on one of my journeys to a rural South Indian village (Koyyalagudam) that I encountered the pit loom and the weaver at its interface within a handloom weaving community setting. I have no conscious memory of having seen this loom and the setting prior to that visit. I had heard about handloom weaving all my life and watched my parents demonstrate how khadi yarn is woven on the small charkha they owned. Upon encountering the pit loom I could not help but notice how "computerlike" the way it worked seemed to me. But this "computer" required the use of the full body. Arms reaching out to pull at the threads and "throwing" the shuttle. Legs moving under the frame of the loom while the weaver sat in a pit dug in the ground inside his home. I remember thinking at that moment about the sari he was weaving:

> *Did the loom make the sari or the sari make the loom?*
> *What kinds of looms allowed what kinds of saris (we know that as they exist looms are structured around the sari concept so it is difficult to adjust them to work with fabric for other garments).*

How did the loom shape fashion and convention.
How does the loom adapt to global fashions coming from a context outside the vision and experience of the weaver's everyday life?

Trying to answer such questions, a few years later, I became an amateur, (individual) weaver and spinner in an attempt to get a sense of the practice of re-introducing older technologies into at least the individual hobby space of a suburban North American daily routine. Therefore, my living room television shares space, at least temporarily, with two four-harness looms and my yarn, roving, spindles occupy an additional room in the house. The most recent "old" technology to arrive in the household was a Saxony spinning wheel in need of repairs and is demanding time and attention from me as its presence and my logic in bringing it into this space struggle to prevent it from becoming an antique museum piece in my formal home spaces.

The re-introduction of such artifacts as productive technologies can only occur if they are used and supported within a community structure. This individualized use of older technologies as hobby is certainly different from the kind of re-introductions done to provide and sustain existing livelihoods under threat, and does not yet carry the urgency for re-examination of discourses of modernity and tradition in the same way as the work of trying to sustain livelihoods of weaver communities in rural South India does.

r Z Starts a Business

In this section I describe rZ's (R's avatar on Second Life) attempts at setting up a "handloom" sari and apparel business on Second Life. R had been exploring Second Life on and off since 2003 when the virtual world was first started. After some initial explorations, in 2004 the avatar that remains currently as R's "alt" had come into being. Based on what this other avatar learned from 2004 to 2006, rZ was brought into being for the main purpose of trying to find Indian culture on Second Life. She wandered around to look for signifiers and images that would somehow remind her of what she knew through her offline experience as "Indian." Her 2004 alt (alternate avatar) had found a temple with South Indian sculptures some time ago (probably an art project) and rZ started by trying to find this project. But she was not able to locate it. She then did a search for India and found an Island named "India." Later she found a "Desi" club and Bollywood and a couple of stores that sold saris amongst other Indian type and international looking garb.

Now, R was curious to know why people on Second Life were creating and selling saris. Perhaps the existence and interest in saris meant there was a visible Indian (diasporic) presence in Second Life? She decided the best way might be to try and build a business and see who came to it. The international designers, the Bollywood builders, the Desi dancers, and the Gor eventually provided quite a customer base for her humble sari business. So she went searching to the stores she had shopped at, for someone to learn from. This is how she discovered that in an environment such as Second Life, skills and literacies are the highest priced commodities. Since she did not have the coding literacies required to build some of the tools needed to make some of the objects that would contribute to the overall sari ensemble that she was envisioning, she had to spend Linden dollars.

To acquire Linden dollars, her offline self had to use US dollars at an exchange rate specified by the owners of Second Life. She then needed to buy a script to help make "flexi" skirts (to create a swirling, flowing skirt through the creation of what is known as a "flexi prim"). There are several free scripting, building and designing tutorials offered by Second Life residents, mostly by those interested in using Second Life for educational purposes. However, they do not teach high-level scripting skills. There are sample templates for basic blouses, skirts and pants and so on available through various Second Life blogs as well. The learning curve and time investment for all this is very steep for someone who does not have much familiarity with code or with using digital imaging software. Therefore, anyone seriously wanting to do business on Second Life needs to invest a large amount of time and energy to the learning process.

Since this was a second profession for rZ's offline self, the one and only body that needed to learn everything was her offline self. rZ was clearly not R G's clone but an online avatar that could function only when R was available to be rZ and the latter's existence depended on the former's ability to log on.

Since 2007 Second Life residents and business owners have noticed more and more sari designers. Since the practice of designing of a sari using Photoshop requires a certain amount of dedicated patience and continued effort in trying to get the detail and shape just right so as to make it look like a sari that an Indian from India would recognize as a sari, this increased production of saris to me indicates at least an increased interest in the consumption of such attire by SL avatars. While the Goreans, a role-playing group that inhabits Second Life (see http://en.wikipedia.org/wiki/Gorean for a quick description of the Gor) are interested in saris, they have not been as particular about how Indian sari-like it should be.

The SL avatar of Indian origin tends to be more knowledgeable of a particular set of practices around sari wearing and this seems to influence what they consider to be apparel worthy of the name "sari." This is reflected in their consumption and production of saris and comments about saris when their avatars are wearing them. Interestingly, then this female attire becomes a certain symbol of "authenticity" of Indianness at the same time as it is still exotic and sexualized through its use by the Goreans on Second Life. There are, of course, instances where both the Gor market and the Indian market are targeted by a sari producer. SL avatar LP, for instance, has at least one store in a Gorean-focused mall and a store in at least one India-focused dance club and shopping center.

She also sells her creations at the now famous House of Style owned by the clothes designer OT. In 2006, O, L, and one or two others were the only sari and Indian apparel designers easily found on Second Life. Now there are several—both well known and not so well known. However, the perception of authenticity of saris on SL has more to do with the offline practice of making the sari through digital imaging and textures from the original textile-based sari material than it does with the authentic Indianness of the SL avatar wearing the sari or the person behind the avatar.

Conclusion

Handwoven cotton fabric has recognition in certain sections of the world as a product of ethnic belonging. The sense of a product from the past as exotic with no sense of continuity, frozen in the past, defines handloom cloth as "ethnic." This notion of handloom cloth is a modern positioning of the product of what is viewed as an old "traditional" technology. Another modern repositioning of the handloom product is its link to eco friendly organic processes that are a response to the modern crises. On the other hand, when the sari becomes digitized as a floating signifier caught in the net of virtual communities, it creates no major direct impact on the modern repositioning except that it creates a generational awareness amongst consumers. How such a floating signifier traveling virtual economies worn by avatars will translate—if at all—into material effects for actual livelihoods in offline worlds remains to be seen.

The present article was not intended either as a celebration or a full rejection of digital space as a possible venue for building value for traditionally produced, ecologically friendly products. The goal of the juxtaposition of the two extremes instead was meant as a way to tell a story about globalization that brings together the "old" and "new" in the telling only to allow the reader to see how these two spaces co-exist uncomfortably in the current global economy.

Notes

1. For a quick account of what a sari is and how it is made go to www.puja.com/sari/ and for a further idea of some varieties of saris available in the sari market, see www.sarishop.com/

2.Also see rad's flickr stream: www.flickr.com/groups/498788@N23/pool/

3. And problematic—but I will not be getting into the details of mapping the notion of digital diaspora in the present article. See work by scholars such as Lily Cho and Ella Shohat to understand some of the nuances of the concept "diaspora" in current times.

4. In his book *Jacquard's Web: How a Hand-Loom Led to the Birth of the Information Age* James Essinger does make the connection between the loom technology and computer technology.

CHAPTER FOUR

FRAMING THE LOOM: AN INDIAN CONTEX

Radhika Gajjala, Seemanthini Niranjana[1] and B. Syamasundari

In this chapter, we focus broadly on the mutual shaping of culture and technology in the context of a particular case in the history of the handloom industry of India through an examination of ruptures made visible in economic practices of consumption, production and marketing. We reflect on the questions raised, not so much from an intervention angle but from positioning what are referred to as "traditional knowledges" in contemporary times while problematizing the very conceptual categories of "traditional" and "modern." We also implicitly and explicitly work against modern-day "received views" about technology (Slack and Wise, 2005, 2); we examine the loom as technology, embedded in everyday life where the interplay between economics and culture is inseparable. Thus, we take seriously the notion of technological cultures as articulated by Wise and Slack, and work through particular contexts and assemblages of handloom technologies—mainly around the pit loom and the frame loom in rural South India.

We will therefore examine socio-economic and cultural practices of weaving fabric in rural South India, focusing on a particular situated case study of how technologies of the frame loom and the pit loom in one Indian context came to be positioned as modern and traditional within a dialectic tension produced through a competing colonial context. In this particular instance, the frame loom (what might be considered as a "traditional" loom technology in the context of European weaving even in present-day Western contexts) came to stand for "modern" in comparison with the pit loom (which is a loom used locally in the contexts discussed, until the introduction of the frame loom as an "innovation" meant to increase productivity).

Laying out particular narratives and descriptions of how these two developed side by side in a certain timeframe in rural South India, we examine structures and hierarchies that emerge as inseparable from practices of production and consumption. Thus our examination will look at the interlinking of markets, community, producer collectives and ideology. The narratives from the rural and urban field in South India serve to highlight the contextual nuances of how well-meaning "development" and "innovation" can, in actuality, function ideologically to shift the focus away from sustainable livelihood. Logics that articulate progress in neoliberal free-market risk based in globalizing hierarchies disadvantage the rural weavers rather than empowering them. Such logics are based in mass production, constant consumption (that in turn relies on a continual production of desire to consume through exposure to cultural media artifacts and explicit and implicit marketing of particular lifestyles) and an ever increasing "growth" paradigm that pays lip-service to equal distribution but politically does not include equity as a practice or serious policy. Thus, for instance, the thoughtless adoption of "new technologies" rather than being somehow progressive and liberatory for the South Indian weaver (as technophiliac storyings of new technologies might suggest), risks further disadvantaging him/her in various ways when close attention is not paid to the socio-cultural context and internal local hierarchies as well as to the relationship between the specific local and the global. In fact, the new technologies that are supposedly introduced in an attempt to upgrade so-called traditional technologies do not simply attempt to "improve" local material conditions. They simultaneously work to convert (homogenize) the thus far perceived "traditional" (subaltern) into the "modern." In other words, digital technologies and related modern technologies are characterized as real Technology with a capital "T." As was noted by a development worker from another context (Indonesia), during one of the co-author's ethnographies in other developing country contexts, for instance, aid programs from the West often privilege the logic of access to new technology and the Internet as the main trajectory of progress. Therefore they tend to develop aid plans that include the donating of new technology (laptops and increased Internet access) to developing world contexts and often end up creating social and cultural problems for local development workers who have been working at the grassroots level trying to introduce social reform in everyday contexts. Such actions, even though well-meaning, contribute to the social issues that are raised by the contradictory ethos of present-day modernity. Thus rather than being helped along and made more efficient through the provision of such access, the task for the development worker gets compounded in a dual struggle against social problems that are already prevalent prior to the insertion of the new technologies as well as battling against the new social problems that get introduced because of the sudden insertion of the new technologies. Thus the work of livelihood creation and capacity building now compels the aid worker to upgrade their own literacies and socio-cultural understandings on multiple levels so they can work against both "modern" and "traditional" social evils and hierarchies.

The examination of "old" and "new" loom technologies in the context of South India in the current chapter is in keeping with the theme of the rest of the chapters in this book. We show how the subaltern is yet again compelled into voicing his/her location in relation to this capital T technology as he/she is shown his/her place within the neoliberal global market hierarchies. Using the case of the handloom and the efforts to sustain the livelihoods of communities of weavers, we examine how technology is located within a developmental discourse. We then proceed to show how a different conceptual framework is needed for the handloom industry to survive. We examine the production and consumption of the handloom as situated technological practice in order to work toward the recognition of different economies that surround technological practice. In the chapter that follows this one, you will see how this situated practice is different in post-modern revivals of craft and weaving in the West such as the handmade only movements and DIY movements that are on the rise in recent years. Thus, while specific production technologies are locally embedded knowledge systems, in a globalizing ethos and digital financializing logic, the directions of these locally embedded knowledge systems are shaped by a different set of audiences/consumers who, as we saw in the case of Kiva.org in the last chapters as well, are situated within different everyday contexts and cultural groups. This privileging of knowledge systems that lie outside the local contexts of the subaltern who lives in developing world contexts leads to the global stretching of relations of labor, capital and consumption. Such a stretching of relations is accelerated in present forms of globalization while reducing the actual involved interpersonal and intercultural interactions and negotiations needed for the successful integration of various locals into global hierarchies that privilege a westernized self.

We thus look at how the weaver is positioned in these systems through a mapping of a particular trajectory of shifts in the handloom industry focused on innovations in handloom technology. This mapping is meant to trouble existing discourses of innovation and progress while pointing to how, in the context of the handloom, the mainstream development discourse of innovation and a particular notion of progress give rise to problematic tensions in relation to policy and practice.

Through this analysis, we also hope to open up a critique of what we see as a methodological blind spot in the way "Technology" is talked about in mainstream development discourse (thus impacting how policy is shaped and obstructing grassroots attempts toward sustainable ecologies). We attempt to reveal the problematic nature of research and practice methodologies that view rural (third-world) communities and their struggles in relation to mainstream globalization and development models as "case studies" by development researchers and workers. Such cases can be used to justify policy and research based in conceptualizations developed in spaces where active and continued engagement with such populations has not been considered to be crucial to the very theory building activity. Thus we tell narratives based in immersive participant ethnographies coming from an engagement as actors in the various contexts we write of. Some of the engagements come from an approach based in "epistemologies of doing" (Gajjala, Rybas and Altman 2007) where one of the authors tried to understand the laboring process by learning to use what in this chapter we refer to as the frame loom.

We begin by underlining the links of knowledge systems with their cultural contexts, asking what happens to particular local technical knowledge systems when they are pushed into different spaces named as modern and how they get characterized as "Traditional," subaltern and Othered. We then proceed to critically examine technology as contextual. We do this by looking at specific technological cultures, which shape mainstream narratives of development and modernity while other technological cultures, such as handloom cultures, are exoticized and placed outside. Thus they continue to remain outside, subalternized and named as "Traditional" as if tradition is frozen in past contexts, while modern practices contain no traditions of practice or hierarchies. Next, we trace the role of macro policy perspectives and directives to show the different ideological frames through which this so-called traditional (but actually located/local) technology gets disembedded and re-positioned in new contexts. We continue our examination by mapping some contexts of handloom technological practice. We use this mapping to highlight ways in which policies on handloom technology attempt to graft a modernization and transnationalization agenda onto existing technologies. Finally, we lay out the challenges in building linkages for weavers.

Knowledge Systems and Their Links with Cultural Context

Knowledge systems in every society form a complicated grid informing practices of all kinds. They include techniques (such as building boats or houses, the way we cook) and beliefs—about ourselves and our place in the world. They also include philosophies that shape our actions, as well as material practices themselves. Many different streams of socio-cultural life feed into knowledge, as do economic, religious, political and other processes. In other words, knowledge systems emerge from experiences of cultures, and are consolidated through practices ranging from the technical to the philosophical. There is a close relation between these knowledge systems and the situations within which they take birth. Ideas of self, their links to the natural and social worlds and their interrelations are articulated within such knowledge systems. This is clearly visible if we look closely at the organization of handloom weaving in the village, the structure of the loom, and weaving practices that are closely linked to caste as well as cultural and ritual contexts. Technique and beliefs coalesce in such knowledge systems, with social relationships and economic practices being built around them.

In a modern environment, links between "natural" and "social" take different forms. "New" technology becomes an important mediator through which these relations are understood. A perspective on technology that views only particular modern technologies as technologies of progress produces and privileges notions of "newness"—equating this "new" with better. This new and better technology comes embedded in a worldview that gains currency and begins to dominate and replace the older framework. The particular context in which this worldview emerged gets obscured, as it is then applied across locales as a homogenized, single form of knowledge. This process is pushed further, in modern times, by the consolidation of technoscience as a worldview.

Behind this consolidation lie developments that emerge from conceptual, methodological and, of course, historical realms. Central to it is the perception that modern science lays the foundation for all knowledge systems, and that modern technology represents the body of substantive scientific knowledge that takes root in society. Modernization of a society is measured, then, by the extent to which such technology pervades all its elements, as technology in this sense holds out a promise as a potential provider of an unending supply of goods. Further, as you see in the other chapters in this book, this has proved attractive to countries outside the immediate socio-economic contexts within which these frameworks arose. In this process, the particular technologies that emerged from within Europe have come to be perceived as universal (and now global) by those societies located outside. Even though within Europe and North America there were struggles over which technologies emerged as modern and there was dissent over shifts (such as in the case of so-called "Luddite" movements during the transition from handloom to mechanization of textile production), those internal struggles gave way to particular technologies as "superior" and these were the technologies that got disseminated elsewhere in the name of progress. It was understood that the diffusion of such innovations in colonized and previously colonized societies would make them truly modern and developed. New technology (whether that meant mechanization of looms in those days or the adoption of wireless and digital technologies in present times) as a knowledge system became the dominant anchor for modernity. To "modernize," societies were expected to follow this path. Technoscience as consolidated in the West soon became the yardstick against which knowledge of other cultures was assessed. In this drive for systematization, standardization and rational understanding, vast bodies of technical knowledge in many non-western countries lost credibility and were equated with the past of modernity (as in premodern). While, as scholars such as Robert B. Kristofferson have pointed out (2007), there were different trajectories through which shifts in craft technologies and textile industries, for instance, moved into mechanization, only the trajectories taken by particular powerful and visible nations (England, in the case of looms and the U.S. in the case of digital technologies) were noted as the ideal linear trajectories to follow toward a path to affluence and redemption from poverty.

This poses a problem for nations, cultures, and of course, the people. Today the idiom of modernity has become the single lens through which we understand the world. This offers a seemingly a universal tool by which to transcend local contexts and aspire for progress. This mystification of particular kinds of technologies as a universal language marginalizes all other forms of knowledge systems, many of which are local systems, having their own rationale, technological or otherwise. In this process the survival of so-called traditional technologies becomes an uphill struggle. The system named as "Tradition" and as "premodern," is then left with no legitimate space for existence. When it is pitted against the parameters of productivity and efficiency, which are central to modernization, such technology falls between the extremes of being an outmoded, inefficient practice that is on its way out or being a part of our heritage that needs to be supported.

In such a context, how do we position these Othered technologies in relation to modernity? The only two positions available for it are either remaining totally outside the modern or trying to find a place within it. In such a situation, when there is a demand from the modern for revival of particular technologies characterized as traditional technologies, the dilemma deepens. It is crucial to see why the opportunity is being offered at this point in time and what would be the pitfalls in entering this modern space now. It is vital to examine the issue in all its dimensions before this technology that carries the label of traditional technology can set foot in modern contexts.

Technology as Contextual

Scholars such as Marvin (1988), Slack (1989) and Sterne (2000) have pointed out how social ideological struggles are negotiated in relation to technologies in specific contexts, and how various practices produce hierarchies around the use, consumption, production, design, reproduction and circulation of such technologies. Further, as Jennifer Daryl Slack (1989) writes:

> Technology is not simply an object connected in various ways to the institutional and organizational structures from within which it emerges to be reconnected in a new context, but . . . it is always an articulated moment of interconnections among the range of social practices, discursive statements, ideological positions, social forces, and social groups within which the object moves. (339)

These articulated moments of interconnections are what we engage in the dialogue that follows as "technology tales" in this article.

However, examining technology as articulated moments of interconnections and situated in community everyday practices should not automatically lead to the conclusion that technology is embedded in specific frozen local cultures. It is impossible to "freeze" practices when communities continually change. This is why the idea of tradition as frozen is actually a myth. Local rural cultures are living organizations—ever shifting and responding to internal and external economic, political and cultural factors that impact their daily lives. They are just as much *located* as urban cultures within "Global Cities" are (see Sassen 1998 for a discussion of Global Cities).

Despite the increased attentiveness to understanding technologies in context, in terms of how technology (as artifact) or technological practices have come to pervade our daily lives, there is an aura around technology that requires some amount of unpacking. Modernity and technology of a certain kind have been considered as synonymous; as modernity travels, particular technologies get reified as universal, often marginalizing what has come to be termed as traditional technologies even though these technologies (as in the case of the handloom) are a source of continuing livelihood for a large number of people. Handloom production is the second largest livelihood in India and comes second to agriculture. IT still only provides a livelihood to not more than 30% of the Indian population. While this is often used as a way to "prove" that India is a developing nation, such a characterization still privileges IT as the forward-looking and modern technology, while ignoring contextual issues and global power relations that privilege IT as a tool for upward mobility. Tracing this matrix of knowledge systems that jostle for space yields a complex picture.

For instance, a way to reveal the problematic nature of mainstream development processes for handloom weavers is to view the handloom as a technology. Viewing the handloom as a technology shifts the way we look at the weavers and their process as opposed to the way that (capital T) Technology often views the handloom and the weavers as merely "nature." When the handloom and the weavers are exoticized as "natural" rural beings, they are positioned in a nature versus technology framework. Thinking in terms of diffusion of technology and of technology as "new" technologies of modernity and post-modernity allows the loom to merge with the weaver pushed into the background of a romanticized rural "natural" backdrop against which modern "new" technologies must be inserted in order for the weaver to become economically upwardly mobile.

Once we start to view the loom as technology, then the weaver too becomes technology in a different sense. The weaver's function in relation to the loom and the loom's function in producing handloom textiles become very clear and visible. The two (loom and weaver) must function together, within a whole community that supports the individual weaver and handloom in production through various necessary functions such as the production and dyeing of yarn and so on. This is the only way to produce handloom material—or there is no "handloom" cloth in existence at all. The weaver being considered technology, of course, has different consequences in the context of globalization and mass consumerism. There will be more on this as one of us (Gajjala) explores the emerging handmade only movements in the westernized strata of the world in a forthcoming book examining globalization and neoliberal dynamics in networked platforms through the increasing ITization and NGOization of socio-economic global space. For now the investigation of the Indian context continues.

The contradiction of modernizing handloom technology when the process is articulated in this way arises even in the simple act of trying to sell in a "modern" market. Practices associated with modernity have connected with older technologies that are now considered traditional, even as hybrid practices have developed at their interface. Yet ideology and policy position them as incompatible. The process can no longer remain what it was as it evolves to cohere with the changing contexts. For example, a handloom product can be placed in a modern national or international market. However, the jostle for space in these markets allows little flexibility for equal or fair bargains for particular products made using such technologies categorized as traditional or old. The problem becomes more complex due to the altered forms of these older technologies, which have to struggle for recognition both among the market segments that carry a memory of the old and those that would like to make place for the "new."

Handlooms are considered "traditional technology" but have had to negotiate with the frames of modernity for decades. Currently, they are in actuality detached from the production community contexts that they were embedded in in the past. The struggle that continues for such Othered technology is more about how to retain its own unique nature, while making changes to become acceptable/closer to mainstream technologies.

There is much written on what happens to the modern technology when it enters the non-modern or the "modernizing" (like developing) contexts. This is what is often referred to as "diffusion of innovation." The impact on the social, the economic and the political has been extensively debated from such a point of view. What has been left out, however, is the discussion on the changes that happen when the reverse happens—that is, when a so-called traditional technology enters the modern contexts. Instances of such older and traditional technology entering modern contexts are not limited to developing world contexts, but happen in first world contexts as well; however, in the latter, they get noted differently—either as alternate, resistant or in some other way. For instance, the do-it-yourself movements, handmade only movements and renaissance of knitting among certain younger generations of women and men in mostly European contexts are noted within discourses of newness and celebrated in ways that differ from what we write about in the present chapter.

In the case of developing world contexts, we are not so much re-inserting the older technologies themselves into communities, but are renegotiating the place occupied by such technological cultures and production communities within modern economies. Mainstream developmental ideologies erase the need to reexamine the importance of such technological cultures and production communities in relation to material upward mobility. These communities exist and continue to provide forms of livelihood in such societies. In fact they continue to be important means of livelihood in various regions of the world. The existence and desirability of these particular old technologies (termed as traditional) in modern contexts is ignored and made invisible discursively through ideologies of material and cultural development as Western-led movements. But making these contexts invisible is equal to ignoring the historical events that affected the people lower in hierarchy and power and concluding that they are powerless to contribute to the shaping of the historical discourse.

As histories of colonialism and modern nation-building began to lean toward notions of a particular kind of teleology of modernization as necessary for progress, technologies such as the handloom were cast as "traditional" with simultaneous negative and romanticized connotations as the past of the modern. Colonizers nostalgic for handloom and craft aesthetics tried to preserve it in a certain form while nationalists in India took it up in a different way as a symbol of authenticity and nationalism following Gandhi's assertion of handloom and cottage industry as Indian. The contradiction, of course, is that simultaneously there was a misunderstanding and even a rejection of the underlying logic that led Gandhi to mobilize the spinning wheel and handloom as technologies of resistance to colonial economics in the first place. Yet, they were simultaneously positioned as anomalous to progress. Thus even while the reality of economic structures (where the handloom provides the second largest means of livelihood in India) required that this so-called traditional technology of the handloom be "inserted" into the postcolonial modernized economic and social structures through which nation-building was happening, the handloom was still positioned as a "backward" technology.

The disembedding of traditional technologies and their rerooting in new contexts is not a smooth process, but fraught with opposing pulls and shifts in economic and social practices. Some of these dimensions are elaborated later in this chapter. We argue, in what follows, that this process of disembedding and rerooting of practices is closely linked to the rearticulations of technology at another level, for instance policy positions mediated through the state.

Rearticulating Location Through Macro Policy Perspectives

In India, development has been coterminous with industrialization, mechanization, productive efficiency, and so on. While the development of large industries (iron and steel, textile mills, for example) fits snugly into this frame, there are smaller industries in the peripheries of this industrial core (for example, artisanal industries such as handlooms, leather, etc), which do not, but whose dynamics have not been examined. The more visible accounts of large-scale industrialization (being perceived as the visible markers of progress) have marginalized the more dispersed and fragmented sites of industrial production represented by the small-scale sector. Yet these dispersed industries, also referred to as the nonformal economy, have sustained local economies/cultures over hundreds of years. This raises problematic questions regarding the frameworks within which economic development and industrialization in India are seen, given the uneven dynamism and scale of different segments. If the standard understandings of this process of development privilege a certain kind of industrial "core," then what of the industries on the peripheries of this logic? How do we think about economic activity considered to be "in the margins" by policy makers focused on teleologies of progress based in post-colonial and globalization/modernization ideologies, but in actuality central to the actual livelihood and sustenance of large communities? More critically, what of the frameworks of knowledge underlying these latter systems?

Westernized Growth Paradigm

In post-independence times, these shifting contexts range from the socio-economic to the political. The socio-economic shifting contexts include new markets and the demand for new products (and hence the search for a particular form of technical innovation). The political shifts include the role of policy perceptions and directives in shaping handloom practices based in how the nation-state must intervene to keep handlooms viable while at the same time presented as traditional, exotic and backward in comparison to modern development initiatives such as manufacturing industries and the IT sector projects.

In a past when handloom technology existed as a socio-economic community formation that was shaped by the local contexts, it was tangibly linked to the local customers that influenced certain changes in the technology based in local market feedback and needs as well as new experiments in design and innovation internal to the handloom-based community. But these were not traumatic in nature as they served as, and through, aids that connected the producer and consumer through local channels and sometimes directly. But in its interactions with contemporary contexts, modern technology demanded a radical transformational change (as opposed to gradual transition) within the socio-economic sphere surrounding the handloom itself because of impacts of the simultaneous privileging of industrialization and urbanization as better ways to move the country out of poverty. Thus rapid and uneven changes came about in the way the handloom production community and its supply-chain linkages functioned. They called for disruptive and violent disengagement with the older contexts and the creation of new environments. The negotiation that happened then between older handloom technology and new modern contexts can be followed in the policy processes that dictated the future directions of the society from time to time. The importance of the policy initiatives in the case of handlooms or other handcrafts is due to the absence of a public/societal ownership of the technology. The rupture from colonial times of the various links that formed an integral part of the traditional technology resulted in a loss of community ownership. The resurrection of handcrafts as an innate element of the country's identity during the struggle for freedom created a legitimate space of ownership for any future governing body in a politically free nation. The perspective of the planners was influenced by the nationalist emphasis on self-reliance.

The national struggle for political freedom never lost sight of the constructive agenda needed for nation-building, both during its initial stages and its strong periods of mobilization. After political freedom there were intense deliberations on the way to move forward to rebuild the nation. The models for the future were available in the examples of European nations and the West in general. The material success of the Western nations, aided by industrialization and intensive mechanization, was phenomenal. There was a significant increase in personal comforts and wealth along with a rise in prosperity of such nations. This was the model in front of our leaders in the post-independence period. In such a background, the argument of Gandhi for developing an indigenous model of development located in the village economy did not find many supporters. On the eve of our independence, Nehru declared that the task ahead for the nation was "the ending of poverty and ignorance and disease and inequality of opportunity" (as cited in Dreze and Sen, 1995). The path to achieving these goals was located in the industrialization model. The main support structures for the course of this journey were provided by science and technology. The progress of a society and nation adopting this route are known to be toward development.

Ideally, the development paradigm should involve the social, cultural, political and economic all together. But the focus in early (immediate post-war) development literature (in the West) has been mainly on the generation of economic growth in the sense of increasing gross national product. In the five-year plans envisaged by India, which were devised as strategies for nation-building and economic development, there is a tacit assumption of this superiority. The indicators telling us how far we have moved ahead in our journey are largely determined by such economic factors. This is the point at which the post-independence Indian process of nation-building can be really said to have moved away from Gandhian thinking on reconstruction.

The emphasis has been on a westernized growth paradigm informing the success of the economy, the polity embracing principles of democracy, the society progressing and the culture forward looking. Growth, which should aim for increasing productivity by efficient use of technology, is supposed to provide the momentum for development in other spheres like the political, cultural and social. Motivated by the positive energy unleashed by this construction of the economic growth ushering in all around development, the concerted national effort was on pushing economic growth high on the agenda. Civil society responded by investing in big industries, supporting large dams and bringing more mechanization into the community at large. Education emphasized the skills required to support these industrial modes of production. Society geared itself toward more centralized forms of production enabled by the use of technology. These developments brought in their wake new networking and inserted different types of everyday practices for sustaining socio-economic activities. This sort of re-routing of socio-economic functions and privileging of literacies within the community affected the existing cultural relations. In the light of this tremendous upheaval, the already existing modes of production, categorized as artisanal, were forced to reinvent themselves to relocate within this altered terrain that was now defined by value chains within national, international and global markets that required extended relations and negotiations of a different sort. They thus had to confront their externally redefined socio-economic value within current technocultures that shifted the way consumers viewed the use-value and social value of their products in the everyday.

Simultaneously, however, the general perspective of planners in the immediate aftermath of India's freedom was dominated by a nationalist ideology with an emphasis on economic self-reliance. Considering the way the population and socio-economic activities of the majority of Indian population and labor force were set up at that time, self-reliance could practically be achieved by mobilizing internal, already existing, livelihood sectors within rural India. This was particularly visible in the way the artisanal sector was approached and dealt with. Promoting the handloom sector in particular was seen primarily as achieving the twin objectives of employment generation and production of cloth for mass consumption.[2] The artisanal sector was supposed to provide rural employment and at the same time uphold the cultural heritage. The handloom sector was seen as a repository of cultural heritage, and support to the sector was seen as part of the need to preserve the country's cultural heritage. But over the decades, this way of seeing the handloom sector dwindled into a formal invocation without any substance, when the focus became creating employment and incomes for the increasing urban masses. Ironically, it was the increase in rural to urban migration that had led to the continuing displaced relocation of rural populations into urban masses. Therefore the increase in urban masses happened because of policies privileging modernity based in ideologies of westernized modernity and industrialization that created a demand for wage laborers. Most of the reports and plan documents approached the issue of the handlooms and handicrafts sector in terms of its potential to generate employment, incomes for artisans, and foreign exchange earnings. However, these objectives are peppered with observations regarding "improving craftsmanship and innovativeness while retaining the foundation of our cultural heritage" and "promoting the economic independence, social status and individual dignity of the craftspersons" for instance, in the report by the working group on handicrafts for the Sixth Plan (Bhasin and Kak, 1983, 24). What is evident is a plethora of objectives and declarations, with no clear indication of how they would be followed through in various programs, and without any clarity on the institutional channels through which this could be achieved.

This situation did not actually create space to address issues of how technology can be engaged in innovating processes and products. The later phase in planning compared existing technologies to the emerging modern technology and started applying the same parameters to each for the purpose of evaluation. The term "technology upgradation" finds favor in all the subsequent planning documents. These documents were focused on diffusion of packaged innovations that came from elsewhere. The efforts in innovating and improving handcrafting socio-economic practices and technologies were now geared toward achieving standards that were to match contexts where such new technologies had the advantage. Thus developing contexts for progress created spaces in which the newer technologies were adopted from external contexts as technocultural assemblages that would automatically contribute to development and poverty relief. Implicit and explicit policies developed within such framings of technology placed handcrafting technologies in the lower rung of the economic development hierarchy. In such a push for standardization of practice in the use of technology and the development of technocultural communities, the different skill levels in traditional technology created a problem. They could not be lumped en masse into one segment and innovated according to formulaic methods developed at the interface of the technological ensembles required for industrialization. The high-skill segment was separated out and the less-skilled section was replaced by mechanical weavers. In earlier times the presence of diverse skills was reflected in the variety of products created and accorded variable social status. There was recognition of higher skill not only through the product woven but in the social status accorded. The point to note however is that there was space for a range of skills in the activity. This range of skills, knowledge, and social status was ignored by policy makers who, in their programs of modernizing, offered support to only the high-skilled segment and advised the rest to move into mechanized weaving.

Along with the plan documents, the various textile policies put out by the state from the 1950s onward also tell a revealing story of how policy pronouncements steered the industry in certain directions. The issue of size (small versus large) looms over these pronouncements, especially with the organized (large) mill sector and the decentralized (small) handloom and power loom sectors jostling for space and attention. While the concern for employment generation and the access of the poor to affordable cloth have been the primary concerns percolating into the textile policies, the way in which this has been addressed has often led to a tussle between sectors. For instance, while it was the mill sector which had to produce cloth for mass consumption in the early decades of Indian independence, now that responsibility has been shifted onto the handloom sector, but without creating adequate institutional infrastructure, such as credit and marketing, to support this new imperative.

Neoliberal Shifts

A significant shift in approach comes around 1985, with the new textile policy that year. Rather than begin with the equity issue (usually articulated in terms of commitment to providing income and employment to the economically weaker sections), the announced objective is one of increasing cloth production, and employment generation is an argument that merely supports this primary objective. There is a much clearer recognition of market forces than before, and several of the "controls" hitherto placed by the government in the interest of protecting the handloom sector—for instance on mills and power looms—are withdrawn, while improving efficiency and competition become important. While paying lip-service to the employment potential, the emphasis on efficiency and increasing productivity points in the direction of neoliberal modernization and globalization through mass production within a postmodern consumer culture, which invariably erodes these existing livelihoods.

Further, contradictory statements emerge at this time, for example, formally stressing the need to expand the rural industry of handlooms, while at the same time encouraging power loom expansion. This does not take into account the complex intersectoral dynamics. For instance, one power loom is said to displace six handlooms: the scale of displacement becomes evident if we look at the lakhs of power looms that have been set up in different parts of the country. Other parallel developments, such as the textile mill strike in the early 1980s (see D'Monte, 2002), also indirectly add to the proliferation of power looms. Similarly, measures like the deregulation of the mill sector and the decontrol of the yarn trade have significant repercussions on sectors like the handloom sector, where there is large-scale disruption due to non-availability of raw materials and marketing support. Reiterating a commitment to the protection of the decentralized handloom sector in the Textile Policies does not make much sense when measures such as decontrol and deregulation are actually countering the State protectionism offered to the small artisanal sector.

The point is that policy directives both frame and steer the traditional handloom industry in certain directions guided by an overarching mechanization agenda. It is this trend that explains the introduction of frame looms and some of the subsequent shifts in organization of production that comes with it.

In the next section, we map some contexts of handloom technological practice, and use this mapping to highlight ways in which policies on handloom technology attempt to graft a modernization agenda onto existing technologies. For instance, through a particular linear telling of the progress narrative, technologies seem to have an almost natural and logical trajectory of growth, development, and diffusion. However, examining the details of the pit loom and frame loom in the south Indian context might help us see how ideologically situated (i.e. not objective and universal) the linear telling of the progress narrative is in actuality.

Mapping Handloom Technological Practices

Handloom Industry

The handloom industry in India is largely rural-based, and is an important provider of rural nonfarm employment. In fact, the handloom industry is the largest employment provider after agriculture.[3] The industry is large in aggregate, and is made up of small, dispersed units that are independent of generated power, thereby avoiding environmental degradation. Handloom weaving is largely done in the weaving families' own homes, on looms owned by them. Being household-based, the production process is inclusive, involving the people otherwise characterized as economically dependant—that is, the elderly and women. In other words, the hierarchies organizing the work flow in this context are significantly different from the hierarchies organizing work flow in a textile mill.

Weaving in the rural South Indian context that we discuss here is presently viewed as a traditional caste-based skill, and continues to be learnt through the everyday routines of production within the community and within the family structure. However, with the increasing pull of IT industry and/or call center work as offering a viable alternative to weaving in the case of the materially better-off weaver families, this sort of learning structure is being disrupted and new weavers learn through different forms of apprenticeships and workshops. Thus, while skills are usually passed on from parents to children, there are also ongoing traditions of apprenticing newcomers and these ongoing traditions are being mobilized currently to recruit weavers.

In a village context where weaving activities still continue to foster weaving communities, looms still occupy significant portions of some of the homes in their everyday living space, joining the labor force that weaves and maintaining the industry infrastructure is comparatively low-capital intensive. Hence the loom is accessible to large numbers of people in and around villages that still carry these networks and infrastructures even though weakening because of market structures. In such a context, entry barriers are low.

The fact that it is a household activity does not mean that weavers are independent producers. They work in co-operative societies where they are shareholders. When work is not readily available, weavers are dependent on master weavers who are present locally and are engaged in the wider trading of handloom cloth. The co-operative society or the master weaver generally supplies yarn and dyes to the weaver. The access to market is in the hands of the society or the master weaver. In many places there are weavers who do not own a loom and weave in sheds owned by the master weaver.

Thus we see that even though these communities have been eroded and disrupted through continuing shifts to the socio-economic and political landscapes in urban and rural India, there is still a community of weavers that provides a context and a lopsided continuity for handloom weaving in South India. Based on Radhika's research in northwest Ohio settings of handloom weaving and spinning in modernity, we know, however, that rebuilding such practices and related supply-chain links that these contexts even now in South India currently sustain—however unevenly—is quite difficult when they are completely annihilated structurally.

The Handloom: Pit Loom

A handloom is an implement used to weave cloth that is operated manually by weavers using their hands and feet. There are two kinds of handlooms—the pit loom and the frame loom—both of which operate broadly on the same principle. The loom is placed in such a way that the weaver can sit comfortably and work. With the pit loom, *gunta maggam*, the weaver sits on the loom and his or her legs are in the pit dug in the ground. The warp of the loom is stretched just above the pit vertically toward the weaver, and parallel to the ground. Thus the weaver would be on an even level with the loom. The shafts of the loom are controlled by a series of foot pedals called treadles. The weaver is able to operate these treadles with his legs comfortably. This ensures that the weaver's hands are free to handle the shuttle. The warp is separated into two layers and then the weft threads in the shuttle are thrown from one end of the warp to the other end. Then the inserted weft is pushed into place by the suspended reed, *acchu*. Such pit looms are used for weaving finer and lighter fabrics like saris, dhotis and fine dress materials.

In the case of a frame loom, the entire operation is on a raised frame above the ground, and the product is usually heavier fabrics like bed sheets and thick furnishing fabrics. Thus the bodily posture and position of the weaver in relation to the technology (the loom) has an impact on what the end product looks and feels like. The cyborg weaver is thus the technology that interacts with different kinds of looms to enable nuances in how the cloth is woven.

The simplest form of weaving on the pit loom would need at least two series of warp (that is, odd and even series) and for the warp to be opened there need to be two sets. So, it is imperative that these two sets need two heddles and two treadles attached to the heddles. By just alternating the lifting of odd and even sets, we would get the simplest weave called the plain weave. There are more complex weaves. By raising the shafts in different combinations, the weaver creates a variety of geometric and artistic patterns.

This extremely complex technology is daily brought to life whenever a weaver sits on a loom. The technique cannot be separated from a way of life. Weavers' weaving practices raise important questions regarding the form in which artisanal skills exist, and how they are acquired and transferred. Most of these skills are part of craft traditions where knowledge/skills have long been passed down through generations. In this context, they constitute a body of tacit knowledge, or noncodified information that has been drawn from and lives through unbroken practice.

Upgrading Technology: Introduction of Frame Looms

Compared to the pit loom, the frame loom seems to have come from practices associated with modernity in colonial and post-colonial India. Frame looms are an integral part of the technology upgrade program of the government. As we have noted, the policies that informed this shift from pit looms saw it as a part of a larger change toward modern technology. The overall plan policy started looking at efficiency and productivity as the basic parameters that define modern technology. In this schema, the speed of the loom becomes the debatable issue. Frame looms resemble the mechanical loom (power loom) closely except that they are hand operated and provide larger warps. As the technology was introduced probably with the motive of slowly moving the entire pit loom production to frame loom and then power loom (a kind of slow transition), the products planned were those that were produced on the power loom like running fabric in lower counts. The government picked up the initial production but the volumes of material produced were ultimately self-defeating since it became difficult to just sell meters and meters of plain fabric without any apparent added value.

Because the loom size was big it could not fit the low roof houses of the weavers and had to be installed in a shed which then had to be supervised by the co-operative. We see this in the rise of the frame loom sheds in co-operatives across the State of Andhra Pradesh. Their number is larger in the Telangana (a region of Andhra Pradesh), where weaving already took a severe beating with the decline of local markets. In the coastal districts of Andhra Pradesh, however, the traditional product still commanded a good immediate market and we see fewer frame loom sheds there. One of the reasons for this is the thriving agriculture in the coastal belt which supported the local economy. On the other hand, in the Telangana region, which adopted more frame looms than the coastal districts, the buying power of the people was absent since the crops in that region were dependent on monsoons and the region is not fed by as many rivers as the coastal districts. As the introduction of frame looms was by and large government-sponsored, they were set up in handloom cooperatives, and not really taken up by master weavers. Master weavers may also have been deterred from the frame looms because the product of a frame loom, unlike the pit loom, does not reflect a unique identity. It is clear that the unique selling point (USP) of a handloom product in India is available today only from a pit loom.

The introduction of the frame loom in this way and in these particular South Indian rural contexts breaks the web of the activities surrounding the traditional pit loom. Setting aside the issues of comparison through matching quality, product variety and so on, the loom brings about a new set of actions both in the preparation of yarn and weaving. The dyers and sizers involved in getting the yarn ready for weaving have to make changes in the way they work, and probably need to increase the scale of their operations to meet the needs of the new loom. The weavers can no longer work within the boundaries of the family but have to go out and work in sheds. This kind of rearranging looks simple on the surface but in reality ushers in an entire new perspective that redefines links between the various actors and slowly may push toward a central point of control to perform the tasks efficiently. The extent of capital investment will also increase and build in new imperatives. The master weavers traditionally performing the function of investment worked informally through kinship networks and managed to build a successful business. To enter the business of setting up frame looms, they had to work with an entirely different mindset and downplay the angle of kinship relations. The alternative to them changing the way they functioned would be for a new set of traders, entrepreneurs, to enter the business. This seems to have happened in weaving villages where the traders oriented the weaving activity to produce for export only. The government export council strongly supported these initiatives and undertook the burden of infrastructure and shipping of the product. In the areas like Kannur in Kerala and Karur, Chennimalai in Tamil Nadu, we find master weavers/traders investing in sheds, competing to produce a furnishing fabric which can come as close as possible to the power loom product.

Frame looms in states like Andhra Pradesh, where traders did not enter the new production processes, remained chiefly an arm of the government, and the entire production was procured by the Apex co-operative (APCO) marketing agency (the federal marketing agency of the co-ops) to supply to government departments like social welfare, women and child homes, and public hospitals. Many a time artificial yarn was supplied by APCO in order to reduce costs of production as this entire activity by now was only a welfare measure. The organic link between natural fiber and a hand-operated loom was also lost in this kind of transaction.

Yemmigannur Co-Operative Society

Frame looms were set up in state-supported handloom cooperatives, but, as explained above, were not always taken up by master weavers. Local histories and market decisions also went into the choice of looms set up. This point can be illustrated with an example from Yemmigannur, which will show how the choice of loom type (pit or frame loom) is related to the kind of organizational structure under which production is taking place (co-operative or master weaver), and to the choice of product and market segment targeted. Yemmigannur is in Kurnool district, in the Rayalaseema region of Andhra Pradesh, which has a number of villages and towns noted for handloom weaving. The products woven across the district are extensive, ranging from cotton and silk border saris to bedsheets and mosquito nets.

Here we find a range of systems and contracts of weaving at work, redefining relationships between the mass of ordinary weavers and the rich "master" weaver. Unlike in other places, there are traditional weaving castes as well as castes/groups that are not traditional weavers, but have taken up weaving as a means of livelihood.[4] This diversity in castes practicing weaving can perhaps be attributed to the fact that weaving was promoted as an income-generation activity when the co-operative was first set up in response to a famine that affected the area in the 1930s. The severity of the famine was such that mass migration of people became very common and attempts by the British government to alleviate the crisis by providing a livelihood through relief-work failed. It is reported that, in 1936, a relief center for agricultural workers was set up at Yemmigannur, but the weavers did not find it suited to their skills and abilities. In 1937, a temporary weavers' relief center was set up, and this succeeded in stemming migratory trends among weavers. Though this was closed down a year later, the weavers had found the center so effective that under the initiative of Machani Somappa, a Kurini master weaver, a handloom co-operative was set up in 1938. Records suggest that not only did this stop the outmigration of weavers to other areas, but attracted weavers from surrounding areas as well. Over the years, there was considerable product diversification, as the cooperative made products to suit changing needs—from weaving bandage cloth during the Second World War to mosquito nets, to carving a distinctive niche for bedsheet production and shirting. As they negotiated new markets, loom technology also changed. For instance, weaving bedsheets and furnishings was undertaken on frame looms that were provided by the cooperative. At the same time, we have to bear in mind that this product was not the traditional product of the region, where the mainstay in weaving was saris, monopolized by master weavers. A distinctive product known as the *gadwal* sari (a cotton sari with an elaborate interweave silk gold zari pallu and border) is the popular product in the market. Because of market demand, several master weavers have taken up this business, and the availability of skilled labor in surrounding areas has allowed an expansion of this market/product.

The point to note is that this sari is woven on a pit loom, and many young weavers produce these saris. An increasing number of women have taken to weaving this as well. A typical scenario in Yemmigannur is one where most of the houses have between two to three looms. Members of the cooperative weave on frame looms (bedsheets and towels being the typical product). They also have pit looms belonging to the master weaver, on which saris are woven. This reinforces the earlier point that master weavers have capitalized on the USP of a handloom product, which comes from the product being woven on a pit loom.

Perceptions from the Frame Loom Technology

Analyzing the reasons for State support and investment in frame loom technology throws up many issues that are problematic. Ostensibly, the technology upgradation program is to help the weaver produce a better quality product from the handloom. But in reality it becomes first a nudge and then a push to conversion to a completely different technological ensemble and resulting product. This is evident in the parameters that are set out to define quality. If productivity and closeness of weave and ability to repeat the same design for thousands of meters define quality, handloom weavers would find them a hard challenge. In a handloom, quality cannot be external to the loom and the weaver on the loom. True, the external factors like quality of thread, color and so on impact the product, but the processes of creating a design and responding to the external environment in order to plan a product are very much a part of the weaver and the loom. The whole ensemble and how it works together define the craft and shape the product. In the new technological ensemble that this particular instance of frame loom adoption is based in, choices and preferences are shaped by illusory links to a so-called international reality, which finds little resonance in the immediate context. The changes in the environment do affect the capacity of the weaver to create a matching product. That is the reason today handloom survival is dependent on the intervention of intermediary agencies (such as an NGO like Dastkar Andhra) for the translation of the market preferences. Also the immediate context of handloom production can no longer be presumed to be local—there are layers of realities today and these are hierarchically arranged where the lowermost becomes a diluted version of the top layer. In terms of market, the top layer is constituted by the export segment and the lower layer is the domestic segment.

The trends in the export market need to be closely followed in order to understand the shifts to be planned in the domestic market. This is true even for handlooms which are not as linked to the international markets. The changes that become acceptable in the domestic market closely mimic the form prevalent in the global market. For example, the markets today are presumed to be influenced by the fashion industry and media. These factors are not located in the immediate weaver context and not immediately discernible by the weaver but are shaped in an environment quite removed from that of the producer. However, consumers are more aware of changing trends through the mass media. Fashion trends pervade different consumer spaces, though not perhaps in the original form. The flip side of the argument is that the producer is also in the related mediated space and can/should be able to perceive the larger trends dictating what we wear and eat, how we live, and so on. But a producer who can translate the information/aspiration into a saleable product needs to be equipped differently. That is, media access or access to spaces of modern consumption does not necessarily empower and equip the producer to decode the desire into a marketable product. The point to note is that consumer preferences are shaped and standardized by dominant ideological paradigms. Take for instance the aspect of color: changing colors for every season with no eye to the specific reality of different locations, places a difficult challenge before handloom technology. For example, the imperative of changing color and texture for every 50 meters to provide the demanded variety involves changing loom accessories frequently and dyeing of small lots repeatedly. All this adds to the cost of the fabric. Producing product that is accepted by those who direct the market (consumers in urban locations) is the key to survival. The translation of the tastes of this segment is needed for the producer to survive in the market. What then happens to the USP of the handloom (even in a pit loom)—does it become totally dependent on the changing tastes of the dominant market? Is the role of influencing the market perception the responsibility of the State and the intervening agencies? We have already seen the government intervention and its adverse effects when the context and knowledge base of the technology formed no part of the decision making. An agency (like an NGO) which wishes to intervene in handloom production, especially one coming from outside the local context and one coming without the legitimacy that the State brings, has to be extra cautious not to fall into the trap of a revivalist ideology or the modern paradigm of efficiency and productivity.

Changing Relations with the Producers

The idea that pit looms are set up against frame looms, interestingly, has not taken root from within local weaver communities. The frame loom as a new technology was accepted and practiced mainly because it was promoted by the State and it still required the literacy of hand weaving. The close links of the frame weave to the mechanical loom and other resemblances to the power-loom-like-increased volumes of uniform production were not immediately perceived. One of the reasons could be related to the variety of the product woven on the frame loom. They were mostly running fabric in a single color for making uniforms. The weavers were possibly untroubled as the typical bordered products (like saris and dupattas), which were possible on a pit loom, continued to sell and their aesthetic appeal retained their loyal consumers. The only problem is that some co-operative societies which adopted or slowly converted to frame loom production were untroubled by the delinking of the product from the market. This resulted in isolated production entirely dependent on the State for support and became a completely subsidized activity. The other side of the story is that outside the co-operatives in the same geographic area, weavers continued to weave traditional saris on pit looms. What becomes evident in this narrative is the clear perception that the co-operative society as an instrument of State and the welfare function emphasized by the State ignores the context of technology and the possibility of long-term sustainability.

The introduction of frame looms also alters the form of organization and, in this instance, brings this decentralized activity closer to an "acceptable" centralized mode. Becoming acceptable refers to the process of finding a place alongside of the mainstream, mechanical technologies. Frame looms organized at a central shed where the weaver has no ownership over the loom and the place while s/he weaves at set hours removes it further from a traditional form of work and moves it closer to a modern factory kind of production. The mainstream form of centralization, while ensuring productivity and promoting efficiency, introduces a new set of hierarchies distinct from the traditional hierarchies. The fact that a staunch advocate of handlooms like Pragada Kotaiah (who has become a well-known figure in Andhra for his advocacy of handlooms) felt that the only way for traditional technology to survive is to imitate the factory mode of production by establishing frame looms in the existing society of his own village, is a telling instance of the faith in the mainstream paradigm for growth. The fact that this happened in the early nineteen twenties, when handlooms were still a household process and the government was positive about promoting traditional industries, is noteworthy. Pragada Kotaiah was an influential leader who came from a weaving background and studied formally to be technically equipped. He became a member of the Congress party and joined the freedom movement. In independent India he was nominated as a member of the Rajyasabha (the house of elders who are nominated and not elected) and consistently raised the issues affecting handloom industry. His contribution is widely acknowledged and a technical institute for handlooms is established in his name in the town of Venkatagiri, Nellore district of Andhra Pradesh.

Changing Structures and Challenges to Traditional Technology

There are other factors to be taken into account when we introduce frame looms. Generally it is only when the entire family works together that production on a single loom can happen. With the fading of a joint family system, weaving activity perforce moved out of the home. It continued with collaborations among neighbours or became a paid activity given to a central unit/person to manage. This changed the relationship of the weaver to the processes that determine the quality and character of the fabric. As the individual weaver became central to the loom, the ancillary activities and their role in understanding and ensuring quality in weaving were slowly getting sidelined. Following this trend the government of Andhra Pradesh passed an order that resulted in the exclusion of family memberships from the co-operative society statistics. It was not done with the recognition of the changes happening within the community structures. The exclusion of family memberships to the society in the reporting of statistics was done so that there could be a precise count of the number of weavers engaged in weaving. It would conveniently exclude the people engaged in support activities without which the weaving on the loom is impossible. This would then enable the government to reduce the budgetary allocations, quoting the reduced number in the sector.

However, leaving out the functions that people in the family or outsiders have to perform and identifying weaving only with "sitting on the loom" denotes a total denial of the way handloom technology operates and the activity is organized. Traditional pit loom production was buffeted by changes in the community structures, while the technology offered by the frame loom introduced a new dimension, the need for a centralization of pre-loom processes. This centralization is conducive to nuclear family structures. The move by the government to bring in a policy (one loom, one weaver member) that goes against the nature and organization of the industry and fosters central control points is an illustration of the bias against an alternative type of industry organization and the move to "mainstream" a non-modern industry.

Apart from the changes in the production process there are new challenges that arise in the marketplace due to the fact that traditional technology has become detached from the contexts in which it was created. In the production process, the weaver is distanced from the production of yarn and the pre-loom processes, changing the logic of the cycle of production. In the market the direct link between the weaver and the people who use the products is broken. The increasing separation of the weaver from the different activities in the chain reduces the stress of engaging in the entire cycle of production, but at the same time it limits the extent of control the weaver can exercise. In the market, the weaver becomes dependent on outside agencies in order to negotiate with the modern context for survival. It is a fact that the seemingly powerless negotiation is balanced by the unique nature of the traditional technology, which has found a way to exist in a modern world. The challenge for the weaver however is to build links with the emerging contexts, which replace the local context and re-establish links with processes of production for ensuring quality in handloom production.

Future Directions: Building New Linkages

The case of the handloom technology illustrates the different ways in which the earlier close links between knowledge systems and cultural contexts shift or even get erased by the dominance of modern technoscientific worldviews and demands. That the homogenization of technology leads to a generic product that then gets positioned across diverse market contexts is a development that needs careful attention. While for some there is immense potential in the market in targeting such global customers, the point to ponder is what back-end work in rebuilding links in production skills, supply chains and familiarity with new aesthetics needs to be done. Seen from the vantage point of these handloom producer communities with limited or no access to the outside and who do not directly participate in the extended relations that form global marketplaces, there are deep breaks, as they are unable to envisage either the final product and consumer, or the modern aesthetic. The older links within local markets and customers having dwindled, the process of building new linkages distant from the local is not an easy process. The role of the master weaver who had his hand on the pulse of the market, and who was not just a trader, has also changed. They have started to look at the possibility of specializing exclusively on only some parts of the overall production process and considering investing exclusively in them, without having to engage in the entire the process of weaving. For example, centralizing pre-loom activities like dyeing and sizing opens up opportunities for business hitherto absent in handloom production. These pre-loom activities—spinning and hand-dying of yarn most especially—are even "mobile" businesses in online micro-transactional networks contributing to and based in a mostly Western handmade only movement (Gajjala, forthcoming). It is interesting, therefore, to see how the breaking up of the overall production process into specialized tasks lends itself to the neoliberal global economy in bits and bytes. On the one hand there is a breaking up of whole communities happening in third-world contexts, while in first-world contexts there is an attempt to build these networks so that the services associated with pre-loom or pre-knitting processes are available online and in specialized craft stores.

People who remained involved in the process of weaving became true managers in that they found it useful to encourage shed weaving for supervising the activity. The cutting up of functions in this linear fashion, where earlier different players were engaged, brought the activities surrounding handloom weaving closer to the mechanical processes. These developments—the consolidation of the trading position of master weavers, their push toward centralization of certain pre-weaving processes, the resultant divorce of the weaver from the different stages of the production process, and even the paths of intervention and support chosen by the government—have all played a major role in dislodging handloom technology from its communal contexts of production, consumption and socio-cultural life. The process of identifying the ruptures in old practices, the points of conjunction where old and new finds place, and the new hierarchies that emerge, enable us to find spaces for the recasting of the evolving connections to build fresh perspectives. This is not to reiterate moments of breaks and ruptures, but to look for ways of going beyond dichotomous perceptions that box handlooms and handloom technology or even the handloom weaver as traditional. To adequately recognize the disjunctures in all their complexities is essential in order to begin to understand what is involved in taking up the immense challenge of building new linkages.

Emerging new markets play a large role in this process of re-linking handlooms to old and new contexts. Yet, considering the changes in the organization of markets, producing and selling handloom material successfully demands the development of different type of linkages. The norms of modern mass markets—like standardization of product and high volume production, which are a function of mechanization and centralization—are directly in contrast with handloom production processes. To successfully operate in such a space (which is governed by a different paradigm), some amount of strategizing is needed, though it is not enough. The main task here is to go beyond merely negotiating the market, to also engage with what can be called "nonmarket" factors. Seen through this lens, handlooms can become a metaphor for a different mode of transacting production and markets. Mass production of goods has introduced a rupture between the producer and product; handlooms offer the space for a re-engagement of producer with product, as well as with the context of production. Negotiating the handloom market also alters the front end of the transaction by making certain demands of the customer. For instance, the transaction goes beyond a purely economic negotiation of buying a product. S/he is paying not for a product alone, but also for recognition of the skills that have gone into preparation of the product. This is qualitatively different from the market logic of paying for a brand name of a firm. In this very act, the handloom customer is also building value of a different sort for handlooms in the market.

What this essentially means is not merely creating markets for a product, but building market and value for the mode of production. In working at the interstices of a traditional technology (the handloom) where everything else (the product, the consumer, the aspirations of the weaver, etc.) is located in increasingly nontraditional spaces, how can this be done? Building value has been done in different ways, but the predominant way has been protectionism or the revival of a traditional skill or art or craft. This raises a number of questions about the context or the politics of revival, and questions the result of sometimes museumizing or exoticizing a way of life. Our attempt in this article to situate the loom within different sets of practices and discourses has helped us to argue not just that handloom weaving takes place within a socio-economic context, but to also ask what happens when these contexts shift into ones where borders are more fluid and ill-defined? Recreating/reviving/protecting a given way of life for the weaver and his technology cannot be the task we address. Rather, the challenge is one of building value for a mode of production within different spaces—these may cut across geographical boundaries, cultures and lifestyles, producers and consumers. Is it adequate to build new communities for the technology and product through new links with the customer? What is the role of the producers in this reconstruction? More importantly, do they see themselves continuing to sit behind the loom (which, after all, remains the only thing that can squarely fit the label "traditional" here)? It is essential to face up to the fact that traditional communities may resist continuing in the occupation for fear of the social stigma of backwardness against the backdrop of high-speed technology. A tough challenge is to motivate communities to stay in the occupation until the stigma of traditional can be removed. The alternative could be to encourage other rural communities to take up hand weaving and enlarge the base of producers by looking out of the traditional boundary of community occupation. Unlike other caste-based occupations, weaving does not pose a major problem in this regard. In its heyday, it formed part of an off-season work for most of the rural communities. With declining local markets, the extent of work was also reduced and this option slowly is disappearing from the rural geography.

The final test would be to find ways of linking the producer and the consumer directly. The whole point of building value for the process and product is to rework the relations between producer and consumer, especially in a context where the individual producer is still able to identify the product of her loom and the consumer comes from a background of understanding this organic link of which she is invited to become a part.

Notes

1. We wrote this chapter over a span of more than two years—and this was only just the writing. We would like to thank Jennifer Slack and Greg Wise for their detailed feedback on previous drafts of this chapter. Seemanthini Niranjana passed away in 2007 from cancer. The surviving co-authors of this article miss her very much, but are grateful for having had the opportunity to write (and work) with her. Also, it must be noted that the content has not been changed—except for some minor additional insights and observations by Radhika Gajjala in 2011—in order to preserve the integrity of our conversations from that period. Therefore, even though there are additional nuances and questions that Radhika can raise and contribute based on her continuing cross-context and international ethnographies, interviews, in-depth engagement with handlooms in northwest Ohio and Indonesia and related fiber crafts (such as knitting, spinning, hand-dying and crocheting in northwest Ohio, quilting in African-American contexts, Batik in Indonesia and so on that shed further light on inter-Asian trade that pre-dates British colonization of India) that will have to be for later publications. Also, since 2006, there has been additional literature published that may shift (although I don't think the main arguments herein get affected significantly) some assumptions made in this article about the case studies used in this article such as work by Abigail McGowan (2009), Prasannan Parthasarathi (2011),

Rebecca Brown (2010), Janet Greenless (2007), Gail Fowler Mohanty (2006) and so on. But then this current project did not start out being about handcrafts and the subaltern—the overall book started out as an exploration of technocultural agency and globalization in relation to "new" technology and Radhika started out with some basic assumptions that in turn took interesting turns along her journey when she encountered how "traditional" technology such as natural dye and other eco-friendly production processes are now being revived as "new" technology in various locations worldwide (Indonesia, U.S.A., South America, India). Once again, Radhika hopes to take up some of these nuances in continuing publications—not as an Indian handloom researcher (as her co-authors in this present chapter are), but as an investigator of globalization, (re)localization and technology. Some of this later investigation would also have helped clarify the traditional and modern binary that we struggle against in this chapter—more on this point in the conclusion to this book.

2. For instance, The All-India Handloom Board, constituted in 1945, had the objectives of meeting the country's clothing needs progressively from the handloom sector to make handlooms an effective instrument of reducing unemployment.

3. It employs 120 lakh weaving families, and handloom production now constitutes about 13% of the country's total textile production (Annual Report, 2005-06, Ministry of Textiles, GOI).

4. In Yemmigannur town proper, the dominant traditional weaving castes are the Kurini and Padmasali (in other nearby villages, we also find Devangula, Togata and Sukrasale castes dominating weaving). The other groups weaving are the Muslims and Malas (in other villages, these are Telagas and Boyas).

CHAPTER FIVE

KENTE CLOTH AND ADINKRA IN THE GLOBAL MARKET

Precious Yamaguchi & Franklin Nii Yartey

Journeying toward Kente (Precious Yamaguchi)

It is the cusp between the spring and summer seasons in Ghana and the weather is over 100 degrees. The windows are all rolled down in our humble *tro tro,* a type of mini-van that squeezes in the maximum amount of people and is an important form of transportation in Ghana. There is heat and sweat from our bodies, dust from the road is flying in through the van, and we are piled into the tro tro. People are sitting on each other's laps and some people's heads are touching the low ceiling of the van, but no one complains about feeling claustrophobic or that it is too hot; we are all just happy to be getting a ride to our destinations. We are on our way to the Kente capital of the world, Bonwire, location where Kente cloth is made and sold. Almost all of the people who live in Bonwire have a relationship with the production of Kente cloth.

In Bonwire, everyone has a role in the production or sale of Kente cloth. As the tro tro approaches Bonwire, local children are waiting ready to guide visitors to the outlets where Kente cloth is woven and sold. When I arrive in Bonwire I am guided to a large wooden building in the town where there are about a dozen weavers at their looms weaving Kente cloth. They are young men, slender, sitting at the bamboo looms in t-shirts, tank tops, and shorts, with little radios perched up on the side of their looms. As soon as they see visitors come inside their building, some continue weaving, and others leave their looms and gather around the visiting individuals to try and sell their cloths. The Kente weavers and sellers are far from being shy; as they hand visitors pieces of Kente and propose prices the bargaining has begun. Many men who are employees of the Kente outlet compete against each other and try to get visitors to buy their Kente.

The cloth is sold in single strips as well as in the forms of ties, key-chains, tunics, and bags. There are some antique Kente cloths made of silk. The warehouse-type room becomes hectic and chaotic as different retailers approach the visitors one by one or sometimes all at once to convince the potential buyers that their Kente is the best. Outside, children yell through the windows at the visitors and try to get people to buy their handmade jewelry. The adults managing the Kente outlet do not allow the children inside, but once a potential buyer steps out of the chaotic Kente outlet building, they are surrounded by children who are begging for people to buy jewelry from them.

The village of Bonwire depends heavily on the production and sales of Kente cloth and is supported by the Kente weavers and the Kente market. Tourism becomes a significant opportunity for the village locals to sell their products and have interactions with visitors from all over Ghana and abroad. Face-to-face bargaining and haggling gives the Kente weavers and salespeople a chance to tell their stories about the cloth, their expertise, the materials used to make the Kente, and build a rapport with the customers. Globalization and the flow of people and services across borders gives international market exposure to the Kente that these weavers produce. But in the process, aspects of the communication, culture, interactions, and stories are flattened, re-ordered, translated and removed from the cultural context that leads to a diminishing of the traditional value of the cloth.

Two Authors Weaving Stories and Research Together

Autoethnography and ethnography are often written from a single-author perspective and location. In this ethnography, there are two authors from different cultures, genders, and nationalities, and we write this piece together, weaving our perspectives, locations, and experiences into globalized and intercultural knowledge. The conversations between both authors who are from different countries and cultures contain many threads that weave themselves throughout this research.

As the first author (Precious Yamaguchi), I am fifth-generation Japanese American. I come from a family of artists, working-class American citizens, and all four of my grandparents were in the World War II internment camps. I have always been interested in the production, craft, and sales of textiles. I am an artist, have my degree in Studio Art, and have an interest in the artists and producers of textiles of the world. In this ethnographic research, I set out to the villages of Ghana where these cloths were made and experienced the role Kente and Adinkra played in the livelihood of villages, tradition, the economy, families, history, and globalization. These cloths and textiles carry embedded narrations of the past and they are also a way of communicating symbolic expressions of the present by the person wearing the cloth.

As a Japanese American, I could relate to the significance, meaning, value, and reasons why certain types of cloths, colors, and symbols are worn, and what it means to own and wear a traditional type of clothing. Like a kimono, Kente carries historical meaning to the wearer and the event in which it is being worn. As much as I studied, researched, interviewed people about Kente and Adinkra, and even participated in the weaving and creation of it, I knew I would never really know what it was like to be from Ghana, and to wear clothing that has had generations and centuries of history connected to a country and culture. I would never experience the same feeling of wearing Kente, the way my co-author

Franklin Yartey did. I could wear Kente, just like Franklin could wear a Japanese men's kimono, but our experiences would be different.

When I returned to the U.S., Franklin Yartey (the second author), who was born in Ghana, and I had many conversations about Ghana, their textiles, and globalization. We had many different and similar perspectives and experiences about the country and an interest in the textile markets of Ghana and believed we could compose an ethnography together based upon our two individual locations joining together to create research. Throughout this ethnography Franklin and I have included our own ethnographies, which are identified in the subtitles of this paper—for example, "Traditions (Franklin Yartey)." In most of this ethnography, such as in the review of literature and the discussions of Kente, Adinkra, and globalization, Franklin and I wrote together. I shared my notes, videos, recordings, journals, and photos with Franklin when I returned from Ghana, and together we conversed, told stories, researched, and wrote together.

Globalizing the Kente Cloth

Globalization is woven into transnational transactions and cultural transactions. This phenomenon is experienced in many countries. In the United States colorful African Kente cloth can be seen at college graduations, churches, cultural events, and sewn into everyday wear such as ties, shoes, and handbags. The meaning of Kente differs from one cultural context to the other. For some North Americans, Kente cloth represents the support of a multicultural or Afrocentric movement, and can also be seen worn as a fashion statement. In the African context, on the other hand, the tradition of Kente cloth is woven deeper for some African people into their culture and is an ongoing negotiation of tradition, identity, and globalization. The history of Kente is recorded from the fifteenth century and its story is still being formed based on all the internal and external issues surrounding this particular cloth from Ghana (Cole, 1990).

In this chapter we explore the role of traditional cloth in the history of Ghana and how present-day issues of globalization have affected the maintenance of culture through traditional cloth such as Kente and Adinkra. Using globalization and critical feminist theory to guide this study, ethnographic methods were used along with informant interviews with people who produced and created Kente and Adinkra. Our method of ethnography also reflects the way in which culture and textiles are observed and translated across time and context. Globalization and critical feminist theory play a large role in this research to show the importance traditional cloth has in the maintenance of a country's identity, economy, history and cultural communication. This research examines the link between Ghana's traditions and culture, and the social organization of Kente and Adinkra in their economic growth and global opportunities.

Traditions (Franklin Nii Yartey)

I clearly remember two weeks before my graduation from Northwestern College, Iowa, my mother opened a suitcase full of Kente cloth, gold chains, and various bangles. With excitement I examined the contents of her suitcase, running my fingers across the woven cloth. I could feel the rich texture of the fabric enhanced with vivid tones of red, yellow, blue, black and gold. Kente is part of my identity as a Ghanaian, and I wear it with a great sense of pride. It re-energizes my identity as an individual from Ghana.

As we stated earlier, a person wearing the Kente cloth communicates beliefs, values, and worldviews that make up the acquired and learned traditions from the past and present. One therefore nonverbally communicates privilege, wealth, access, wisdom, well-being, beauty, self-confidence, an aura of importance, and much more without uttering a word. There is so much meaning embedded in adorning yourself with rich Kente cloth.

As my mother (Naa Manye Aforkor Omaeduro II) explained to me, it takes a long time to weave a strip of handmade Kente cloth, and because this cloth is expensive it was especially an honor and privilege to own one in the olden days. Now quite a lot of people can afford it. According to my mother, Kente has in many ways lost its beauty and value in the eyes of many Ghanaians because globalization and the influx of imitated Kente on the global market has cheapened the value that some Ghanaian's attach to this cloth. This is because the cloth is now being mass produced in factories and it is used for making handbags, table cloths, and other items.

In the previous chapter, Radhika Gajjala, B. Syamasundari and Seemanthini Niranjana looked at globalization, culture and the innovation of handloom technologies in the context of India. In this chapter we specifically focus on the role of traditional cloth in the history of Ghana and how present-day issues of globalization have affected the maintenance of culture through traditional cloth such as Kente and Adinkra. While Radhika Gajjala, B. Syamasundari and Seemanthini Niranjana examined how the adoption of new technologies by traditional weavers in India has sometimes resulted in disadvantages to the weaver, we examine how the mass production of Kente with advanced technologies is affecting local weavers in Ghana. The common theme that runs through these two chapters is the displacement that weavers experience with the introduction of new technologies that are supposed to help increase production and eventually increase revenue for these weavers. For example, the traditional weavers in Ghana are unable to compete effectively on the global market because their traditional tools that help produce carefully handwoven fabric cannot keep up with the technological and mechanized looms/sewing machines that spit out woven fabric at lightening speeds in countries such as China. This is reminiscent of how weavers and merchants in South Indian Coromandel regions faced challenges in trying to meet the increased demand for cotton cloth when the British Colonizers wanted to export Indian cotton to England (see Parthasarathi 2009). Further, the face-to-face acts of bargaining, negotiating, and haggling at the art markets and Kente festivals where such cloth is usually sold is an important component of the traditional textile retail market. The change in modes of marketing of such products affects the way in which the products are priced, consumed and how the weaver's labor is valued. Such issues, once again, are similar to those faced by South Indian weavers in their encounter with the British officers in the 17th century Indian context (see Parthasarathi 2001).

These industrialized nations have the privilege and access to the tools of mass production whereas the traditional and master weavers of countries such as Ghana where the production of the Kente or Adinkra is more localized are put at a disadvantage because they do not have to mass produce their textiles and effectively market them on the global market. Not only do they not have the tools to mass produce Kente, but the act of mass producing such a traditional and rich cloth would go against the beliefs and cultural values that go into the weaving. We therefore argue that globalization and the transnational movement of mass produced Kente in the industrialized countries is having adverse effects on the livelihood of Kente weavers in Ghana. We also argue that the modern practices of mass producing "unauthentic" Kente, as one weaver called it, and Adinkra misrepresent the meanings crafted into these treasured fabrics. In Ghana, the Akan (an ethnic group) communicate knowledge and indefinable truths through Adinkra symbols (Opoku 1997).

In this chapter, we take a close look at history of Kente cloth and its present day story and note how the identity of Kente is being formed and transformed from its traditional status. Issues of gender and the global market play a large role in the creation, meaning, and marketing behind Kente. Through an ethnographic engagement with the contexts, we began to understand how certain individuals' lives and livelihood revolve around Kente and other African cloths such as Adinkra. From the basic manufacturing of the thread to the weaving of the cloth and finally, the marketing of the cloth, the process of Kente is an intense craft that often involves a community of people and global cooperation.

Through visits to the Volta region of Ghana and the village of Bonwire where Kente cloth is made and sold we learned how the creators of Kente and Adinkra incorporate the cloth into their everyday life, tradition, and livelihood. We learned how these crafted forms played into cultural identity formations and displacement (Massey, 1994) in present day Ghanaian society. In addition to the cloth producing communities and labor forces, the role of bargaining practices and the bazaar—like market—spaces where face—to—face interactions between the buyer and seller take place are important to the sales of such handcrafted textiles. In a time where the Walmarts of the world strive to hide the stories of the people who produce materials and items due to unsatisfactory labor conditions, children working in factories, and employees who receive too little pay, face—to—face bargaining, haggling, and negotiating aims to do the opposite.

Economic Development and Ghana

The Republic of Ghana has had both a bright history filled with art and culture, and a dark past tracing back to times of colonization and slave trade in this country formerly known by its British colonizers as the Gold Coast. It became the first sub-Saharan country to gain its independence on the 6th of March 1957. In 1981, due to political conflict, there was a suspension of the constitution that was not restored until 1992, when Lt. Jerry Rawlings became president. A 2009 *New York Times* article explains that Ghana now enjoys rapid growth in its economy and many investors flock to Ghana due to the peaceful climate that exists (*New York Times*, 2009). Some of the resources of Ghana include gold, timber, cocoa, and diamonds.

Ghana is a country of approximately 24,791,073 people with a high mortality rate due to HIV/AIDS. In Ghana there are over 260,000 people living with AIDS and in 2009 there were estimated to be 18,000 HIV/AIDS deaths. Health and employment are important issues. The unemployment rate is 11% of its population and over 28.5% of its citizens are living below the poverty line (C.I.A. World Factbook, 2011). Ghana is dependent on international financial and technical assistance. It participates in the United Nations Heavily Indebted Poor Country (HIPC) program and strives to reduce poverty and improve its social services. Inflation is one of the country's most significant problems in coherence to its economy (C.I.A. World Factbook, 2011).

With products such as gold, timber, and cocoa, as well as its traditional arts such as wooden carvings, furniture, small boats, Adinkra, drummaking, and Kente, Ghana has created an identity for itself in the global market. According to development theorists Biggart and Guillen (1999), a global marketplace exists and competition plays a vital role. The idea of competition in a global market becomes more complicated when traditional arts such as Adinkra and Kente become international commodities. The concerns that arise are not only the basic supply and demand, but also the transformation of the meaning behind art as a commodity and the issue of traditional art as a mass-produced product. Now that we have provided a brief history of Ghana it is important to highlight the origins of the Kente and Adinkra cloth, tracing the history of these cultural treasures.

Ghanaian Traditional Cloth

The origins of Kente cloth and Adinkra come from the country of Ghana. Kente and Adinkra originate from the Asante people of Ghana. Kente can also be found in various regions produced by traditional weavers who also contributed to the historical and cultural identity of Kente.

Adinkra is a cloth that is made from a homemade black, brown, red, or purple dye with a grid of black stamp designs placed in a pattern on the cloth with symbols representing proverbs, people, or logos. The cloth is mainly worn at funerals (Opoku, 1997; Boateng, 2011). However, its usage also goes beyond just funerals to formal gatherings (Opoku, 1997). The word *Adinkra* means "saying goodbye to one another" to the Asante people. Adinkra on white cloth is worn for the post-burial celebration. Adinkra symbols are used by institutions of higher learning including the University of Ghana, and also by social clubs, commercial vehicles (tro tros), taxis, churches and some government agencies (Opoku, 1997). The popularity of Adinkra began during the reign of the former king of Cote D' Ivoire in the nineteenth century when he wore the stamped cloth in the battle against the Asante in the early nineteenth century. Although the king died his son was taken prisoner and taught the Asante how to make the cloth if the Asante agreed not to kill him. However, we do not know *who* first created Adinkra, though the Asantes are identified as the people who have kept the tradition and production of the cloth alive. Since the event of the king and his battle, Adinkra is a special traditional cloth that is used for celebrations, funerals, weddings, and can also be displayed around the house or for the pleasure of wearing the cloth casually. It is important for the person to be aware that almost all Adinkra communicates a message through its traditional symbols and colors (www.marshall.edu/akanart/Adinkracloth.html, 2006). The Asante people also introduced more colors in the weaving and production of the Kente cloth. Like Adinkra, Kente is a traditional cloth that communicates through symbols, patterns, and colors. Communication is embedded in the symbols of the cloth and at events at which the cloth is worn. The origins of Kente cloth can be traced back to Ghana's first president, Kwame Nkrumah. There is disagreement as to when Kente first started; some scholars say it started with the Asante and Ewes in the seventeenth century (Anonymous, 1997), while others trace it back to before the 1500s (Cole, 1990). Kente was first worn by the kings, queens, and important political figures of Northwest Africa. Now Kente can be seen worn by students during graduation ceremonies, cultural events, or parties. True traditional Kente has always been hand-woven, though in the present day Kente can now be produced by machines. It is one of the traditional fabrics from Africa and the process of making Kente is very complex, from the building of the loom, to the careful consideration of thread, the concern for design and color, the craftsmanship of the weaving; and finally the marketing of Kente is not only a skill of a Ghanaian weaver but it also includes the participation of many Ghanaian villages and communities (Cole, 1990).

Kente Woven into the Modern

For African Americans today, Kente is worn to make a political statement or to show cultural pride. In the 1960s during the civil rights movement, Kente became more widely seen and worn to support a new awakening of cultural pride, along with other African-originated wear such as dashikis (Dunabar 1991). The colorful material has also integrated itself into the international fashion world, where designers are always looking toward multiculturalism for inspiration. In times where ethnic pride has assimilated into fashion, Kente wearers often feel like they are making a connection with their heritage through wearing Kente. Unlike the dashikis, which were worn as "a sign of rebellion" in the United States (Dunbar, 1991), Kente has become a way of displaying African pride. In subtle ways it is sewn into ties, bags, belts, and scarves. Though some feel a sense of "placement" or an establishment of connection to their heritage through the use of accessories such as bags and belts, others feel the meaning infused with the production of this cloth is lost through the processes of commercialization and modification of Kente. The Kente fabric is traditionally made squares about three inches wide and is hand-woven with cotton or silk thread. The word *Kente* means "basket" or "woven basket." The Kente woven strips are then sewn together to make outfits such as tartans, blouses, and traditional wear. In general, Kente clothing is supposed to fit loosely and be displayed on the body as a multitude of Kente cloths woven together to make a single piece of clothing. The patterns woven into the different Kente strips usually contain proverbs or have specific meanings (Dunbar 1991).

The appreciation of Kente has not gone unnoticed by ambitious entrepreneurs. From Disney, that incorporated the use of Kente cloth in the costumes for their promotional events for *The Lion King* motion picture (Parrott, 1994) to the Kente cloth importers in New York City (Dunbar, 1991) and Los Angeles (George, 1993), Kente cloth is readily available for purchase in the United States in many forms of clothing, accessories, and even furniture. The state of Virginia is even home to a furnishing company that includes Kente cloth in their upholstery of sofas, pillows, wall hangings, and tables (Anonymous, 1999). The influence of Kente has gone beyond its traditional interpretations in Ghana and has become a cultural influence, and a fashion statement in America. For art historians and collectors, traditional craftwork, textiles, and art from Africa are particularly valuable. The symbols used in Adinkra and Kente can be presently seen in modern-day Ghanaian art such as that visible on clothing, advertising, and media. The way the imagery has existed throughout Ghanaian history and is now being transferred and displayed in contemporary media creates much interest in the research of art historians (Ross, 2000). The symbolic images tell stories of the culture and the skillful work in Adinkra, Kente, woodcarving, and mask-making come from a deep-rooted lineage of Ghanaian artisans, craftsmen, apprentices, and cultural masters. It is important to know how these cultural artifacts (e.g. Kente and Adinkra) are being protected by the government of Ghana.

Protecting Ghanaian Artifacts

In 1973, Ghana attempted to protect cultural artifacts like Adinkra and Kente with a textile design registration law which was passed under the country's industrial property law (Boateng, 2011). In 2003, Ghana introduced the Geographical Indications Act (ACT 659) "an indication which identifies a good as originating in the territory of a country, or a region or locality in that territory, where a given quality, reputation or other characteristic of the goods is essentially attributable to its geographical origin; 'goods' mean any natural or agricultural product or any product of handicraft or industry and includes Kente" (World Intellectual Property Organization, 2012). In spite of the measures put in place to protect cultural artifacts such as the Kente cloth, Adinkra and Kente have been mimicked throughout the history of modern Ghana (Boateng, 2011).

Context

The ethnographic sites that we draw on in this chapter consisted of four different locations in Ghana where Kente and Adinkra were made: Kopeyia, Medie, Ntoso, and Bonwire. The weavers, teachers, and sellers involved in the creation of the Kente and Adinkra cloths were interviewed, observed, and one of us (Precious) even took private lessons from some of the Kente masters on weaving Kente cloth. With the use of the ethnographic methods, the individuals were selected through the community organizations, art centers, and networks as well as from acquaintances and friendships made while journeying through Ghana and the art villages. These individuals came from small villages where both Kente and Adinkra originated from and continued to be produced and sold.

Scholars who research economic development in developing countries such as Ghana have argued development depends on successfully linking a country's historical patterns of social organization with opportunities made available by global markets (Biggart & Guillen, 1999). Ghana's textile industries are spaces where culture is historically embedded and communication takes place in relation to their traditional African cloth industry within the global market. The role of traditional cloth such as Adinkra and Kente remain as cultural symbols, rooted in historical and political stories, proverbs, and craftsmanship. These cultural symbols have experienced changes due to globalization and modern influences. The interactions and conversations about the Kente cloth started in Kopeyia.

Kopeyia (Precious)

Kopeyia was the first placed I studied and researched in Ghana. In this small village in the Volta region where the Ewe people lived, I resided at an art school where traditional art, music, and dance were taught. The Kente master at this art school in Kopeyia was the first Kente master to teach me the basics of Kente and the process of applying all four limbs (both hands, and both feet) to control the intricate weaving tools on the loom. For several days I lived with the Ewe people in the village of Kopeyia where many of the people support their livelihood as agriculturalists or "culturalists," as they call themselves.

Nani Agbeli, a culturalist, who owns the Dagbe Cultural Center, told me about the Ewe people and explained how practices such as Kente, drumming, dance, and art are all significant ways the Ewe people have communicated throughout history. The drums were ways people would communicate to one another and Kente also holds many symbols communicating how a person is feeling at a specific moment, such as feeling prideful or in mourning. The Kente master was only four years old when he learned how to weave Kente from his older brother:

> I learned Kente from my older brother when I was four years old, which came from the Asante region. It was my favorite thing to do. Good quality Kente has no smell. The fake ones have a smell, also if you put fake Kente in water, the color comes out. Real Kente has color that won't come out, especially the yellow. People who make real Kente dye it themselves and trade or sell it for clothing. Some of the dye comes from a small nut, like a coconut. There are symbols that are very specific to us in our clothing and culture. Umbrellas and combs are for chiefs, also stools are important. One day I would like to teach many people Kente and I get to know other countries.

He was very informative and patient in showing me how to weave the colored threads dyed from various natural products such as local plants and nuts into Kente cloth. The Kente master stated the meanings behind the symbols are weaved in the cloth. Symbols such as combs, stools, or umbrellas are common imagery in Ghanaian art and represent chiefs, kings, or royalty. An important issue for the Kente master in Kopeyia was *how* to tell qualities of authentic hand-woven, traditional Kente apart from fake or nontraditional Kente. Before he began to tell me how to tell if a piece of Kente cloth was fake or not, he went and picked a cocoa nut to show me that yellow dye comes from this very important nut. Almost all Kente has the yellow or, as they call it, a "gold" color in it, which is a beloved color of Ghanaians. The Kopeyian Kente master then explained that many Ewe people like him take part in the total and full creation of Kente, from the dying to the weaving to the selling processes. Mass production of Kente does not exist because real Kente should be commissioned and individually made, where each piece is authentic, unique, and one of a kind.

Kente is used for clothing, accessories, and decoration. The Kopeyian Kente master stressed what makes authentic Kente cloth valuable is all the hard work and time that goes into its creation and more so, the act of passing the knowledge of weaving from one person to another through generations and history. Part of the tradition of Kente is having an elder master accept and teach a dedicated student (who eventually becomes his apprentice) how to dye, weave, and sell Kente cloth. As he explains in the extract above, quality authentic Kente cloth should have "no smell" to it. He brought out a piece of "fake" Kente and a traditional authentic piece of Kente that he wove and showed me the differences.

The fake Kente did have a synthetic smell to it, while the authentic Kente the Kente master produced had absolutely no noticeable or strong smell. He mentioned that Kente that "comes from other countries" smells of chemicals and will lose its color when it's washed, but quality authentic Kente will never smell and lose its colors and the quality of the weave will last for a lifetime. When I asked the Kente master what countries produce fake Kente he responded, "China."

While residing in the small Volta region village, I learned the complex process of Kente weaving and how the three-inch-wide strips of cloth take numerous hours to make, even for experienced Kente masters such as the one I interviewed. With all the work the weavers put into the process of dying the thread, setting up the loom, weaving, ironing, and then finding a market to sell it in, it is very understandable to see how fake Kente or mass-produced Kente, can have a negative effect on the global market for quality hand-woven Kente made by the Ewe. As the Ewe Kente master expressed, most Ghanaians know how to tell the difference between traditional Kente and mass-produced Kente, but it is the international traders who buy Kente from nontraditional outlets who do themselves a disservice of purchasing poor-quality Kente. Buying knock-off Kente cloth also causes the Ewe people harm by not supporting their livelihood as Kente masters, weavers, and Kente community members.

Ntonso

Ntonso is a village near Kumasi, Ghana, specializing in the creation and selling of Adinkra. Ghanaian locals and culturalists informed me that when a person wants to buy Adinkra cloth, she or he knows to go to Ntonso. I arrived in Ntonso and throughout the village large pieces of Adinkra cloths were displayed on clotheslines for sale in front of peoples' houses along the highway.

The residents of Ntonso were very kind and welcoming. They were friendly and eager to show their art, yet not too pushy. After spending some time in other parts of Ghana prior to arriving in Ntonso, I had observed in the marketplaces many retailers trying to sell their products and some of them aggressively trying to convince foreigners to buy their goods. Oftentimes, numerous retailers flocked around individuals to sell their products to them. In Ntonso I met a young man who was learning the art of Adinkra. He was 21 years old and had been making Adinkra for several years. According to this Adinkra maker, Adinkra was founded during the eighteenth century when the king of Gyaman was conquered by the Asante people. He went on and explained the process of making Adinkra:

> I live in a village and what we do right here is take the bark of the tree and then we boil it for some time, after we boil it and then get out the liquid and then we boil it again...and use it as an ink. We weave it right here, we have one of the biggest weaving towns around the Asante region. It's a wonderful and so many

> people come here, both in and outside the country. This is the real home and the village of Adinkra.

Does everybody make Adinkra?

> No, it's limited to people right here, so only people around this town have access to Adinkra. We have our own way to dye clothes. The whole thing revolves around the 18th century when we conquered a king, the king's name was Adinkra and after we killed him, we brought his subjects here and they taught us the symbols and the meaning of the symbols, so we got this from war.

The responses from the Adinkra producer affirm the degree to which this woven cloth is treasured in Ghanaian culture: "This is the real home and village of Adinkra." The respondent alludes to the fact that Ntonso is the authentic or genuine producer and place of the Adinkra cloth and s/he takes pride in that. The symbols of Adinkra are carved out of dry gourd (calabash) and strong pieces of palm leaves are formed into handles. The symbols are then dipped into a dye (*badie*, a black dye from the bark of a tree) then pressed on pieces of cloth with iron (Opoku, 1997). The tools used to extract the dye and design the cloth into its final product are technologies rooted in Ghanaian culture and knowledge systems, and as the respondent said, this knowledge and art is protected within the Ntonso community: "No, it's limited to people right here, so only people around this town have access to Adinkra." So mass producing this cloth on the global market demeans the local cultural systems that produce them.

Globalization and its impact on Adinkra are similar to those of Kente cloth. As the Adinkra cloth is exposed to the processes of globalization and trade it is subjected to all kinds of positive and negative elements including the possible replication of the Adinkra with industrialized tools that may take away the original meaning behind the production of these fabrics. Like Kente, when Adinkra is mass produced in factories it has adverse effects on the local master weavers in Ghana. In the global marketplace the original Kente or Adinkra cloth may be displaced by mass-produced ones.

The village members of Ntonso introduced me to the Adinkra master, who showed me the process of Adinkra. The people who make Adinkra in Ntonso participate in every step of its creation, from the dying process to the stamping, cutting, and marketing. The creators of Adinkra are mostly men and some children. A local Adinkra maker told me women are included in the Adinkra production process, but only to boil the bark that comes from the local trees for their special dye. The segregation in sexes in traditional art is seen widely throughout Ghana.

The Adinkra makers I met told me that almost all Adinkra is produced and sold from Ntonso and as far as they knew there was not much of a problem in people trying to make knock-off Adinkra or nontraditional Adinkra because Adinkra is known for reflective black dye which can only be obtained by boiling the bark from the local trees. The cloth is very heavy and in the hot temperature of Ghana, it is hard to imagine people wearing such dense cloth. Regardless of its weight and the hot weather, Adinkra is the main attire worn at funerals and sometimes weddings, and the means by which Ntonso exists.

Bonwire

As described in the introduction, Bonwire is the internationally-famous location where Kente cloth is made and sold. Almost all of the people who live in Bonwire have a relationship with the production of Kente cloth and it is one of the villages where the locals approach visitors to try and get them to buy their Kente cloth. The village of Bonwire depends heavily on the production and sales of Kente cloth and is supported by the Kente weavers and the Kente market as one of the weavers explained:

> We sell at the Art Center in Accra too. Hopefully the same customer(s) come every month. We (combined weavers) try to sell 24 pieces a month. It is difficult to sell more. Sometimes eight pieces of Kente can make a woman's shirt. A man's shirt can take up to 18 pieces. White men buy Kente at the Art Center in Accra.

As the gentleman explained in the extract above, it can sometimes be difficult to sell 24 pieces of Kente strips a month because it is a daunting task since it takes such a long time to complete a strip of Kente. The weaver affirmed that "A piece like this (holds out a long piece, almost 2 ft. long), takes three days." How much a person pays for Kente is dependent on the quality of Kente and their bargaining techniques in the art markets and outlet where it is sold.

Medie

The Kente master weaver was at the music and arts center in Medie, about an hour outside of the country's capital of Accra. The music and arts center is known as a small private cultural school and center founded by its internationally known percussionist who specializes in the rhythms of the gil (a Ghanaian xylophone) and the Djembe. He offers students and visitors opportunities to learn the arts of Ghana, including the skills of Kente weaving.

In Medie, I stayed at the cultural center's compound and met with the Kente master on a daily basis. During the period when I collected ethnographic data, the Kente master (Lawson) was 27 years old and had been a Kente master for two years. He told me he did not have a last name and when I asked him if he learned Kente from his father, brother, or relative he informed me that he did not have a family and was an orphan. When he finished his time at school as a student, he found a Kente master and was an apprentice for the Kente master for two years. Within the time he was an apprentice, he lived with his teacher and learned the process of Kente weaving. He learned how to make two different types of looms, dye the thread, and learned how to gain his own clientele. He narrated his experiences below:

> If you do well, making good Kente, you will have more customers. At the Art Center is not easy to sell because some people have low prices. When I first started selling Kente, I had no customers, nobody ordered from my first time. Everything in Ghana has increased (prices). I began to get customers in November 2005. A traditional loom is made out of bamboo, an artificial (non-traditional) is made out of wood. . . . When I first started selling Kente, I had no customers, nobody ordered from my first time.

The Kente master shared his experiences and narrated that it was not that easy starting off because there was a lot of competition among the weavers—some strategically had low prices so they could sell more Kente stripes. The National Arts Center is one of the main attractions in Accra. Though it is more of a craft market, there are so many cultural artifacts that one can see and buy including Kente and Adinkra. The Kente master I spoke with enjoyed talking about the history of Kente and how it is considered as a very special fabric for rich men.

In Akokepe, Ghana, there is a festival each year honoring Kente from September to October, which Lawson looks forward to. He sees it as great opportunity to sell his cloth to people. For the Kente master in Medie, Kente is very challenging but is a significant part of his identity. "I am a Kente master," he said, and he told me how his life is based on creating Kente and teaching students how to weave the cloth.

The Kente master of Medie informed me that although he teaches visiting female students at the music and arts center how to make Kente, that Kente weaving is traditionally a man's role or occupation. This does not surprise me because all through the Volta region, Bonwire, and in Medie I had not seen any female Ghanaian Kente weavers. It will be interesting to note how this may have changed since this ethnography was conducted.

The market for Kente cloth is competitive. The Kente master in Medie said, when he first graduated from his Kente apprenticeship, he had to find clients to make his skill a worthwhile living. Like most young Kente masters, he went to the art center in Accra, the city's capital, to sell his Kente. He told me it is a necessity to sell Kente in a market first so people can see the products he made and then once they can see that he made quality Kente, he can then gain individual clients. Successful Kente masters do not have to go to the art center to sell their Kente, the Kente master told me, because they have their own individual clientele and are commissioned on their projects. On average, it takes the Kente master in Medie a little over a day to make one piece of cloth and when his clientele is good he is making about 24 pieces of Kente a month and receives two million cedis for it (two million cedis is the equivalent of $200 U.S. dollars). In our conclusions we summarize the rich ethnographic encounters while elaborating some of the key issues raised by the master weavers that are influencing the culture and traditions of the Kente cloth.

Bargaining and the Spaces Where Cultural Exchange Takes Place (Precious)

When I first arrived in Ghana, I did not know how important bargaining and negotiating were in purchasing, selling, and financial transactions. Coming from a culture where the majority of items and services purchased are marked with a set price I was not used to, and even intimated, to state a price and discuss a price. The act of bargaining and negotiating always felt like I was arguing with the seller since I was not used to it. As time passed and I gained more experience in the art markets and working with weavers I found that bargaining was not arguing at all. The act and transaction of participating in making a deal with a person helps the buyer and seller become acquainted with each other, gain respect for each other, and is the start of a possible lifelong business relationship.

Throughout my time in Ghana, I became more and more used to being able to price textiles accurately and bargain with sellers. When I returned to the United States, I had to adjust once again, to looking at the price tags, knowing there would be no negotiations involved. It was not until I invited Franklin, my co-author, to my Interpersonal Communication class to talk about the culture and communication of Ghana, that I was reminded of how important bargaining and negotiating are in the ways of how items and services are bought and sold in Ghana.

In our Interpersonal Communication class Franklin spoke about the politics, history, foods, and textiles of Ghana. He spontaneously demonstrated how bargaining takes place, jokingly asking a student sitting in the front row, "how much for your cellphone?" The class laughed and the student, who was usually very talkative and boisterous, automatically became very shy. The student smiled nervously and finally stated a price. In response, Franklin, confidently and sincerely replied, "help a brother out, how about $60?" The student said a lower price and gradually they reached an agreement. This was just a hypothetical situation and no cellphone was actually bought or sold, but an important act of communication took place between Franklin and the student.

In the Volta region of Ghana, I was taking percussion lessons from a music teacher. We got to know each other well and enjoyed having several discussions with each other. He never tried to sell me anything other than the percussion lessons and throughout time we became close friends. One day, he took me on a walk through his village; it was very small and he took me to the one-room house with a dirt floor and hardly any furniture where his family lived. He introduced me to his mother and showed me some weaving she made. I did not decide to buy the Kente cloth right then and there, but later I thought about the cloth, how it was made, who it was made by, and the conditions of the weaver.

The deep friendship we had and getting to know my friend's family made me want to buy cloth from his mother, not just because of its quality and craft, but more so because of the personal friendship and ties I had with him and his family. Meeting the weaver face-to-face and seeing her house, her family, and conversing with her was meaningful to me. Knowing the weaver and the person selling the cloth was important in my decision of purchasing the cloth. We still bargained with each other as a way for her to tell me about the cloth, how long it took her to make it, the materials it was made of, and for me to respond.

Bargaining does not always happen because people are looking to rip each other off, but it is a way for people to converse, tell their story, talk about the quality, and eventually reach an agreement that makes both the seller and the buyer happy. Negotiating and conversing creates empowerment between both of the people in which the item for sale becomes the link between the transaction and the relationship that is built.

In the United States, it is rare for a store manager and customer to bargain in a store, but bargaining, bidding, and negotiating are not unfamiliar to our culture. Corporations and businesses participate in negotiations, bids are placed on eBay, and wholesalers and people offering services will also ask "to help a brother out." The ways in how we conduct and communicate business in person, online, through credit, and cash are all negotiations, though it is less common for a customer to have the power to directly ask a waiter at a fancy restaurant, "Can you give me a better price?"

In the sales of Kente and Adinkra, the face-to-face aspect of bargaining is important partially because it gives the weaver a chance to tell his story of how he made his cloth. The stories, histories, and cultures woven into cloths can be seen in many cultures. For instance, the color of a kimono can communicate the marital status of a woman in Japanese culture, or take a moment to browse through such do-it-yourself websites like Etsy.com, and you will see the stories embedded in the items people make.

Technology plays a role in how traditional textiles such as cloths from Ghana are sold. As one weaver from Bonwire said, "Asians come with technology and mass produce Adinkra and Kente." The weavers talk about how this negatively affects their source of livelihood and the weavers who are used to selling at the outlets and art markets are at a disadvantage.

The Role of Communication in Bargaining for Ghanaian Textiles (Franklin)

The production of textiles and cloths woven by individual weavers who are used to creating a rapport with their customers diminishes in globalization. A rapport consisting of a complex process of communication between a seller and a buyer, as Precious stated, may initiate a long-term business relationship and for these Kente weavers to be successful they have to build relationships with their customers. During the process of haggling or bargaining body language is being observed by both seller and buyer, and it takes practice to master the art of negotiating a price that will be mutually beneficial for seller and buyer. Sometimes things don't go as smoothly and you may end up paying a higher price for a strip of Kente when you could have gotten it cheaper somewhere else, or a seller may end up making a loss by selling a strip of Kente cheaper than the selling price (but ends up building a relationship that will attract more customers through referrals). However, this is a system that works in the Ghanaian cultural setting and it makes buying and selling more exciting and actually adds value to the transaction—that extra human touch, and immediacy in communication. When bargaining takes place it is not only the price that is negotiated, but the quality of the product is part of the negotiation as well.

Factors that determine the quality of weaving are single, double, or triple weaving techniques; the higher the number, such as a triple-woven Kente, the higher the price. The length, colors, and material content are also important qualities that contribute to the price of Kente. Silk Kente is more expensive and often seen by weavers as "an antique" and has an heirloom type of quality that gets passed down through generations of a family.

The weavers in Bonwire work vigorously to produce traditional cloths and textiles for the Kente festivals that happen in the late summer and early fall seasons. One of the weavers said, "Many people send Kente to their hometowns, some people don't have family members to teach them [how to weave] Kente so it is very special." Art markets and festivals are extremely important opportunities for Kente weavers and communities, such as Bonwire, to participate in and sell as much Kente as possible. The art markets and festivals are a place where potential lifelong customers, networks, and negotiations happen.

Personal relationships between the buyer and seller are replaced with order forms, Paypal accounts, invoices, and faxes. The empowerment between both people of reaching an agreeable price in person changes in globalization. Without the act of bargaining and negotiating back and forth, the buyer has no choice but to pay a set price that is posted on a price tag.

Maintaining the Culture and Traditions of Kente

Through the ethnographic methods of spending time in Ghanaian environments where African cloth is produced informant interviews were conducted. Spending time with Kente masters in the Volta region and Medie revealed that the basic creation of Kente continues to be executed through its most traditional roots and processes. The Kente master in the Volta region showed the cocoa nut from which he makes his yellow dye for the thread and the intricate meaning behind the symbols and colors that he and many Kente masters still use to weave the cloth today. The Kente master in Medie showed how the building of two different kinds of traditional looms has not changed for hundreds of years. An "artificial loom," which is a temporary loom, is made out of wood and is different from the "traditional loom" because the traditional loom is more sturdy, and built out of bamboo, which is handmade by the weavers. There seems to be a consensus shown by both Kente masters and the weavers in Bonwire that Kente cloth remains three inches wide and then it is sewn together to make larger pieces of fabric for clothing. This is not an unyielding rule but overall it seems to be part of the tradition in Kente weaving.

Another way in which the culture and tradition of Kente cloth has been maintained is not only through visitors and tourists buying Kente, but also by many locals supporting the Kente weavers as well. Kente weavers such as the Kente master in Medie gain a consistent clientele from Ghanaians who commission weavers to make cloths for them. The traditions and culture of Kente weaving are expressed through the maintenance of the unchanging process in the clothmaking by the Kente masters who make a conscious effort to do so and maintain their high standards of quality and authenticity. Although there may be subtle changes in the process such as weavers going to the store to buy their thread rather than making it, the looms that are operated by their hands and feet appear traditional in relation to the mass production sewing machines used in industrial cloth factories. Though kings and queens have limited power now, the same symbols and imagery that define royalty are still used and communicated, as well as the use of timeless proverbs that have existed in Ghanaian culture throughout generations.

The Globalization of Kente

The contributing factors globalization has had on African cloth were discussed in the interviews with the Ghanaian textile makers and sellers. Bergen (1998) studied the assimilation of women entering into the Kente weaving tradition. Though some Ghanaian women's groups have included themselves in the tradition of Kente weaving, the weavers in the village of Bonwire and the Kente masters I encountered were all men. When the men I interviewed were asked if Ghanaian women participated in weaving all of them said women do not usually weave, although there may be the occasional one or two they knew who have become Kente masters.

In the transformation of globalization, many developing countries have encouraged women to participate in the national workforce. From my time spent in Ghana and through the interviews, women, in general, were not commonly expressed as cultural teachers or "culturalists," by the Kente masters, though they are seen in the markets selling products. As Bergen (1998) asserted, the gender role of women in Ghana is still commonly seen as the caregivers of the children, family, and the home.

The main threat Kente weavers face, more so than Adinkra creators, are the establishment and sales of fake Kente, as the Kopeyia Kente master mentioned. Kente is a product that has entered into the international market and is a fabric worn by people in many countries. This issue is coherent to the interests of

Boateng (2002; 2011), who researched Ghanaian folklore and art as intellectual property and the challenges of it being controlled in an international arena. The concept of Kente cloth being mass-produced in China and by people who weave fake Kente through untraditional methods becomes significant to people like the Kente masters interviewed in this study and the Bonwire weavers who depend on the sales of Kente as their livelihood for themselves, their families, and their villages.

In relation to globalization, Kente cloth is at risk of having the Ghanaian cultural symbols, traditions, and Kente cloth techniques depreciated through the process of mass production. Ghanaian Kente weavers thoughtfully place traditional and cultural symbols in their cloths to tell a story or signify a feeling in order to communicate their culture. The mass production of Kente cloth takes away from the respected skills and steps the Kente masters follow in the methods of their weaving.

Issues of gender, intellectual property, and mass production play a role in the culture of Ghanaians through their cloths and textiles. The characteristics of globalization include the changing and transformative influences on culture through the constant negotiation of socialization, economics, and technology. Ghana is part of the United Nations HIPC program. This organization encourages international dependence and economic development and plays a role in the future changes of how cultural and traditional values will be tied to the process, sales, and meaning of African cloth. Kente and Adinkra remain important treasures of Ghanaian culture. In this chapter we have demonstrated how these cloths are deeply woven into the Ghanaian culture and the threats that Kente weavers face from the production of fake Kente by countries such as China. The globalization of the Kente cloth has thus been riddled with issues that scholars should continue to theorize and discuss to help explore ways we can draw more attention to some of the contradictions of the global marketplace (the physical and the virtual).

CONCLUSION

MULTIPLE INTERFACINGS WITH THE SO-CALLED SUBALTERN: TO BE CONTINUED

I started work on this book during a post dot.com socio-economic era, soon after I had completed my last book. The last book (Gajjala, 2004) that was based fully on my own research endeavors and collaborations drew on the work I'd done both for my dissertation and toward tenure, during the mid to late 90s. Since then I have done several co-edited books and this is the second book that is based fully on my own research investigations and conversations. In the midst of the last book project and this current one (and I anticipate the same for the next one I am embarking on as I shut the covers on this one), shifts have occurred. These shifts have reaffirmed for me that what I was observing at these cross-sections is indeed impacting our presents and futures in ways that compel us to reseat ourselves from disciplinary comfort zones. What is discussed in this book that you are reading the "conclusion" of, for instance, does not just impact our social and cultural lives as if those were separate from the political and the economic. These online/offline intersections are changing the way we need to respond to situations around us—whether in our domestic everyday or in the worldwide political milieu. What is most compelling is not that there are shifts or that change continues to happen—these are givens in any era. Our urgent attention and reflexive engagement is needed to observe carefully how this so-called speed of change allows a loss of memory that permits layers of status quo hierarchies to be unchanged generation after generation. While bodies and cultural objects are coded as interchangeable and made visible as agents of difference, democracy and multiculturalism codes are standardized and these individual agents of so-called change are placed on naturalized technical platforms.

Code is made invisible. Does this mean that the coders—the labor that codes—have the power? Does this mean that the complex literacies involved in producing the platforms and networks are created by the labor force that codes them? What configurations of practices, literacies and assumptions underpin how this labor force is trained and simultaneously rendered powerless while they labor to produce "us" in the interface? Should the Humanities and Social Sciences be left out of these kinds of interdisciplinary practices of standardizing socio-cultural financial codes named as "technical" and "Technology"? How out of touch are we in disciplines such as communication, for instance, when all we focus on is how to find the "new" (lo and behold—another social network emerged and they're tweeting about how people from the third world are using it to fight off dictatorships!) to re-insert disenfranchised peoples of the world into the same group of editorial collectives and reviewers, in the same formats that mainstream academic groups remain familiar with through the years.

In continuing work my call to fellow researchers is to scrutinize closely every practice, every code, every interface, woven designs, crochet patterns, spoken word for what seems seamless. We have been looking at and reveling in the discovery of "ruptures" and celebrating them or pointing to them as evidence of hopeful change. But we are missing what hides in the background of the ruptures we see "popping up." What are the nonchanging factors that are hidden by the fast appearing manner in which the "newness" of the place/space/time/body intersections seems to have the potential for reproducing "old" oppressive regimes in brand new bytes of great speed and less time for reflection and contemplation?

How do we "upgrade" the lens that sees the world and its problems? What do we look for and why? How is an "unscripted entry" (here I refer to a recent podcast interview of Larry Gross where he talks about the unscripted entry of Justin Bieber and the likes into the mainstream)[1] into the mainstream actually a product of status quo production mechanisms that have shifted and been hidden through the continual and simultaneous upgrading and standardization of layers of access and literacy. What do we write and publish for and why—if we reproduce consistencies in the name of discovery of newness? What are we as scholars celebrating as unscripted entry? Here, situated in a westernized academy, what do we see and how do we name it? Do we bother to hear other ways of speaking and understand other ways of doing? What is the difference, for instance, between Justin Beiber's unscripted entry into public internet space and that of Norman the "dancing cop" from Indonesia[2] or the unscripted multiple localizations of Dahler Mehndi's "tunak tunak" video[3]?

Further, in a climate where technology service industries such as those that recruit and "traffic" in immigrant programmers are becoming increasingly crucial to the functioning of a "Global" digital economy, what are the socio-economic and cultural contradictions that emerge? The digital economy operates against an optimistic (euphoric) backdrop. Objectives of the architects of digital capitalism are "to develop an economy-wide network that can support an ever growing range of intracorporate and intercorporate business processes" (Schiller, 1999). Various transnational issues occur at the intersection of configurations of power that emerge out of digital capitalism and transnational labor flow. Therefore, what might be the dominant socio-cultural patterns and directions embedded in digital capitalism? Will the implicit structuring of digital finance and e-commerce allow for any kind of empowering or even "subversive" uses of technology as is being claimed by various technophiliacs around the world?

The chapters in this book differently examined multicultural cyborg subject positions that e-merge within current modes of globalized, integrated, networked, digital, risk society, through multiple methods of investigation and drawing on online and offline ethnographic encounters and interludes and textual analyses of websites. The project, thus, relies on analyzing and understanding the semiotic implications of visible corporatization of the subaltern through relational frameworks set up through online socio-financial environments, be they socially networked websites such as kiva.org or immersive three dimensional virtual worlds such as Secondlife. E-commerce, E-philanthropy, and their role in the social construction of financial instruments and risk in the transnational digital economy in turn contribute to a discourse on globalization which privileges specific hierarchies and cultural processes over others. In relying on semiotic analysis however we do not restrict ourselves to sitting behind the desktop computer for our method: each of the contributors has developed relational, praxis-based ethnographic and experiential understandings of the contexts that we examine. This book brings together analyses of these environments through theoretical/philosophical lenses situated in feminist studies, cultural studies and political economy.

The purpose of this book in general, therefore, is to open up some theoretical considerations for continued attempts at mapping these connections. It is my belief that such connections can be mapped at various local/global intersections and that every such contextual analysis will reveal the various ways in which these work together and contribute to the production of power relations within which discourses and practices of globalization are situated. These rely on a complex layering of discourses related to information technologies, lifestyles based on the celebration of globalizing consumer cultures as well as on the seemingly contradictory invoking of nationalist cultures in transnational and global cyberspaces.

It is possible for an upwardly mobile digiratti class to celebrate a romanticized "multiculturalism" and diversity in cyberspace. From this class location, it is possible to view information communication technologies as magical tools for establishing a new, democratic Utopia or the Global Village. This global village is seen as a space where all men, women and children will enjoy the benefits of a modemized, networked liberal humanist society with its implicit underpinning ideologies. Here, network is bandied about as metaphor rather than network as technical and as a coded platform that excludes and includes (see Galloway, 2004). But what is missing from these technologically deterministic narratives about the "new" electronic communication technologies and about cyberspatial Utopias is any concerted sense of new electronic communications technologies as part of a long history of rich and often wayward social *practices* [italics in the original] (including the interpretation of these practices) through which we have become socially acquainted with these technologies (Leyshon and Thrift in "Money/Space").

Despite modernist teleologies and linear causal constructions of the history of science and technology, the "origin" story of electronic technologies is not a singular, linear, inevitable and "upward" progression from the "primitive" to the "modern." In fact, we might argue there is no singular origin story for the development of digital technologies, but that the growth of the phenomenon now known as the Internet owes its existence and fast-paced growth to various political and economic "drives" (power struggles and negotiations) as well as social and cultural appropriations and uses.

Further, historical change leading to the development of various digital technologies and to the establishment of the digital economy is made up of complex sets of negotiations, power struggles, cultural and political decisions. As Carolyn Marvin (1988) has argued, the history of electronic technologies is less a revolution of technical efficiencies in communication than a series of arenas for negotiating issues crucial to the conduct of social life: among them, who is inside and outside, who may speak, who may not, and who has authority and may be believed. She suggests that we focus on "the drama in which existing groups perpetually negotiate power, authority, representation and knowledge with whatever resources are available," rather than merely focus on the instrument (the technology) as central to social change. She further writes:

> New media intrude on these negotiations by providing new platforms on which old groups confront each other. Old habits of transacting between groups are projected onto new technologies that alter, or seem to alter, critical social distances. New media may change the perceived effectiveness of one group's surveillance of another, the permissible familiarity of exchange, the frequency of and intensity of contact, and the efficiency of customary tests for truth and deception. Old practices are then painfully revised, and group habits are refined. New practices do not so much flow directly from the technology that inspires them as they are improvised out of old practices that no longer work in new settings. Efforts are made to restore social equilibrium, and these efforts have significant social risks. In the end, it is less in new media practices, which come later and point toward a resolution of these conflicts (or, more likely, a temporary truce), than in the uncertainty of emerging and contested practices of communication that the struggle of groups to define and locate themselves is most easily observed. (Marvin, 5)

The chapters in this book also clearly raise the question of whether "cyberspace" as a cultural concept can be separated from "cyberspace" as situated within an economic system. The global information society, therefore, is implicated in the production of transnational communities of production, especially since cyberspace is increasingly *the* site for commercial exchanges and financial transactions that in turn further influence software and hardware "directions" such as the continued development of integrated digital financial database systems.

Transnational/travelling subjects at the present time in history come into being at the intersection of traveling analogue and digital contexts within what has come to be termed as the digital economy. Thus we are all transnational, global and local in some way—each formed within slightly or extremely variable configurations of transnationality, globality and locality. Constructs of identity and ignorance occur within communities of production and practice that privilege certain skills and knowledges over others within an increasingly digital economy. Thus, constructs of identity and ignorance occur within a discursive framing of the Internet and digital technologies that allows the "'unconnected' in the present" to be negatively equated with the "'illiterate' of the past" (Warnick, 5). "Ignorance" and "knowledge" therefore, are constructed relative to specific socio-cultural and economic contexts, within various power fields.

Dan Schiller, in 1999, published his work on "Digital Capitalism" where he described how the digitalization of financial practices and systems plays into a globalizing of neoliberal economic systems through the increased digitalization of finance. Clifford Bob, in his work on marketing rebellion noted how transnational corporate marketing processes and logics underpin advocacy and activist movements online. Linking these arguments to Spivak's concern about transnational literacy and cyberliteracy, we see the micro-transactional abilities of the social networking interface allow for the simultaneous globalizing of particular situated forms of participatory practices and representational practices. Such practices work in sync with evolving marketing practices based in the mainstreaming of selected alternative and parallel modes of production through the online marketing interface.

The dual processes of global "NGOization" and "ITization" produce global communities of production and consumption at this coded interface. Visually and aesthetically they are reproduced to connect to disembedded affects and aesthetics. The coded interface, on the other hand, structures the practices in very specific ways even as liberal discourse points to the rampant "multiculturalism" online as evidence of progress and democracy, while in coded fact this multiculturalism is almost accidental, yet shaped by a labor force that is based in a tiered hierarchy of layered literacies and material access. Identity production and technocultural agencies and subjectivities are shaped through the interplay of multiple offline and online contexts, histories and literacies. Thus, as Mark Andrejevic notes, even the interactive interface provided by digital media reconstitutes public space in a manner that scatters the collective into individual scattered spaces. Networks in fact keep us away from each other as we work alone toward similar goals, so that we can't physically be digging at the same path. But we do indeed share a feel-good virtuality that makes us seem connected. The binary that then emerges begs the question—"are you in my 'networks' or are you in my everyday life"—not, "are you real or are you virtual." As Hayles (1999) notes, "[t]his construction necessarily makes the subject into a cyborg, for the enacted and represented bodies are brought into conjunction through the technology that connects them" (xiii).

What might all this mean for continuing processes of globalization and the transnationalization of labor forces? Such questions need to engage the historical formations of transnational ("local" and "global") communities of production in relation to specific contexts of technological design and use. Therefore, socio-cultural descriptions of technological environments as well as their political and economic situatedness are essential to the study of transnational technological environments.

Notes

1.http://culturalstudies.podbean.com/2011/03/29/a-conversation-with-larry-gross-about-the-social-sciences-communication-humanities-and-sol-worth/#
2. See www.youtube.com/watch?v=iLwY_PbVENs
3. See www.youtube.com/watch?v=s9qvCTdBLDs)

GLOSSARY

Adinkra – Hand-printed fabric from Ghana usually worn at important events and traditionally made for royalty.

Agency – The ability to actively participate online/offline using the required tools.

Gamer as cyborg – The digital role-playing individual whose capabilities are enhanced or reduced through technology. The individual has biological and artificial parts (the digital medium and avatar also become an extension of the self).

IT worker as cyborg – Refers to having biological and artificial parts. The information technology worker's capabilities are augmented or diminished through technology. The technology the IT worker engages with becomes an extension of her/himself.

Kente – One of the traditional clothes of Ghana worn on special occasions, it is made out of interwoven strips of cloth. Kente was traditionally made for royalty.

Moo-er as cyborg – Refers to the text-based online virtual reality player as having biological and artificial parts. The artificial part refers to the technology that is being used.

Networks and space – The online and offline spaces occupied by physical and virtual networks.

Power tactics and strategies – Refers to the various means used to negotiate.

Production of community through offline placing and community through online networks – The creation of communities offline and digitally online.

Production of identity – The creation of new or replicated identities through the engagement with technology.

Production of socio-economic processes – Refers to any of the social and financial online/offline processes affecting the well-being and development of a people.

Subaltern – Individual who does not have the tools or the agency to actively and freely participate in a social order. The subaltern is also deemed as not to have the voice to speak for her/himself.

Technoculture – Refers to the relationships and interactions between technology and culture.

Technocultural agency – Refers to the capability to actively participate or act having the technological and cultural know-how or the tools.

Technocultural agent within each community – The technological forces that influence change in a community.

Weaver as cyborg – Refers to the human weaver's capabilities augmented or diminished through technology. The weaver is said to have biological and artificial parts (the loom becomes an extension of the self).

Bibliography

Alcoff, Linda. "The Problem of Speaking for Others." *Cultural Critique* 36, no.11 (Winter 1992-1992): 5-32.

Alcoff, Linda, and Elizabeth Potter. "Introduction." In *Feminist Epistemologies*, edited by Linda Alcoff and Elizabeth Potter, 1-14. New York: Routledge, 1993.

———. "*Feminist Epistemologies*." New York: Routledge, 1993.

Amelia Ubilluz Mejia's Group. "Kiva.org." www.kiva.org/app.php?page=businesses&action=about&id=40584 (accessed April 14, 2009).

Anarbaeva, Mamatova, S. "Samarita Ibannez: An identity journey from first life to second." *Journal of Virtual Worlds Research, 5*, no.1(March 2012): 1-14.

Anderson, Benedict R. O. *Imagined Communities: Reflections on the Origin and Spread of Nationalism*. Rev. and extended ed. New York: Verso, 1991.

Andrejevic, Mark. *ISpy: Surveillance and Power in the Interactive Era*. Lawrence, Kansas: University Press of Kansas, 2007.

Anonymous. "Stretching the national fabric." *The Economist, 342,* (1997): 93 – 95.

Anonymous. Connecting with Kente. *Smithsonian, 30* (1999): 36 – 40.

Anonymous. Kente for home. *American Visions, 13* (1999) 10.

Apps for Development. http://appsfordevelopment.challengepost.com/ (Accessed November 15, 2011).

Appadurai, Arjun. "Global Ethnoscapes: Notes and Queries for a Transnational Anthropology." In *Recapturing Anthropology: Working in the Present*, edited by R. Fox, 191-210. Santa Fe, N.M.: School of American Research Press, 1991.

———. Disjuncture and difference in the global cultural economy. Theory, Culture & Society, 7, (1990): 295-310.

Arundathi. "Saris With a Twist [Blog Post]." 2007. http://arundathi-rediscovery.blogspot.com/2007/02/sarees-with-twist.html. (accessed April 15, 2011).

Asante, Molefi, K. "The rhetoric of globalization: The Europeanisation of human ideas." Journal of Multicultural Discourses, 1 (June 2006):152-14.

Balqees Serwat. Kiva.org. www.kiva.org/app.php?page=businesses&action=about&id=19162 (accessed April 18, 2009)

Boateng , Boatema, Akosua. "African culture in the global marketplace: The case of folklore and intellectual property in Ghana." (PhD diss., University of Illinois at Urbana-Champaign, 2002).

Boateng, Boatema. "*The Copyright Thing Doesn't Work Here: Adinkra and Kente Cloth.*" MN:University of Minnesota Press, 2011.

Barthes, Roland. *Mythologies*. New York: Hill And Wang, 1972.

Best, K. Rethinking the globalization movement: Toward a cultural theory of contemporary democracy and communication. *Communication and Critical Cultural Studies*, 2, no.3 (September 2005): 214-237.

Bergen, Elizabet M. Kente cloth weaving among the Asante in Ghana: A West African example of gender and role change resistance. (Doctoral dissertation, University of Alberta). *Master Abstracts International, 38/03,* 937. (1998).

Biekart, Kees., & Alan Fowler. "Civic Driven Change: A Concise Guide to the Basics." The Hague, The Netherlands: Institute of Social Studies. (accessed April 18, 2009).

Biggart, N.W. & Guillen, M.F. Developing differences: Social organization and the rise of the auto industries of South Korea, Taiwan, Spain, and Argentina. American Sociological Review, 64, (1999): 722 – 748.

Bhasin, B.B. and K.K. Kak. *Towards an Objective for the Handicrafts Sector - An Examination of the Five Year Plans*. Unpublished paper, New Delhi, 1983.

Black, Shameen. "Microloans and micronarratives: Sentiment for a small world." *Public Culture, 21*, no.2 (Spring 2009): 269-292.

Blair, Kristine, Radhika Gajjala, and Christine Tulley. "*Webbing Cyberfeminist Practice: Communities, Pedagogies, and Social Action*." Cresskill: Hampton Press, 2009.

Bob, Clifford. "*The Marketing of Rebellion: Insurgents, Media, and International Activism*." New York: Cambridge University Press, 2005.

Bob, Clifford et al. Media Spaces: Innovation and Activism, www.global.asc.upenn.edu/docs/CSY08ch10.pdf (accessed May 26, 2012).

Boellstorff, Tom. "*Coming of Age in Second Life: An Anthropologist Explores the Virtually Human*." Princeton: Princeton University Press, 2008.

Boyd, D.M, and N.B. Ellison. "Social Network Sites: Definition, History, and Scholarship." *Journal of Computer Mediated Communication* 13, no. 1 (2007): 210-230.

Bratich, Z. Jack. "From embedded to Machinic Intellectuals: Communication Studies and General Intellect" Communication and Critical/Cultural Studies, 5, no. 1 (March 2008): 24-45.

Brinkerhoff, Jennifer M. "*Digital Diasporas: Identity and Transnational Engagement*." New York: Cambridge University Press, 2009.

Brown, M. Rebecca. "*Gandi's Spinning Wheel and the making of India*." New York, NY: Routledge, 2010.

Calabrese, A.. "The Promise of Civil Society: A Global Movement for Communication Rights." *Continuum: Journal of Media & Cultural Studies* 18, no. 3 (2004): 317-329.

Carroll, Thomas F. "*Intermediary NGOs: The Supporting Link in Grassroots Development*." West Hartford, CT: Kumarian Press, Inc., 1992.

Castells, Manuel. "*The Rise of the Network Society, The Information Age: Economy, Society and Culture Vol. I*." Cambridge, MA: Blackwell, 1996.

Castells, Manuel. "*The Power of Identity, The Information Age: Economy, Society and Culture, Vol. II.*" Cambridge, MA: Blackwell, 1997.

Castells, Manuel. "Communication, Power, and Counter-Power in the Network Society." *International Journal of Communication* 1 (2007): 238-266.

Castree, Noel. "Differential Geographies: Place, Indigenous Rights and 'Local" Resources." *Political Geography* 23, no. 2 (2004): 133-167.

Chandrasekara, Ishani. "Why is Finance Critical? A Dialogue with a Women's Community in Sri Lanka." *Ephemera: Theory & Politics in Organization* 9, no. 4 (2009): 300-317.

Chickens for When the Rains Don't Come. "Kiva stories from the field." http://fellowsblog.kiva.org/2009/04/13/chickens-for-when-the-rains-don%E2%80%99t-come/ (accessed April 20, 2011).

Cho, Lily. "The Turn to Diaspora." *Topia* 17 (2007): 11-30.

Chopra, Rohit. *Empire Redux: Imperial Indifference and the Normalization of Empire in the Global Present* (2011).

———. Global primordialities: "Virtual identity politics in online Hindutva and online Dalit discourse." *New Media & Society*, *8,* no.2 (April 2006): 187-206.

C.I.A. World Factbook – Ghana. https://www.cia.gov/library/publications/ the-world-factbook/geos/gh.html. (accessed March 13, 2011).

Clarke, Kamari Maxine. "*Mapping Yoruba Networks: Power and Agency in the Making of Transnational Communities.*" Durham, NC: Duke University Press, 2004.

Cole, Herbert M. "Kente: a Meaningful Tradition in Cloth," *American Visions* 5 (October 1990): 18-22.

Collier, Mary J., and Milt Thomas. "Cultural identity: An interpretive perspective." In Y. Kim & W. Gudykunst (Eds.), *Theories of intercultural communication* (pp. 99-120). Newbury Park, CA: Sage, 1988.

Collin, P. "Building and Connecting to Online Communities for Action: Young People, ICT and Everyday Politics." International Journal of E-Politics (IJEP), 1, (2010): 1-18.

Cooks, Leda M., and Kirsten Isgro. "A Space Less Traveled: Positioning Gender in Information and Communication Technology." *Feminist Media Studies* 3, no. 3 (2003): 347-351.

Couldry, Nick. "*Why voice matters: Culture and politics after neoliberalism*" London: SAGE, 2010.

Couze, Venn. "Neoliberal Political Economy, Biopolitics and Colonialism: A Transcolonial Genealogy of Inequality." *Theory, Culture, & Society* 26, no. 6 (2009): 206-233.

Custard, Holly A. "The Internet and Global Civil Society: Communication & Representation Within Transnational Advocacy Networks." *Global Media Journal: Mediterranean Edition* 3, no. 2 (2008): 1-11.

D'Monte, Darryl. "*Ripping the Fabric: The Decline of Mumbai and Its Mills.*" New Delhi: Oxford University Press, 2002.

Deetz, Stanley. "Corporate Governance, Corporate Social Responsibility, and Communication." In *The Debate Over Corporate Social Responsibility*, edited by S. May, G. Cheney, and J. Roper, 267-278. New York: Oxford University Press, 2007.

Dirlik, Arif. "Introduction." In *Pedagogies of the Global: Knowledge in the Human Interest*. Boulder: Paradigm Publishers, 2006. 3-18.

Donnette Dunbar 'Everybody wants a piece of Africa now' culture: Kente, a cloth rich in color and tradition, weaves its way into wardrobes of African-Americans. *Los Angeles Times,* pp.5. (1991, October 27).

Dreze, Jean, and Amartya Sen. *India: Economic Development and Social Opportunity*. Delhi: Oxford University Press, 1995.

Dunbar, D. "Everybody wants a piece of Africa now culture: Kente, a cloth rich in color and tradition, weaves its way into wardrobes of African-Americans." Los Angeles Times, pp.5. (1991, October 27).

Elliott, Carolyn M.. "Introduction: Markets, Communities, and Empowerment." In *Global Empowerment of Women: Responses to Globalization and Politicized Religions*, edited by Carolyn M. Elliot, 1-23. New York: Routledge, 2008.

Enteen, Jillana. "Spatial Conceptions of URLs: Tamil Eelam Networks on the World Wide Web." *New Media & Society* 8, no. 2 (2006): 229-249.

———. "*Virtual English: Queer internets and Digital Creolization*." New York, NY: Routledge, 2010.

Escobar, Arturo. "*Encountering Development*": *The Making and Unmaking of the Third World*. Princeton, N.J: Princeton University Press, 1995.

Esha Shah. "Telling Otherwise: A Historical Anthropology of Tank Irrigation Technology in South India." Technology and Culture, 49, no. 3 (July, 2008): 652-674.

Essinger, James. "*Jacquard's Web: How a Hand-Loom Led to the Birth of the Information Age*." Oxford: Oxford University Press, 2004.

Everett, Anna. "*Digital Diaspora: A Race for Cyberspace*." Albany: SUNY Press, 2009.

Fawcett, Michelle, "The market for ethics: Culture and the neoliberal turn at UNESCO." New York University. September 2009. Publishing. (PhD diss., New York University, 2009).

Friedman, L. Thomas. *The world is flat: A brief history of the 21st century*. New York: Farrar, Straus & Giroux, 2005.

Fürsich, Elfriede and Melinda Robins. Africa.com: The self-representation of sub-Saharan nations on the World Wide Web. Critical Studies in Media Communication, 19, no. 2 (2002): 90-21.

Gajjala, Radhika, and Annapurna Mamidipudi. "Cyberfeminism, Technology, and International "Development"." *Gender and Development* 7, no. 2 (1999): 8-16.

Gajjala, Radhika. "*Cyber Selves: Feminist Ethnographies of South Asian Women*." Walnut Creek, CA: AltaMira Press, 2004.

Gajjala, Radhika, and Melissa Altman. "Producing Cyber-Selves Through Technospatial Praxis: Studying Through Doing." In *Health Research in Cyberspace: Methodological, Practical and Personal Issues*, edited by P. Liamputtong, 67-84. New York: Nova Science Publishers, 2006.

Gajjala, Radhika, Natalia, Rybas., & Mellissa, Altman. "Epistemologies of doing: E-merging selves online." *Feminist Media Studies, 7*, 2, (June 2007): 209-213. [commentary and criticism section]

Gajjala, Radhika, Natalia Rybas, and Yahui Zhang. "Producing Digitally Mediated Environments as Sites for Critical Feminist Pedagogy." In *The SAGE Handbook of Communication and Instruction*, edited by D.L. Fassett and J.T. Warren, 411-436. Los Angeles: SAGE Publications, 2010.

Gajjala, Radhika. "Placing South Asian Digital Diasporas in Secondlife." In *The Handbook of Critical Intercultural Communication*, edited by Rona Tamiko Haluani and Thomas K. Nakayama, 517-534. Oxford: Wiley-Blackwell, 2011.

Gajjala, Venkataramana. "The Role of U.S.-Based Indian Diasporas in the Entrepreneurship and Globalization Processes in the IT Industry." In *South-Asian Technospaces*, edited by R. Gajjala and V. Gajjala, 25-36. New York: Peter Lang, 2008.

Gajjala, Venkataramana. "Role of US-based Indian diasporas in the entrepreneurship and globalization processes in the IT industry" in Brij Maharaj, K. Laxminarayan and Dave Sangha (eds.) Indian Diaspora: Retrospect and Prospect, New Delhi: Sage Publications, (2006).

Gajjala, Venkataramana, Radhika Gajjala, Anca Birzescu, and Samara Anarbaeva. "Microfinance in Online Space: A Visual Analysis of Kiva.org." *Development in Practice* 21, no. 6 (2011): 880-893.

Gajjala, Radhika., & Mamidipudi, Annapurna. "Cyberfeminism, technology and international "development." *Gender and Development*, 17, 2, (1999): 8-16.

Gajjala, Radhika. "An interrupted postcolonial/feminist cyberethnography: Complicity and resistance in the "cyberfield." *Feminist Media Studies*, 2, no. 2 (July 2002): 177-193.

Gajjala, Radhika, Yahui Zhang, and Phyllis Dako-Gyeke. "Lexicons of Women's Empowerment Online" *Feminist Media Studies*, 10, 1(March 2010): 69-86.

Giddens, Anthony. "*Modernity and Self-Identity: Self and Society in the Late Modern Age.*" Stanford: Stanford University Press, 1991.

Gonzalez, Jennifer. "The Appended Subject: Race and Identity as Digital Assemblage." In *Race in Cyberspace*, edited by B.E. Kolko, L. Nakamura, and G.B. Rodman, 27-50. New York: Routledge, 2000.

Greenless, Janet. "Female Labour Power: Women Workers' Influence on Business Practices in the British and American Cotton Industries, 1780-1860" Ashgate Publishing, 2007.

Gumucio-Dagron, Alfonso. "Six Degrees and Butterflies: Communication, Citizenship, and Change." In *Civic Driven Change: Citizen's Imagination in Action*. The Hague: Institute of Social Studies (ISS), 2008. 1-10.

———. "Playing With Fire: Power, Participation, and Communication for Development." *Development in Practice* 19, no. 4-5 (2009): 453-465.

Haraway, Donna J. "*Simians, Cyborgs, and Women: The Reinvention of Nature*." New York: Routledge, 1991.

Hayles, Katherine. "*How we became Posthuman: Virtual Bodies in Cybernetics, Literature and Informatics*." Chicago: The University of Chicago, 1999.

Hay, Colin and Rosamond, Ben. "Globalization, European integration and the discursive construction of economic imperatives." *Journal of European Public Policy*, 9, no.2 (April 2002): 147-167(21).

Hedge, S. Radha. Postcolonial Scholarship – Productions and new directions: An interview with Gayatri Chakravorty Spivak." *Communication Theory*, 12, no. 3 (2002): 271-286.

Herold, Kurt, D., Shirley, Minocha, and Natalia Rybas. "An Assembled Issue" *Journal of Virtual Worlds Research*, 5, no. 1 (May 2012): 1-4.

Hine, Christine. *Virtual Ethnography*. Thousand Oaks, CA: SAGE Publications, 2000.

Hudon, Marek. Norms and values of the various microfinance institutions. *International Journal of Social Economics*, 35, (2008): 35-48.

Huesca, Robert. Conceptual contributions of new social movements to development communication research. *Communication Theory*, 11, no. 4 (November 2001): 415-433.

Jackley, Jessica. Jessica Jackley: "poverty, money and love." www.ted.com/talks/jessica_jackley_poverty_money_and_love.html (accessed April 14, 2011)

Jayati, Ghosh and Chandrasekhar, C.P. "Agrarian crisis in Andhra Pradesh." www.macroscan.org/fet/oct04/print/prnt041004Agrarian_crisis.htm (accessed April 1, 2011).

Kamat, Sangeeta, Ali Mir, and Biju Mathew. "Producing Hi-Tech: Globalization, the State and Migrant Subjects." *Globalisation, Societies and Education* 2, no. 1 (2004): 5-23.

Kaplan, Caren. "Transporting the Subject: Technologies of Mobility and Location in an Era of Globalization." *Publications of the Modern Language Association of America* 117, no. 1 (2002): 32-42.

Kevorkian, Martin. "*Color Monitors: The Black Face of Technology in America*." Ithaca: Cornell University Press, 2005.

Kiva Lender: Connor. "*Kiva.org. Loans that change lives*." www.kiva.org/lender/connorb (accessed April 21, 2009).

Kiva Lender: Katie. "*Kiva.org. Loans that change lives.*" www.kiva.org/lender/katiekonrath (accessed April 21, 2009).

Kiva Lender: Meagan. "*Kiva.org. Loans that change lives.*" www.kiva.org/lender/meagan9783 (accessed April 21, 2009).

Kiva Lender: Tyler. "*Kiva.org. Loans that change lives.*" www.kiva.org/lender/tyler7579 (accessed April 21, 2009).

Kiva Lender: Charles. "*Kiva.org Loans that change lives.*" www.kiva.org/app.php?page=lender&action=view&name=charles4234&pageID=3 (accessed April 21, 2009).

Kiva Lending Team. "*Kiva.org. Loans that change lives.*" www.kiva.org/community/viewTeam?team_id=94 (accessed April 21, 2009).

Kiva. Kenya Agency for Development of Enterprise and Technology (KADET). from www.kiva.org/partners/133 (accessed June 2, 2011).

Kiva. "Kenya Rural Agency for Development." www.kiva.org/partners/33 (accessed April 21, 2009).

Kiva. "Ghana Women's Trust, Inc." www.kiva.org/partners/54 (accessed May 23, 2012).

Kiva. "Ghana, Kraban Support Foundation." www.kiva.org/partners/19 (accessed April 15, 2011).

Kiva. "Poverty Isn't Always Pretty *Kiva stories from the field.*" http://fellowsblog.kiva.org/2009/04/08/poverty-isnt-always-pretty/ (Accessed April 15, 2009).

Kiva. "You Have Internet, but No Running Water? *Kiva stories from the field.*" http://fellowsblog.kiva.org/2009/04/16/a-study-in-contrasts-2/(accessed April 20, 2009).

Kolko, Beth E., Lisa Nakamura, and Gilbert B. Rodman. "Race in Cyberspace: An Introduction." In *Race in Cyberspace*, edited by Beth E. Kolko, Lisa Nakamura, and Gilbert B. Rodman, 1-14. New York: Routledge, 2000.

Kristof, Nicholas. D. (a) "You, too, Can Be a Banker to the Poor." *The New York Times*, March 27, 2007. http://select.nytimes.com/2007/03/27/opiion/27kristof.html?_r=1&scp=1&sq=You,%20Too,%20Can%20Be%20a%20Banker%20to%20the%20Poor&st=cse (accessed April 3, 2011).

———. (b) "Answering Your Questions on Micro-Finance." *The New York Times*, March 28, 2007. http://kristof.blogs.nytimes.com/2007/03/28/answering-your-questions-on-micro-finance/ (accessed April 17, 2011).

Kumar, Amitava. "Temporary Access: Indian H-1B Workers in the United States." In *Technicolor: Race, Technology, and Everyday Life*, edited by A. Nelson, T.L.N. Tu, and A.H. Himes, 76-87. New York City: New York University Press, 2001.

Kurian, Priya A., and Debashish Munshi. "Terms of Empowerment: Gender, Ecology, and ICTs for Development." *Feminist Media Studies* 3, no. 3 (2003): 352-355.

Landow, George P. "*Hypertext: The Convergence of Contemporary Critical Theory and Technology.*" Baltimore, Md.: Johns Hopkins University Press, 1992.

Latour, Bruno. "*Reassembling the Social: An Introduction to Actor-Network-Theory.*" Oxford: Oxford University Press, 2005.

Latour, Bruno. "Visualization and Cognition: Thinking with Eyes and Hands." *Knowledge and Society: Studies in the Sociology of Culture Past and Present* 6 (1986): 1-40.

Lazar, Sian. "Education for Credit: Development as Citizenship Project in Bolivia." *Critique of Anthropology* 24, no. 3 (2004): 301-319.

Lender Profile: Mallory. www.lendwithcare.org/profile/index/558 (accessed April 30,2011).

Lewis, Jonathan. "Microfinance Leaders Debate Future." *The Huffington Post (New York)*, January 3, 2011. www.huffingtonpost.com/jonathan-lewis/microfinance-leaders-deba_b_803324.html (accessed January 3, 2011).

Leyshon, Andrew, and Nigel Thrift. "*Money/Space: Geographies of Monetary Transformation*." New York: Routledge, 1997.

Lingam, Lakshmi. "Domains of Empowerment: Women in Microcredit Groups Patriarchies." In *Global Empowerment of Women: Responses to Globalization and Politicized Religions*, edited by C.M. Elliott, 119-140. New York: Routledge, 2008.

Lourenco Rafael Vilanculos. "*Kiva.org*" www.kiva.org/app.php?page=businesses&action=about&id=66316 (Accessed April 19, 2009).

Mackinnon, Rebecca "*Consent of the Networked: The Worldwide Struggle for Internet Freedom*." New York: Basic Books, 2012).

Mallapragada, Madhavi. "Home, Homeland, Homepage: Belonging and the Indian-American Web." *New Media & Society* 8, no. 2 (2006): 207-227.

Mamidipudi, Annapurna, and Radhika Gajjala. "Juxtaposing Handloom Weaving and Modernity: Building Theory Through Praxis." *Development in Practice* 18, no. 2 (2008): 235-244.

Martin, Randy. "*Financialization of Daily Life*." Philadelphia: Temple University Press, 2002.

Marvin, Carolyn. "*When Old Technologies Were New: Thinking About Electric Communication in the Late Nineteenth Century*." London: Oxford University Press, 1988.

Massey, Doreen B. "Don't Let's Counterpose Place and Space." *Development* 45, no. 1 (2002): 24-25.

Massey, Doreen B.. "*Space, Place, and Gender*." Minneapolis: University of Minnesota Press, 1994.

Mcgowan, Abigail. "*Crafting the nation in colonial India*." New York: Palgrave Macmillan, 2009.

Miller, Daniel, and Don Slater. "*The Internet: An Ethnographic Approach*." Oxford; New York: Berg, 2000.

Mitra, Rahul and Radhika Gajjala, (2008). "Queer Blogging in Indian Digital Diasporas: A Dialogic Encounter" in special issue of *Journal of Communication Inquiry*. 32 no. 4 (October 2008): 400-423.

Mohanty, Chandra Talpade. "*Feminism Without Borders: Decolonizing Theory, Practicing Solidarity*." Durham, NC: Duke University Press, 2003.

Mohanty, Chandra Talpade. "Under Western Eyes: Feminist Scholarship and Colonial Discourses." *Feminist Review* 30 (1988): 65-88.

Mohanty, Chandra Talpade. "Under Western Eyes: Feminist Scholarship and Colonial Discourse." *Feminist Review 30*, (1988): 60-88.

Mohanty, Fowler, Gail. "*Labor and Laborers of the Loom: Mechanization and Handloom Weavers, 1780-1840*."Routledge, 2006.

Nadesan, Majia Holmer. "Enterprising Narratives and the Global Financialization of Microlending." *Women and Language* 33, no. 2 (2010): 9-30.

Naficy, Hamid. "An *Accented Cinema: Exilic and Diasporic Filmmaking*." New Jersey: Princeton, (2001).

Nakamura, Lisa. "*Cybertypes: Race, Ethnicity, and Identity on the Internet*." New York: Routledge, 2002.

Narayan, Uma. "*Dislocating Cultures: Identities, Traditions, and Third-World Feminism*." New York: Routledge, 1997.

Narayan, Uma. "Essence of Culture and a Sense of History: A Feminist Critique of Cultural Essentialism." In *Decentering the Center: Philosophy for a Multicultural, Postcolonial, and Feminist World*, edited by U. Narayan and S. Harding, 80-101. Bloomington: Indiana University Press, 2000.

New York Times. http://topics.nytimes.com/top/news/international/coun triesandterrito-ries/ghana/indexhtml?scp=1&sq=Ghana%20economic%20boom&st=cse (accessed March 16, 2012).

Opoku, K. A. "*Hearing and keeping: Akan proverbs*." Pretoria: University of South Africa, 1997.

Owens, Lynn and L. Kendell, Palmer. Making the news: Anarchist counter-public relations on the World Wide Web. *Critical Studies in Media Communication*, 20, no. 4 (2003):335-361.

Pandey, Gyanendra (editor). "*Subaltern citizens and their histories: investigations from India and the USA*." London: Routledge, 2010.

Parameswaran, Radhika. "The Other Sides of Globalization: Communication, Culture, and Postcolonial Critique." *Communication, Culture & Critique* 1, no. 1 (2008): 116-125.

Parrott, S. BC. "Fabrics helps Disney promote film." *Journal Record*, no page citation, 1994.

Parthasarathi, Prasannan. "The transition to a colonial economy: Weavers, merchants and kings in south India, 1720-1800." New York:Cambridge University Press, 2001.

———. "Cotton textiles in the Indian subcontinent, 1200-1800." In *The Spinning World: A Global History of Coton Textiles, 1200-1850*, edited by Giorgio Riello and Prasannan Parthasarathi, 17-42.

Peterson, V. Spike. "*A Critical Rewriting of Global Political Economy: Integrating Reproductive, Productive, and Virtual Economies*." New York: Routledge, 2003.

Pickard, W. Victor. Assessing the radical democracy of indymedia: Discursive, technical, and institutional constructions. *Critical Studies in Media Communication*, 23, no. 1 (March 2006):19-38.

Puttu, Guru. P. *The forgotten saga of real madras hand kerchiefs: A great southern Indian's handloom tradition.* Paper presented at UGC National Seminar, Chirala, Prakasam District, A.P. www.scribd.com/doc/18382306/real-madras-handkerchiefs-the-forgotten-saga-of-RMHKFull-Paper-on-RMHK . (accessed April 15, 2009).

Rheingold, Howard. "*Virtual Reality*." New York: Touchstone, 1991.

Ross, Mariama. Symbols of identity: Akan art in the popular culture of Ghana and its educational implications. (Doctoral disseration, Indiana University, 2001). *Dissertation Abstracts International=62/02,* 293, 2000.

Sassen, Saskia. "*Globalization and Its Discontents: Essays on the New Mobility of People and Money*." New York: New Press, 1998.

———. "Local Actors in Global Politics." *Current Sociology*, 52, no.4 (July 2004): 649-670.

Schiller, Dan. "*Digital Capitalism: Networking the Global Market System.*" Cambridge, Mass: MIT Press, 1999.

———. "*Digital Capitalism: Networking the Global Market System.*" Cambridge, MA: MIT Press, 2000.

Schultz, Lisa, Jose Roberto Guevara, Samantha Ratnam, Ani Wierenga, Johanna Wyn, and Charlotte Sowerby. "Global Connections: A Tool for Active Citizenship." *Development in Practice* 19, no. 8 (2009): 1023-1034.

Sengupta, Rajdeep, and Craig P. Aubuchon. "The Microfinance Revolution: An Overview." *Federal Reserve Bank of St. Louis Review* 90, no. 1 (2008): 9-30.

Sharma, Aradhana. "*Logics of Empowerment: Development, Gender, and Governance in Neoliberal India*." Minneapolis: University of Minnesota Press, 2008.

Shiv, Ganesh and Kirsty Barber. "The silent community: Organizing zones in the digital divide." *Human Relations*, 62, no. 6 (June 2009) 851-874.

Shohat, Ella, and Robert Stam. "*Unthinking Eurocentrism: Multiculturalism and the Media*." New York: Routledge, 1994.

Shome, Raka and Radha Hegde. Culture, communication, and the challenge of globalization. *Critical Studies in Media Communication, 19*, no.2 (June 2002): 172-189.

Slack, Jennifer Daryl. "Contextualizing Technology." In *Rethinking Communication: Paradigm Exemplars*, edited by B. Dervin, L. Grossberg, B. O'Keefe and E. Wartella, 329-345. Newbury Park, CA: SAGE Publications, 1989.

Slack, Jennifer Daryl, and J. Macgregor Wise. "*Culture + Technology: A Primer*." Berne: Peter Lang, 2005.

Soja, Edward W. "*Thirdspace: Journeys to Los Angeles and Other Real-and-Imagined Places*." Cambridge, MA: Blackwell, 1996.

Sosale, Sujatha. "Pre-Modern" Online: Converging Discourses of Globalization and Development." *Journalism & Communication Monographs* 9, no. 1 (2007): 1-52.

Spivak, Gayatri Chakravorty. "Cultural Talks in the Hot Peace: Revisiting the 'Global Village'." In *Cosmopolitics: Thinking and Feeling Beyond the Nation*, edited by P. Cheah and B. Robbins, 329-448. Minneapolis: University of Minnesota Press, 1998.

Spivak, Gayatri Chakravorty. "*A Critique of Postcolonial Reason: Toward a History of the Vanishing Present.*" Cambridge, MA: Harvard University Press, 1999.

Spivak, Gayatri Chakravorty. "Can the Subaltern Speak?" In *Maxism and the Interpretation of Culture,* edited by C. Nelson & L. Grossberg, 271-316. Urbana: University of Illinois Press, 1988.

Spivak, Gayatri Chakravorty. "Questioned on Translation: Adrift." *Public Culture* 13, no. 1 (2001): 13-22.

———"Can the subaltern speak?" in Cary Nelson and Lawrence Grossberg (eds) Maxism and the interpretation of Culture London: Macmillan, 1988.

Sterne, Jonathan. "Bourdieu, Technique and Technology." *Cultural Studies* 17, no. 3/4 (2000): 367-389.

Sterne, Jonathan, and Carol Stabile. "Using Women as Middle Men: The Real Promise of ICTs." *Feminist Media Studies* 3, no. 3 (2003): 364-368.

Strom, Stepanie. "Confusion on Where Money Lent via Kiva Goes" www.nytimes.com/2009/11/09/business/global/09kiva.html (accessed April 15, 2011)

Sundén, Jenny. "*Material Virtualities: Approaching Online Textual Embodiment.*" New York: P. Lang, 2003.

Terranova, Tiziana. "*Network Culture: Politics for the Information Age.*" London: Pluto Press, 2004.

Thrift, Nigel, and Shaun French. "The Automatic Production of Space." *Transactions Institute of British Geographers* 27 (2002): 309-335.

Tirthankar, Roy. "Out of Tradition: Master Artisans and Economic Change in Colonial India." *Journal of Asian studies*, 66, no. 4 (2007): 963-991

Tubella, Imma. "Television and Internet in the Construction of Identity." In *The Network Society:From Knowledge to Policy*, edited by M. Castells and G. Cardoso, 257-269. Washington, D.C.: Center for Transatlantic Relations, 2006.

United States Department of Labor. www.dol.gov/ (accessed April 16, 2012).

United States Census Bureau. www.census.gov/ (accessed April 16, 2012).

Wade, R. H. (2005, May). *The March of Neoliberalism and What to Do About It.* Draft paper for plenary talk at the conference Beyond 'Deregulation': Finance in the 21st Century, University of Sussex. Cited in Orhangazi, O. (2008). *Financialization and the US Economy.* Cheltenham, UK: Edward Elgar.

Walker, Rob. www.nytimes.com/2008/01/27/magazine/27wwln-consumed-t.html (accessed April 15, 2011).

Williams, Raymond. "*Marxism and Literature*." New York: Oxford University Press, 1977.

Wood, Andrew F., and Deanna L. Fassett. "Remote Control: Identity, Power, and Technology in the Communication Classroom." *Communication Education* 52, no. 3/4 (2003): 286-296.

World Intellectual Property Organization (WIPO). www.wipo.int/wipolex/es/text.jsp?file_id=223004 (accessed March 6, 2012).

Woolsey, Biggart, Nicole and Mauro F. Guillén. "Developing differences: Social organization and the rise of the auto industries of South Korea, Taiwan, Spain, and Argentina." *American Sociological Review, 64,no.5* (October 1999): 722 – 748.

Index

Contributor Bios

Anca Birzescu is a doctoral candidate in the School of Media & Communication at Bowling Green State University, Ohio. Her research interests include postcolonial theory, feminist cultural studies, ethnic identity, gender and communication, digitally mediated communication and globalization, and mass media discourse in Eastern and Central Europe. Her current doctoral research focuses on Roma minority identity negotiation in post-communist Romania. Anca is also an adjunct faculty at Bowling Green State University, Firelands Campus.

Radhika Gajjala (PhD, University of Pittsburgh, 1998) is professor of media and communication at Bowling Green State University. Her book *Cyberselves: Feminist Ethnographies of South Asian Women* was published in 2004. She has co-edited collections on *South Asian Technospaces*, *Global Media Culture and Identity*, and *Webbing Cyberfeminist Practice.* She is currently working on two interrelated projects—one on microfinance online and money in virtual worlds and social media in relation to the ITization and NGOization of Global socio-economic work and play environments, and the other on coding and placement of affect and labor in digital diasporas, while also working on an edited collection on digital diasporas and globalization.

Seemanthini Niranjana, PhD is the author of Gender and Space Femininity, Sexualization and the Female Body (2001) and was an Independent Researcher. She also worked as an officer in Dastkar Andhra, INDIA.

B. Syamasundari, PhD (University of Hyderabad) is currently an independent researcher, activist and also an officer at Dastkar Andhra in Hyderabad India. Her academic work is in the area of development and education in relation to voluntary organizations. Her interests include writing in Telugu, translating children's literature into Telugu for use in schools. She is s a member of the Anveshi (Research Center for Women's Studies in Hyderabad) Executive Committee and is also associated with Centre for Learning (CFL) Secunderabad, a voluntary organization offering quality education for children and contributes to a journal *edu care* which provides a forum for reflecting on issues of education and development, published by CFL. She has co-edited a book on "Traditional Industry in the New Market Economy" with Kanakalatha Mukund and also published work in journals such as *Yojana* and *Economic and Political weekly.*

Precious Yamaguchi, PhD. Is currently a tenure-track Assistant Professor of Communication at a women's liberal arts college, Cedar Crest College, in Allentown, Pennsylvania. She has doctorate in Communication Studies from Bowling Green State University's School of Media and Communication Studies with research emphases in Critical Studies and Cultural Studies. Her academic research is interdisciplinary, focusing broadly on issues of culture, identity, generation, transnational labor, art, social media, and international textile markets. She has experience teaching at a private university, a public (state) university, an international university, a community college, a culinary institute, and a women's college with diverse populations of students and faculties.

Franklin Nii Yartey, (PhD, Bowling Green State University, 2012) Franklin Nii Amankwah Yartey holds a B.A. in communications from Northwestern College, IA, and an M.A. in Communications from Indiana State University. Franklin's research focuses on Digital Media & Globalization/Social Media with a secondary focus on Intercultural Communication. His research interests include online microfinance and its impact on third world women, health communication, media ethics, and globalization. He has held an assistant professor position at the University of Dubuque, Iowa in August 2012.